Eric E. McCollum, PhD
Terry S. Trepper, PhD

Family Solutions for Substance Abuse
Clinical and Counseling Approaches

Pre-publication
REVIEWS,
COMMENTARIES,
EVALUATIONS . . .

"**A**fter decades of working with substance-abusing families, it is refreshing to move away from the disease model of dysfunction to a more positive focus of strength and competency.

For students, here is a readable text that paves the way from the beginning of treatment through its termination. Although the work is complex, this book presents a clear and complete model as a pathway. It leads everyone involved out from under the shameful cloud of addiction, through the process to healthier functioning.

This is an installation of hope for the hopeless and for the clinician a course based upon joining rather than opposing. It gives the responsibility and the respect to the families because these authors trust them to establish their course. How empowering! How enriching and yes, refreshing!"

Jean Seelig, MEd, CAC
Family Therapist,
Alcohol and Drug Services
of Fairfax County, Virginia

The Haworth Clinical Practice Press
An Imprint of The Haworth Press, Inc.
New York • London • Oxford

Family Solutions for Substance Abuse
Clinical and Counseling Approaches

HAWORTH Marriage and the Family
Terry S. Trepper, PhD
Executive Editor

Parents Whose Parents Were Divorced by R. Thomas Berner

Multigenerational Family Therapy by David S. Freeman

Therapy with Treatment Resistant Families: A Consultation-Crisis Intervention Model by William George McCown, Judith Johnson, and Associates

Developing Healthy Stepfamilies: Twenty Families Tell Their Stories by Patricia Kelley

Propagations: Thirty Years of Influence from the Mental Research Institute edited by John H. Weakland and Wendel A. Ray

Structured Exercises for Promoting Family and Group Strengths: A Handbook for Group Leaders, Trainers, Educators, Counselors, and Therapists edited by Ron McManus and Glen Jennings

Making Families Work and What to Do When They Don't: Thirty Guides for Imperfect Parents of Imperfect Children by Bill Borcherdt

Family Therapy of Neurobehavioral Disorders: Integrating Neuropsychology and Family Therapy by Judith Johnson and William McCown

Parents, Children, and Adolescents: Interactive Relationships and Development in Context by Anne-Marie Ambert

Women Survivors of Childhood Sexual Abuse: Healing Through Group Work: Beyond Survival by Judy Chew

Tales from Family Therapy: Life-Changing Clinical Experiences edited by Frank N. Thomas and Thorana S. Nelson

The Therapist's Notebook: Homework, Handouts, and Activities for Use in Psychotherapy edited by Lorna L. Hecker and Sharon A. Deacon

The Web of Poverty: Psychosocial Perspectives by Anne-Marie Ambert

Stepfamilies: A Multi-Dimensional Perspective by Roni Berger

Clinical Applications of Bowen Family Systems Theory by Peter Titelman

Treating Children in Out-of-Home Placements by Marvin Rosen

Your Family, Inc.: Practical Tips for Building a Healthy Family Business by Ellen Frankenberg

Therapeutic Intervention with Poor, Unorganized Families: From Distress to Hope by Shlomo A. Sharlin and Michal Shamai

The Residential Youth Care Worker in Action: A Collaborative, Competency-Based Approach by Robert Bertolino and Kevin Thompson

Chinese Americans and Their Immigrant Parents: Conflict, Identity, and Values by May Paomay Tung

Together Through Thick and Thin: A Multinational Picture of Long-Term Marriages by Shlomo A. Sharlin, Florence W. Kaslow, and Helga Hemmerschmidt

Developmental-Systemic Family Therapy with Adolescents by Ronald Jay Werner-Wilson

The Effect of Children on Parents, Second Edition by Anne-Marie Ambert

Couples Therapy, Second Edition by Linda Berg-Cross

Family Therapy and Mental Health: Innovations in Theory and Practice by Malcolm M. MacFarlane

How to Work with Sex Offenders: A Handbook for Criminal Justice, Human Service, and Mental Health Professionals by Rudy Flora

Family Solutions for Substance Abuse
Clinical and Counseling Approaches

Eric E. McCollum, PhD
Terry S. Trepper, PhD

The Haworth Clinical Practice Press
An Imprint of The Haworth Press, Inc.
New York • London • Oxford

Published by

The Haworth Clinical Practice Press, an imprint of The Haworth Press, Inc., 10 Alice Street, Binghamton, NY 13904-1580

Client identities and circumstances have been changed to protect confidentiality.

Cover design by Marylouise E. Doyle.

Library of Congress Cataloging-in-Publication Data

McCollum, Eric E.
    Family solutions for substance abuse : clinical and counseling approaches / Eric E. McCollum, Terry S. Trepper.
       p. cm.
    Includes bibliographical references and index.
    ISBN 0-7890-0622-7 (hard : alk. paper) — ISBN 0-7890-0623-5 (soft : alk. paper)
    1. Substance abuse—Patients—Rehabilitation—Case studies. 2. Substance abuse—Patients—Family relationships—Case studies. 3. Substance abuse—Prevention—Case studies. I. Trepper, Terry S. II. Title.
RC564 .M326 2000
616.86'0651—dc21
                                             00-040765

CONTENTS

**Chapter 1. Why Work with Families
in Substance Abuse Treatment?**   **1**

   "Like a Zoom Lens . . ."   3
   What This Book Is About   7

**Chapter 2. Understanding the Family in Context:
Family Systems Theory and Practice**   **11**
     Wendy Snyder

   Interdependence: The Family and Individual
     Development   12
   Systems Theory: The Basis for Understanding
     Interdependence   13
   Human Systems in Perspective: Family, Culture,
     and Society As Context   16
   Major Schools of Family Therapy   22
   Goals and Techniques: What and How Family
     Therapists Help People Change   26
   Family Therapy Misunderstood: The Issues
     of Parent Blame, Biologically Based Disorders,
     and the Disease Model of Addiction   30
   Family-Centered Treatment in a Variety of Settings   33

Chapter 3. What Makes a Difference in Treatment?   **39**

   Client Contributions   40
   The Therapeutic Relationship   48
   Hope and Expectancy   50
   Therapy Models   52
   A Final Word   52

Chapter 4. Working with Families: Basic Skills   **55**

   Power Dynamics in Family Therapy   56
   Emotional Intensity in Family Therapy   57

Learning to Join with Families   58
Moderating Intensity   64
The REM Approach to Working with Conflict   66
Domestic Violence and Safety   69
Using Goals to Frame Counseling   82
Attending to Process   83
Summary   85

Chapter 5. Assessing Motivation   **87**

What Is Motivation?   88
Visitors   95
Complainants   103
Customers   108
Working with Visitors and Complainants
    in the Same Family   113
Summary   116

Chapter 6. Negotiating a Contract for Therapy   **119**

A Vision of the Future   120
Making Goals Measurable   123
Resolving Conflicting Goals   125
Contract Problems   134

Chapter 7. Problem and Solution Sequences   **139**

Defining Problem Sequences   141
Solution Sequences   150
Summary   156

Chapter 8. The Ups and Downs of Change   **159**

Making Change Bigger   161
When Change Gets Derailed   172
Troubleshooting Relapse Work   178
Summary   179

Chapter 9. Ending Treatment   **181**

Structure of the Sessions   182
Difference Punctuating Interventions   182

Strategies to Maintain Change   190
Plan for Posttreatment Challenges   195
Termination Interventions   200
Booster Sessions   201
Termination   207

References   **209**

Index   **217**

ABOUT THE AUTHORS

Eric E. McCollum, PhD, is Associate Professor and Clinical Director in the marriage and family therapy program at Virginia Tech's Northern Virginia Center. He is a licensed clinical social worker and a licensed marriage and family therapist in the state of Virginia. Dr. McCollum has spent the past ten years doing research and training in the area of family therapy of substance abuse, including consulting to the state of Washington and being co-investigator on a five-year NIDA-funded research project in Phoenix, Arizona. His work has appeared in publications including the *Journal of Marital and Family Therapy,* the *Journal of Substance Abuse Treatment,* the *American Journal of Family Therapy,* and the *Journal of Family Psychotherapy.* He is on the editorial boards of the *Journal of Marital and Family Therapy* and the *Journal of Family Psychotherapy* and is a contributing editor for *The Family Therapy Networker.*

Terry S. Trepper, PhD, is Director of the Family Studies Center, Professor of Psychology, and Professor of Marriage and Family Therapy at Purdue University Calumet in Hammond, Indiana. He is an APA Fellow, an AAMFT Clinical Member and Approved Supervisor, an AASECT Certified Sex Therapist, and a Diplomate in the American Board of Sexology. He is Editor of the *Journal of Family Psychotherapy* and Editor-In-Chief of The Haworth Clinical Practice Press, an imprint of The Haworth Press, Inc. Dr. Trepper is the co-author (with Mary Jo Barrett) of *Systemic Treatment of Incest: A Therapeutic Handbook; Treating Incest: A Multiple Systems Perspective* (Haworth, 1987); *101 Interventions in Family Therapy* (with Thorana S. Nelson) (Haworth, 1993); and *101 More Interventions in Family Therapy* (with Thorana S. Nelson) (Haworth, 1998).

Chapter 1

Why Work with Families
in Substance Abuse Treatment?

Sixteen-year-old Dylan has had two stays in a residential drug treatment program as well as trips through several outpatient programs in the past three years. He began smoking marijuana when he was eleven and currently uses any drug he can get, although he prefers crack. He is in trouble with the law for a variety of things—possession, dealing, and breaking and entering. Despite his problems, Dylan has a pleasant smile and a winning personality. Lots of people are rooting for him to stay out of trouble. At their last meeting, his probation officer [PO] told him, "Dylan, if you keep going like you are, you're going to end up at the detention center, and the judge is going to make you serve out all your suspended time. If it gets to that point, there won't be anything I can do about it. You've got to get your act together." When he reads his weekend arrest report this morning, Dylan's PO spots Dylan's name right off. "Damn," the PO says to himself. Dylan has been arrested on another breaking-and-entering charge.

Maria is thirty-two. She is the mother of twin daughters who have been placed in foster care because of her alcohol use. Most afternoons find Maria in front of her television set, drinking vodka until she passes out. She has tried all the treatment programs she could find in her county. She has not been sober for more than three weeks since she was twenty-three. Her social worker tells Maria over and over again that she has to stop drinking if she ever wants to get her daughters back. But every time she comes for a home visit, it is clear to the social worker that Maria has not even decreased her rate of drinking.

To see Tyrone on the street, you would never guess that he has two years of community college under his belt, or that he used to work as the night manager at a fast-food place to save money for the rest of his college courses. He wears a knit stocking cap pulled down over his forehead against the autumn chill and a tattered flannel shirt. He no longer makes much effort to cover the needle marks on his arm.

Traditionally, substance abuse treatment, similar to most other forms of mental health and medical treatment, viewed the individual with a drug or alcohol problem as the focus for intervention. The causes of drug abuse and addiction were sought in qualities of the individual and historically have included such things as moral failure, psychological distress, and genetic predisposition. Even the disease model of addiction encourages a focus on individuals; diseases are something that individuals get, after all.

The individual focus in substance abuse treatment seems sensible. Clearly, Dylan, Maria, and Tyrone are making daily choices that keep them mired in addiction. No one is holding a gun to Maria's head and making her drink, for instance. So, it is only logical to try to understand why people use drugs, and what they can do to stop, by closely examining the users themselves. Our experience, however, as well as the research literature, tells us that the individual view alone is only half the story and omits important resources that can help drug abusers in treatment. For that reason, we have spent more than ten years working with people who abuse substances *and their families* in treatment.

As family therapists, we knew that working with whole families was effective with any number of problems that we usually think of as individually based.* We believed that the same would be true in substance abuse treatment. Our experiences include two large research projects—one focused on drug-abusing adolescents and the other on women and their partners. In addition, we have been involved in a series of smaller projects for which we taught substance abuse counselors the principles of working with families from a family systems perspective. Based on all these experiences, we are convinced that including families in substance abuse treatment is essential if we want to provide the best service to our clients. However, to do so, sub-

---

*The October 1995 issue of the *Journal of Marital and Family Therapy, 21*(4), contains an excellent series of review articles on the marriage and family therapy outcome literature.

stance abuse counselors or others who work in substance abuse treatment need to learn some special skills and ways of thinking about drug and alcohol problems. The purpose of this book is to present those skills and ways of thinking.

"LIKE A ZOOM LENS . . ."

Moving from an individual focus to a family focus is much like zooming a camera lens from a close-up to a wide-angle view. In wide-angle mode, things come into the frame that are not visible in the close-up. To illustrate this change in perspective, we will look at Dylan, Maria, and Tyrone's situations in turn to see what a wide-angle view might add to our understanding of why they use drugs and what a family approach might add to their treatment.

Dylan—An Adolescent Drug User

As we pull back from an individual focus to a family focus, we come to understand more about the circumstances that surround Dylan's drug use. Dylan's mother and father have never gotten along. Although they no longer have the violent physical fights they used to have, the constant tension in the house regularly erupts into screaming matches. Much of the time, the fights are about Dylan. Dylan's dad thinks Dylan is lazy and no good.

"I was working nights to support my family when I was your age," he often tells Dylan, "plus going to high school. I never thought a son of mine would grow up to be such a bum."

Dylan's mother, on the other hand, tends to be softer with her son and defends him when his father criticizes him.

"Leave him alone, Frank," she says. "Can you blame the boy for being in trouble when he's got a father like you?"

As their fight escalates, Dylan usually slips out the back door and heads downtown, hoping to score and hook up with some of his friends. If he is lucky, his parents will be asleep by the time he comes home.

What does the wide-angle view tell us about Dylan's drug use? Does his parents' conflict make him take drugs? Of course not. Many kids grow up in unhappy homes and never resort to drug use, while other kids with severe drug problems live in homes that are relatively untroubled. What this view does tell us is that Dylan's drug use occurs in a unique context—a context in which he is the focus of his parents' corrosive and bitter conflict—and that for Dylan to stay clean and sober, that context must change. Although changing how Dylan and his parents get along will not automatically change Dylan's drug use, it will free him from having to shoulder the burden of his parents' troubles, thereby creating some calmer space for Dylan to think about his addiction and what he wants to do about it.

Including parents and other family members in the treatment of adolescents with drug and alcohol problems makes perfect sense in many ways. Adolescents usually live with their parents, and it is often at the parents' behest that the adolescent comes to treatment in the first place. Further, despite growing independence, adolescents are both emotionally and financially dependent on their parents. Thus, parents play a key role in adolescents' lives and have much to offer as part of substance abuse treatment. However, in a number of the adolescent treatment agencies where we have consulted, parents were not involved at all in their children's treatment. This was surprising to us in light of the research that shows how useful family involvement in adolescents' drug treatment can be. Szapocznik and his associates (1988) found that including an adolescent's family members increases the adolescent's involvement in treatment. Obviously, if parents or other family members support treatment and attend with the adolescent, there is a greater chance the adolescent will attend and become involved. Not only does family involvement help get adolescents involved in treatment, it also keeps them there. Diamond and colleagues (1996) report, based on a review of the family therapy outcome and process literature, that family members' involvement in adolescent drug treatment lowers the adolescents' rates of attrition. In other words, an adolescent is less likely to drop out of treatment if family members are involved. Finally, various studies suggest that family treatment approaches for adolescents are more effective than individual or group-only approaches (Friedman, 1989; Henggeler et al., 1991; Joanning et al., 1992; Lewis et al., 1990). And one study (Schmidt, Liddle, and Dakof, 1996) found that parents who were involved in family therapy with their drug-abusing adolescents changed their parenting practices in ways that appear to be associated with their children's decreases in substance use. So, not only does it make intuitive sense to include an adolescent's family members in treatment, it is also effective. One of the missing pieces in Dylan's many attempts at treatment may have been the participation of his parents.

Maria—An Adult Alcoholic

At first glance, it is more difficult to see how family counseling might help Maria. She is an adult, after all, and not dependent on her husband the way Dylan is dependent on his parents. However, spouses of adult substance abusers and addicts often contribute significantly to the problems of their partners. This certainly seems to be the case for Maria. According to her, Paul, her husband, is "always on my case about something. The house isn't clean enough for him, or he doesn't like what I cook, or he thinks I should get a job. If he'd just leave me alone, life wouldn't stink so much. Who can blame me for drinking?"

As you might guess, Paul has a different view. He feels caught between having to work to support the family and wondering if he and Maria will ever be able to get their daughters back.

"I'm doing my best to help," he explains. "If Maria would just stop drinking, I could relax, and we could focus on getting our kids back. My boss is hassling me at work because all I can think about is Maria and whether or not she's doing anything to stop drinking. I've been calling her all the time, and that's starting to interfere with my job. Every day that I can't see our girls is like torture for me. I just don't know what we're going to do."

The wide-angle view gives us a different picture of Maria's drinking. Although Paul's worry does not cause Maria to drink, both of them are caught in an escalating pattern of nagging and withdrawing that centers on alcohol. The more Paul nags at Maria to stop drinking, the more she withdraws through continued drinking. This pattern makes change difficult for both of them.

An extensive body of research literature describes the benefits of including the family members of adult substance abusers such as Maria in treatment. For one thing, the onset of drug abuse and the occurrence of drug overdoses are often precipitated by family events (Duncan, 1978; Krueger, 1981; Noone, 1980). This connection is especially strong for women. Anglin and colleagues (1987) reviewed the literature on the couple relationships of female opiate addicts and concluded that "women are commonly introduced to narcotics and maintained in their addiction by men, especially when the women are involved in an intimate interpersonal relationship with male addicts" (p. 500). Williams and Klerman (1984), in a similar review of the literature concerning the couple relationships of alcoholic women, note that "[w]omen are . . . more likely than men to cite marital instability and family problems as reasons both for problem drinking and for seeking treatment" (p. 291). Gomberg (1993) and Wilsnack, Wilsnack, and Klassen (1984) both report similar findings.

Once adults get to treatment, involvement of their partners improves engagement in treatment as well as retention and outcome (see, for example, Atkinson, Tolson, and Turner, 1993; Fals-Stewart, Birchler, and O'Farrell, 1996, 1999; McCrady et al., 1986; O'Farrell, 1989, 1991; O'Farrell and Feehan, 1999). Not only does the inclusion of spouses or other adult partners in treatment improve substance abuse outcomes, it also results in higher levels of relationship satisfaction (Fals-Stewart, Birchler, and O'Farrell, 1996; McCrady et al., 1986) and lower levels of spouse abuse (O'Farrell, Van Hutton, and Murphy, 1999). Finally, a significant connection exists between family relationships and relapse (McCrady et al., 1986; O'Farrell et al., 1998), another argument in favor of including partners in the treatment of substance-abusing adults.

Including partners in treatment results in better outcomes, but the benefit does not stop there. The social costs of alcohol and drug abuse are reduced when family members are involved. Such costs include, for example, further substance abuse treatment, involvement with the criminal justice system, lost work days, public support payments, and so forth. Fals-Stewart, O'Farrell, and Birchler (1997), for instance, found that the cost of providing couples treatment to male alcoholics was not significantly different from the cost of providing individual treatment, but the subsequent savings in social costs between the two modalities was dramatic. Couples treatment provided a net yearly savings of $6,628 versus a net savings of $1,904 for individually based treatment in the year following treatment. O'Farrell and associates (1996) found a similar reduction in social costs when couples therapy was included as a part of treatment. Overall, then, not only will a client such as Maria have the best chance for a good treatment outcome in a program that also involves her husband, but society's interest is well served by this approach as well.

Tyrone—A "Loner" Addict

People such as Tyrone pose the greatest challenge to the wide-angle view. Who seems more cut off from family than a heroin addict who is focused almost constantly on finding the next dose? Most of us see "street people" and assume that they must be isolated from everyone and everything in their past. While this is an easy assumption to make, it does not reflect reality. Tyrone, for example, sees his sister a couple of times a week when he goes by her house to take a shower, get a hot meal, and sometimes borrow money. Although Tyrone's sister worries about him and wonders if helping him is somehow enabling him not to face his addiction, she also feels that she is the only real support he has, and that if she does not help him he might engage in even more high-risk behavior, such as burglary or mugging, to support his habit. Tyrone sees his mother every couple of weeks, but when he does, they simply fight with each other. She tells him she is disgusted with him and his life and that she cannot imagine what Tyrone's deceased father would say if he knew his son was an addict. However, she, too, often gives him money and food when he comes by her house.

Tyrone's situation is not unusual. Although young-adult drug addicts (age thirty-five or younger) often appear to be cut off from their families, 60 to 80 percent of them either live with their parents or are in daily contact with them, while up to 95 percent have weekly contact with at least one parent (Cervantes et al., 1988; Stanton, 1997). Family members can be influential in involving these young adults in treatment (Garrett et al., 1997, 1998, 1999) and helping them complete it. Stanton and Shadish (1997) report that opiate-addicted adults in individual treatment drop out at a rate of 64 to 95 percent, while adding a family component reduces the dropout rate to 33 percent. Finally, as in the cases of Dylan and Maria, research does indicate that Tyrone will have a more successful treatment outcome if his sister or mother is also involved in his treatment (Stanton, Todd, and Associates, 1982).

We have examined the cases of Dylan, Maria, and Tyrone both to illustrate the differences between a close-up (individual) and a wide-angle (family system) view and to summarize the research literature on the advantages of including family members in substance abuse treatment. For each case, the research suggests that family involvement would help get the substance abuser involved in treatment, help keep the person in treatment, and result in better outcomes than an individually focused program alone.

WHAT THIS BOOK IS ABOUT

While we are convinced that it is important to involve families in treatment, we also know that many substance abuse counselors do not believe that they have the skills or training they need to do so. The need for family counseling training for substance abuse counselors was highlighted by the Substance Abuse and Mental Health Services Administration's 1998 publication of *Addiction Counseling Competencies: The Knowledge, Skills, and Attitudes of Professional Practice* (SAMHSA, 1998). This document delineates eight core competencies for addictions counselors, one of which involves the skills and knowledge to provide family counseling. Specifically, counselors should have the following skills in order to work competently with families:

1. Understand the characteristics and dynamics of families, couples, and significant others affected by substance use.
2. Be familiar with and appropriately use models of diagnosis and intervention for families, couples, and significant others, including extended, kinship, or tribal family structures.
3. Facilitate the engagement of selected members of the family, couple, or significant others in the treatment and recovery process.
4. Assist families, couples, and significant others to understand the interaction between the system and substance use behaviors.
5. Assist families, couples, and significant others to adopt strategies and behaviors that sustain recovery and maintain healthy relationships. (SAMHSA, 1998, p. 122)

This book is designed to provide addictions counselors with a set of skills that will allow them to meet these competencies. We do not intend this book to turn substance abuse counselors into family therapists. As with substance abuse treatment, family therapy is a broad field with a depth of knowledge and skills that cannot be learned in one course or through one book. However, we see the connection between family therapy and substance abuse treatment as a cooperative, not a competitive, one. In other words, we feel that by lending our knowledge about families to substance abuse counselors we can help them improve their work, just as our association with the addiction treatment field has made us better at seeing and working with clients who come for family therapy but who have substance abuse problems. By learning how we can work together, and respecting the unique knowledge each field possesses, we can do our best for our clients.

In the next chapter, we describe family systems theory and give a brief history of the field of family therapy. This chapter provides the knowledge foundation for making the switch from the close-up view to the wide-angle view that we discussed earlier. In Chapter 3, we present the factors that help people change in treatment, factors drawn from the research literature. We have based our model on these factors. Chapter 4 describes the set of skills that counselors need to manage family counseling sessions, regardless of the theoretical model they are using. Working with families is different from working with any other kind of group because family members have ongoing and intense emotional relationships with one another. Substance abuse counselors must be familiar with these differences and possess the skills to deal with them.

The remainder of the book presents a model for working with families that many of the counselors we have trained have found useful in their daily practice. The model is based on the pioneering thinking of the solution-focused approach to therapy developed by Steve de Shazer, Insoo Kim Berg, and their colleagues at the Milwaukee Brief Therapy Center. The solution-focused approach is based on the belief that it is more useful to look at clients' strengths and abilities than it is to focus on their problems and liabilities. We have modified the solution-focused approach somewhat based on our experiences in working with people who abuse substances and their families. In particular, we have introduced the concept of solution sequences to add an interactional component to the model, and we have expanded the notion of motivation to include the stages of change model that has come from substance abuse treatment. However, we want to be clear about the debt we owe to the creative clinicians who first developed the solution-focused approach.

Although the solution-focused approach differs from the traditional disease model of addiction treatment, it is not necessarily incompatible with it. Osborn (1997) surveyed 284 alcoholism counselors, for example, and asked them to rate how much they agreed with several statements that were representative of solution-focused thinking. The majority of the respondents (79 percent) indicated that they agreed or strongly agreed with the solution-focused questionnaire items, including the respondents who also strongly endorsed the disease concept of alcoholism. Osborn concludes that her results "suggest that the alcoholism treatment field may be 'ripe' and amenable for [solution-focused brief therapy]" (p. 26). We think Osborn is right and that the time is right for a focus on strengths and competence in working with families in substance abuse treatment.

Chapter 2

Understanding
the Family in Context:
Family Systems Theory and Practice

Wendy Snyder

Family systems therapy is an exciting approach to working with drug and alcohol abusers. Its appeal is in part due to the reliability of systems theory as a guide to intervention. Family systems principles lead the therapist to attend to observable phenomena and to develop a clear plan for treatment based on those observations. The theoretical model allows the therapist to conceptualize how a variety of agents and forces figure into the picture presented by the substance abuser and his or her family. Family systems therapy is flexible enough that it can often mesh with other approaches and techniques and forms the basis underlying our competency-based counseling program.

This chapter will first explain some of the principles of family systems theory and then briefly describe prevailing models of family systems therapy. The aim is to give the reader an understanding of the basics, so that he or she may better understand the family treatment model presented in the rest of the book.

This chapter is adapted from Snyder (1992).

Wendy Snyder is a licensed marriage and family therapist and a registered nurse with many years of experience helping families in recovery from substance abuse. She has a master's degree in Public Health from Johns Hopkins University and a master's degree in Marriage and Family Therapy from Virginia Tech University, where she currently teaches and does clinical supervision. She is in private practice in Vienna, VA.

INTERDEPENDENCE:
THE FAMILY AND INDIVIDUAL DEVELOPMENT

The alcohol, drug abuse, and mental health professional relies on theories of human development and human behavior to guide the assessment of adolescents and adults, and to inform the therapeutic interventions employed with individuals in treatment. Traditional individually oriented theories focus primarily on the intrapsychic (inner) processes of the individual. Family systems theory is considerably different from these. It focuses on the *interaction* among family members and can be seen as a theory of both family functioning and human development and behavior because these processes are so interrelated. Indeed, systems theory sees all aspects of a person's environment as a context that creates meaning and influences the person, even as it is redefined and influenced by him or her.

Traditional developmental theories have explained the needs of a developing child and the historical importance of the family in meeting these needs. By its very presence, the family provides the child's earliest definition, the definition of himself or herself as a separate individual. The family provides food, shelter, and a nurturing buffer between the less powerful child and the more powerful world. Family members react to events and persons and, through these reactions, create meaning for the child. The focus is always on outcomes for the child.

The individually oriented focus of traditional developmental theories leads them to exclude an important phenomenon, however. That is, while the family fills a role of utmost importance in the life of the developing child, the family is at the same time transformed by the participation of the child. The arrival of a child defines family members in new ways, as mother, father, sister, brother, grandparent, and so on. The family responds to the child, and the child responds to the family. Each child within a family is responded to differently by different members. It is apparent that these interactions have no real beginning or end; they are ongoing, circular, and continuous feedback processes (Minuchin, 1985).

Of course, every family is not an intact, smoothly functioning, warmly involved group. All families, in fact, fail to meet some needs of their members at some times. All families vary over time in their ability to work together and respond to the challenges of daily life. Detached, abusive, and even absent family members affect and influence one another. While the content of issues may differ from family to family, the *interdependence* of behaviors and the importance of the family in the continuing development of individuals remain constant.

The recognition and understanding of this interrelatedness of behavior is the hallmark of family systems theory. In counseling, it leads to a focus on what goes on *among and between* people, rather than what goes on *within* them. This focus is useful because interpersonal transactions are directly observable to the therapist, whereas intrapersonal processes are not.

SYSTEMS THEORY:
THE BASIS FOR UNDERSTANDING
INTERDEPENDENCE

During the first half of the twentieth century, the family was seen primarily as a collection of individuals and the focus of mental health research and treatment was on the characteristics of individuals. In the 1960s, developments in several scientific fields set the stage for change. In biology and physics, interest began to focus on the *relationships* among the parts of a whole, rather than on the parts themselves, to better understand how machines and living things worked. *Cybernetics* theory emphasized the importance of feedback among parts of a whole. The "whole" was seen as a "system," or a complex of interacting parts and the relationships that organize them within some kind of boundary.

This led to a radically new and different way of looking at the concept of "cause." When mutual feedback among parts of a whole was recognized, an alternative to the existing linear view of causality—"A causes B"—arose. (See Figure 2.1, Systems Theory: An Ecology of Influence, for an example of the influence of various systems on an individual adolescent.) In the old view, cause could be represented by a straight arrow between two events—the cause pointing to the effect. In the new view, though, the events could be seen as mutually determined. This phenomenon could be represented as "A causes B causes A." Both A and B were at the same time cause and effect. The arrow now curved around in a circular pattern pointing from A to B and back to A. The circular pattern defied the traditional notion of cause and effect altogether (Weiner, 1948, 1954).

The diagram titled Systems Theory: An Ecology of Influence illustrates this new view. A person who is abusing substances influ-

FIGURE 2.1. Systems Theory: An Ecology of Influence

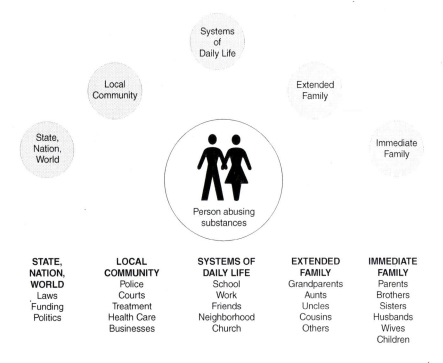

STATE, NATION, WORLD	LOCAL COMMUNITY	SYSTEMS OF DAILY LIFE	EXTENDED FAMILY	IMMEDIATE FAMILY
Laws	Police	School	Grandparents	Parents
Funding	Courts	Work	Aunts	Brothers
Politics	Treatment	Friends	Uncles	Sisters
	Health Care	Neighborhood	Cousins	Husbands
	Businesses	Church	Others	Wives
				Children

Source: Based on Snyder, 1992, p. 17.

ences and is influenced by a number of systems. In addition, each of these systems interacts with the others. The immediate family both influences and feels the effects of substance abuse. This is transmitted to the extended family, who may try to help and who also experience the worry and concern of the immediate family members. Some attempts to help may be useful, while others may interfere. The substance-abusing person is also involved in daily interactions with work or school. With an adolescent, the school may try to involve the immediate family in managing the difficulties the adolescent is having. State and national laws limit the actions that can be taken to deal with the person who is abusing substances (e.g., the family cannot lock the child in the basement to keep him or her from using drugs), and community resources determine what treatment options are available. Although the focus of this book is on individuals and their families, counselors must always keep in mind the number of other systems that are involved in the life of anyone who uses substances.

At the family level, the circular pattern of interactions is like a dance. As the old saying goes, "It takes two to tango." One person cannot "do" a tango to another person. Each must make coordinated and cooperative moves for the pair to tango. And if the dance is to change—if the tango turns into a waltz, for example—both partners must eventually alter their part in the sequence of steps. If one partner waltzes while the other tangos, stubbed toes and bruised shins are likely to result. The problems that bring families to treatment can also be thought of as part of a dance, or a pattern of interactions, and the solutions to those problems ultimately require changes on the part of all members of the family system. Often, families express this circularity through mutual blaming. The classic example is the nag-and-withdraw cycle seen in couples: "I wouldn't nag you all the time if you'd only listen to me," one partner says. "I'd listen to you if you weren't nagging all the time," the other partner replies. In fact, both partners have a piece of the truth. Each is doing the steps in an interactional dance with which neither is satisfied. Although one partner can initiate change, eventually *both* must change their parts in the dance to arrive at a satisfactory solution.

Although the idea of circular causality sheds new light on family interactions, it still does not provide us with a complete picture. Families do not exist in a vacuum, and many factors outside the family influence the patterns of interaction that families develop. In this sense, families represent "open" systems—systems whose boundaries are open enough to admit the influence of outside factors (von Bertalanffy, 1968). To look only at the influences that arise from within the family is to miss many important aspects of the pattern the family brings to treatment. Individuals are situated within larger and larger systems—families, communities, nations, and cultures. At the same time, many physical parts and biological and psychological processes interact in a systematic way to "create" an individual.

Thus, an individual can be conceived of as a system, and a family can be conceived of as a system, made up of several smaller systems. Likewise, a school and a church can each be seen as a large system made up of smaller ones, as can a neighborhood or a country. Individuals are members of many systems simultaneously. The systems nest within each other or overlap, yet each has a set of interacting parts that respond to feedback from one another within some kind of defining boundary. All human systems are open to some degree; that is, they must exercise some exchange with their environments.

HUMAN SYSTEMS IN PERSPECTIVE: FAMILY, CULTURE, AND SOCIETY AS CONTEXT

This set of interrelated systems, which constitutes an ecology of influence, is diagrammed in Figure 2.1. Surrounding the individual, and his or her biological and psychological processes, are the other systems in which he or she lives. The circle on the far right represents the immediate family, and next to it, is the extended family. The next circle includes the family's daily contacts, including workplaces, schools, churches, and neighborhoods. As we move to the left, we find the local community, including the health care, justice, and social service systems. Finally, we come to the circle representing society and the influence of laws and governmental activity. The set of beliefs and values known as ideology and culture constitutes an overlay, as it affects all the systems within the ecology. Family, community, and society constitute levels in a hierarchy of systems making up the context of the individual; each level is influenced and largely defined by cultural beliefs and values. All the systems represented by the circles interact with and influence one another to varying degrees. It is through his or her interaction with others in this context that the individual derives meaning, develops an understanding of the world outside himself or herself, discovers the scope and limits of his or her ability to influence this world, and develops his or her capacities.

One important clinical implication of the systems view is that an individual may behave very differently in different *contexts*. Thus, a teenager may be rude and out of control in a classroom run by a permissive teacher but a model of good behavior in an authoritarian-structured home, or an adolescent may be self-centered and self-absorbed with parents but sensitive and empathic with peers.

Focus on the Family System

Family systems theory recognizes and respects the importance of each system in the ecology of the individual, from his or her own internal processes to the social and cultural forces many "circles" removed. The theory focuses attention on the family because the interactions in the family are among the most powerful forces in a person's life and are most easily available for observation and intervention. The family context therefore provides a unique resource for creating change. In addition, family therapists increasingly intervene in other important systems as well—for example, schools, churches, courts, and social service agencies—as part of an effective therapeutic strategy with a family.

In a family-centered approach, the therapist may see an individual alone or with other members of the immediate or extended family. The approach dictates that the primacy of the family should be respected, and that the family should be in charge of involving others in treatment. The therapist's role is to empower the family and help everyone to behave responsibly and helpfully.

Some families may be concerned, caring, and hard-working in their efforts to help a troubled member; others may be unconcerned, uncaring, uninvolved, and even abusive. When family members are detached or abusive, they are still important to treatment and cannot be ignored or discounted. Direct contact with as many family members as possible is important to assess their role in the problem and their potential to be involved constructively in working toward a solution. While the nature and degree of the family's involvement in treatment may vary, its importance to the process will not.

Definition of Family

In discussing family members in treatment, it is necessary to stop for a moment to consider what is meant by "family." Who is included? Who is excluded? There is wide variation in what might reasonably be called a family. In the past, the definition of a family was generally limited to parents and children living together. However, the extensive social changes of the past few decades make that definition too limiting.

A rising divorce rate means that members of a traditional nuclear family are now more likely to be separated than they were some years ago. In other cases, the parents of a child may not be married and may not live in the same household. Indeed, some families have no household; they have no home at all and may or may not live together, wherever they are. Along with the increase in divorce has come an increase in the number of single-parent families and the number of remarried or "blended" families. Each is a family just as surely as the mother-father-son-and-daughter type is. The members have the same needs to be loved and cared for. They face the same challenges in supporting one another's growth and development. When they do not conform to the traditional view of what a family is, in fact, they face additional challenges because society is organized around its own stereotype of a family.

The modern conception of family must account for an increasing variety of human situations if today's substance abuse professionals are to help their clients effectively. In each case, the treatment professional must evaluate who is of importance in a given system—that is, who is considered family—and who should therefore be included in treatment.

Family Functioning

Family therapists have found several concepts helpful in describing the patterns they observe in families. These universal patterns are found in all families, not just families who are having difficulties. The following is an overview of common patterns of family functioning, including discussion of rules, roles, communication, proximity, and boundaries and hierarchy.

Rules

All families operate according to a recognizable set of principles and have unspoken as well as spoken rules. For instance, it might be openly stated and known to everyone that no one may interrupt Mom when she is talking; it might be unspoken but equally known to everyone that anyone can interrupt Dad. The rules themselves will differ from family to family; the fact that rules exist does not.

Roles

Roles, too, are a universal aspect of family operation, defining each member's function in the family. For example, a thirteen-year-old girl might be a student, the caretaker of the family pet, the family heroine who inspires familial pride through her success in school, and the family "switchboard" who carries messages from person to person.

In assessing family functioning, the counselor should look at the degree of rigidity in family rules and roles. Some families so rigidly adhere to rules and roles that it is difficult for them to adapt to the changing needs of family members or changing circumstances in the environment. On the other hand, other families may flexibly alter rules and roles when they encounter changing needs, thereby preserving order while adjusting to change. In some families, rules and roles are so flexible and ever-changing that chaos results. No one knows who is in charge, whose job it is to feed the dog, pay the bills, or make sure the children get to school on time.

Communication

Family members perpetuate rules and roles by communicating their intentions and needs through a variety of means, both verbal and non-verbal. Their communications may be generally clear and consistent, or vague, confusing, and inconsistent. The pattern of communication in a family is itself a powerful message to family members. When parents communicate to their child what behavior is acceptable and what is not, they also communicate the more subtle, but far-reaching message that they are in charge. Conversely, of course, when the child tells the parents what he or she will do (or fails to consult them at all), this pattern establishes that the child is in charge. Confusion arises when the parents say they are in charge but the transactions make it clear to all that they are not. A kind of ambiguity is set up that makes it difficult for family members to trust their own perceptions, contributing to a sense of unreality in the family.

Proximity (Closeness and Distance)

Relationships are established and constrained by the family's patterns of communication. Some relationships are close, and the family members are quite available to one another. Other relationships are distant, and the members would not think to call on one another for help and support. In most families, closeness ebbs and flows in relationships. A marriage may experience times of closeness, when much energy goes into the relationship, and times of more distance, when each individual focuses on his or her own needs and development. A small child requires a great deal of closeness and access to his or her parents, whereas an adolescent will strive to create distance and independence. Issues of proximity become problematic when the relationships become rigid or interfere with the developmental needs of family members. A teenager who still has the amount of closeness with and dependence on his parents that one would expect to see between parents and a three-year-old will have difficulty meeting the demands for autonomy that come with adolescence.

Boundaries and Hierarchy

Some family members display appreciation of one another as distinct beings and respect one another's rights to this individuality. Others seem confused about their separateness and become anxious when family members think or act independently. These abstract demarcations between individuals are called boundaries. Boundaries also exist between the subgroups in a family. For example, the generational boundary between the parent and child subsystems may be clear, with the parents demonstrating their difference from the children by exercising authority in the family. The boundary is said to be unclear when the children hold more authority than the parents; that is, confusion arises regarding the distinction between parents and children in the family. This distribution of power demarcated by subsystem boundaries is referred to as the family hierarchy.

The Long View of the Family: The Family Life Cycle

Although families can be characterized in terms of the previous concepts, such a description is a static "slice-in-time" look at a family. A family does not simply come into existence as it is, nor will it necessarily stay the way it is. Families come to be as they are over time. They pass through developmental stages much similar to the stages that define individual development. The family systems view of the life cycle, though, focuses on the reciprocal nature of role definition and personal development. A couple marries, and the man becomes a husband and the woman, a wife. They must renegotiate their relationships with their respective families of origin to allow for the presence of the spouse. If they cannot form a solid boundary around themselves as a new couple, the marriage will be threatened. A baby is born, and the woman becomes a mother, the man, a father. They must now adjust their marital relationship to make room for the child and again realign their relationships with their parents to allow for the new parenting and grandparenting roles. When the child leaves home, the couple must again change their roles, leaving behind mother and father as primary roles and again emphasizing the primacy of the spousal relationship. The repetition of these realignments over the generations puts the family in its historical context.

When a family fails to negotiate a transition successfully or to resolve a major issue, the family members will carry with them the messages inherent in that failure, and they may pass along these messages in their parenting of the next generation. Thus, a process develops whereby the family attempts to work out similar issues over the generations. If one generation solved the struggle of a child's leaving home by the child leaving precipitously through some sort of trouble (a teen pregnancy or involvement with the justice system, for instance), oftentimes a child in the next generation will have similar difficulties at the same transition point.

Each stage in the life cycle presents a challenge to all involved. Negotiating the transitions is a mutual undertaking. The success of an individual in meeting his or her challenges in these transitions depends in part on the success of the other family members in meeting their own. In this respect, each transition represents a potential snag in the fabric of individual and family development.

Summary

When counselors meet with families, it is important for them to remember that the people sitting in the room with them represent only the tip of the iceberg of the system in which they are trying to make a change. The family is a system nested within other systems, and it is made up of individuals who themselves can be seen as systems. Family therapists try to identify the patterns of interaction between family members that are hindering the proper functioning of the family and then try to change those patterns. However, it is important to remember that the patterns of interaction observed in the present represent the tip of another iceberg. The family is not a static entity; it changes over time. The problematic interaction patterns that bring the family to treatment have a unique history, and their resolution will have a positive impact on the future. Helping such a complex enterprise as a family change its habitual patterns of interaction, and thereby solve its problems, is not an easy task. The following section considers the various schools of family therapy to see how this task can be accomplished.

MAJOR SCHOOLS OF FAMILY THERAPY

Family therapy is a dynamic, evolving discipline, and not all the models contained in it fit neatly into schools. However, some recognizable approaches to working with families can be considered schools of family therapy. A variety of such schools is described here to give the reader a sense of the breadth of the field of family therapy. The model presented in this book is based primarily on an approach known as solution-focused family therapy—a school of family therapy described in detail later.

Intergenerational Family Therapy

Intergenerational family therapy is based on the work of Murray Bowen (1978) and others who focused on the processes among generations in families. Problems are seen as the product of intergenerational patterns of unresolved issues and inadequate emotional separation among family members. The therapist helps family members to recognize the patterns, to understand the family legacy, and to see that they are not at fault and are free to change their own behaviors.

A widely used technique in this kind of family work is the construction of a family genogram, a kind of family tree that includes information about major events, losses, relationships, and other factors of importance to the family's issues. The genogram elucidates the family's intergenerational patterns. In the Bowen model of intergenerational family therapy, the therapist keeps the affective level of the sessions low and acts as a coach to the family members working on behavior change. Even therapists who primarily apply other models of treatment in their work draw on the concepts and constructs from the intergenerational school and frequently use genograms in their work with families.

Structural and Strategic Family Therapy

The structural and strategic family therapy approaches are distinct but closely related and compatible. They are commonly referred to together, as they are here, and represent a major school of therapy within which a number of specific models can be categorized. The structural approach is the offspring of Salvador Minuchin (1974; Minuchin and Fishman, 1981) and his colleagues at the Philadelphia Child Guidance Clinic, including Jay Haley (1976, 1997), whose work with Cloe Madanes (1981, 1984) later spawned the strategic approach. Strategic work is very problem focused and does not aim to achieve understanding or insight but to resolve the presenting problem. As in structural therapy, it focuses on the here-and-now family organization as defined by the observed patterns of interaction.

Similar to family therapists in general, structural and strategic therapists see the interactive behaviors of family members as communications. Patterns in these communications govern the functioning of family members, defining for them a range of behavior and influencing their further interactions with one another. From a structural point of view, a functional family organization is one that supports the members' individuality while still providing a sense of belonging. It reflects a clear understanding of the distribution of authority. When there are problems in a family, the boundaries are often unclear and the distribution of authority is confused and incongruous. Problems arise in part because the family's worldview constrains it from seeing the situation differently and conceiving of alternative responses.

Structural family therapy aims to reorganize the family into a more functional structure in order to solve the presenting problem. Interventions aim to challenge the family's view of the problem and expand its options for response. They also alter the family's interactions to clarify boundaries and authority. Classic structural interventions include reframing situations to change perceptions and beliefs. Identification and enactment of both spontaneous problem-related interactions and alternatives in the sessions are also commonly employed.

Strategic therapy shares a concern about organization with structural approaches, but it focuses on more circumscribed patterns, called interactional sequences. Sequences are the specific patterns of interaction that surround problem behavior. Strategic interventions are very directive and are aimed at disrupting the interactional sequences that lead to the presenting problem. In this approach, the therapist takes much responsibility for inducing change. Strategic interventions employ creative "reframes"—new ways of looking at situations—and many interventions involve the use of play and pretense to disrupt ingrained patterns of behavior. Strategic work also employs paradoxical interventions, in which a directive seems in some way contradictory to the desired change but actually puts the individual or family in a kind of therapeutic bind, thereby inducing change. Some people characterize the directiveness of the strategic therapist and the frequent use of paradoxical techniques as manipulative, but this approach is extremely effective in solving specific presenting problems, and because that is the goal of therapy, as Haley points out (1976), the therapist is serving the family.

Experiential and Communications Family Therapy

Experiential family therapy approaches are difficult to classify and describe precisely because they are so experiential and spontaneous in nature. Experiential family therapy is the least theoretical of all the approaches. The most widely known family therapist whose work is clearly experiential is Carl Whitaker (Connell, Mitten, and Bumberry, 1999; Napier and Whitaker, 1978; Whitaker and Bumberry, 1988), a psychiatrist who, with his colleagues in Atlanta in the 1950s, pioneered the experiential approach to psychotherapy. Whitaker stresses what he sees as the danger of theory as the basis for psychotherapy and instead emphasizes the importance of intuition and creativity. By avoiding theory and technique, Whitaker believes that he forces families to develp their own theoretical basis for living. He stresses the importance of the therapist being genuine with the family as it struggles to solve its problems. Whitaker is known for insisting that many family members from all living generations be involved in the therapy.

Personal growth of the individual members within the supportive context of the family is emphasized in this approach to family therapy. Although Whitaker works with large family systems in the room, he and other experiential therapists often focus attention on the family members one at a time, rather than working back and forth or facilitating interaction among the members of dyads or groups, as the structural and strategic therapists do. This is reflective of the Gestalt influence in experiential family therapy. Therapeutic change comes about through enhanced awareness, which expands each person's sense of choice in his or her own behavior.

Whitaker advocates the use of a cotherapist and quality supervision because he believes that it is personal support, not theory and technique, that allows the therapist to do his or her best work.

Virginia Satir (1972, 1983) is sometimes classified as an experiential therapist, although her work is just as often called communications therapy. In spite of her involvement with the highly theory-based communications people in Palo Alto, she focused more on dynamic work with families than on theory and so is difficult to place squarely within one school of thought or practice. She believed that low self-esteem, reinforced by family members, is the basis for dysfunction.

Satir used creative techniques that were very experiential in nature, including family sculpting, in which the family members are helped to assemble themselves into physical configurations that reflect their perceptions of their relationships and their roles in the family. This technique is illustrative of Satir's focus on helping family members become more aware of their experience of themselves and one another.

Social Learning and Cognitive and Behavioral Family Therapy

A number of family therapy models (for example, see Falloon, 1988; Fishman, Rotgers, and Franks, 1988) draw on learning theories and extensively use cognitive and behavioral techniques to effect change. These models often focus on identifying the specific skills that family members need to solve their problems and then teaching those skills. Finally, efforts are made to ensure that the skills are used by practicing them, reinforcing their occurrence, and changing the cognitive processes that prevent them from being used. Cognitive and behavioral approaches are the basis of parent training, which can be helpful in the treatment of some adolescent problems. The social learning approach has also been used to teach couples communication and problem resolution skills.

Feminist Family Therapy

Although the leaders of the movement point out that feminist family therapy is a perspective rather than a school of therapy or a new method, its impact on the practice of family therapy warrants mention here.

Within the context of the feminist consciousness that arose in the early to mid-1970s, four prominent family therapists, Marianne Walters, Betty Carter, Peggy Papp, and Olga Silverstein (Walters and The Women's Project in Family Therapy, 1988), came together to critique the family therapy leadership for its gender biases. Building on a groundbreaking work by Hare-Mustin (1978), they defined for themselves a feminist framework that recognized gender as an organizing principle in society, in general, and in family life, in particular. They sought in this framework to include the experience of women in all formulations of human experience and to eliminate the dominance of male assumptions. Their conception of feminism did not blame individual men for the patriarchal social system but attempted to understand the system as it existed.

These four family therapists formed The Women's Project in Family Therapy. They explored ways in which family systems theory and family therapy had failed to acknowledge and deal with the impact of gender and examined family systems concepts for indications of patriarchal assumptions. For example, the notion of "overcloseness" in relationships as problematic may simply reflect an undervaluing of the more traditionally feminine way of relating to others and an assumption that the more distant, traditionally male way of relating is better. Another aspect of the same issue is the tendency to assume that the mother who is "overclose" to a child in the family is keeping the father distant, rather than responding to a legitimate fear of the vacuum that might exist if she retreated or backed off.

The current and ongoing work of the feminists is the development of nonsexist and feminist systemic interventions and revision and adaptation of traditional interventions to take gender into account. These interventions are informed by a set of feminist guidelines that serves as a reminder of the reality of female experience. That is, these guidelines remind the therapist to recognize the real limitations of female access to social and economic resources and the dilemmas and conflicts of childbearing and child rearing in our society. They also encourage affirmation of the values and behaviors characteristic of women and recognition of the basic principle that no intervention is gender free.

Feminist thought cuts across the schools of family therapy and can be applied within different theoretical and practical frameworks and in different settings. It has changed how many therapists look at their clients and the options they conceive for them.

GOALS AND TECHNIQUES:
WHAT AND HOW FAMILY THERAPISTS
HELP PEOPLE CHANGE

The schools of family therapy vary somewhat in their definitions of therapeutic goals, although they generally focus on the resolution of problems, as opposed to the restructuring of personality. By virtue of its focus on problem resolution, much family therapy is relatively short-term work. Indeed, some models of family therapy are designed to be conducted in very few sessions. For example, in a survey of selected American Association for Marriage and Family Therapy (AAMFT) clinical members, it was learned that 42 percent of family therapy cases are terminated within ten sessions, 68 percent within twenty sessions, and 88 percent within fifty sessions. Families are often told that it is not unusual to hit a "snag," resolve the issues with a little help, and then move on, to return later if they again need help. Of course, the duration of treatment varies with the nature, severity, and chronicity of the presenting problem and the characteristics of the family.

Family therapy is an approach that can be applied to a wide variety of problems. When indicated, family therapists work in conjunction with other professionals, including psychiatrists, to set appropriate goals and manage cases of great complexity.

One of the ways family therapy differs most clearly from other approaches is its understanding of how people change and the therapeutic techniques derived from this understanding. Family systems theory leads to the assumption that people can change in response to changes in their here-and-now interactions with others.

Other differences from traditional treatment approaches are often more ones of emphasis, rather than absolute differences. For example, family therapy is less reliant on insight than psychodynamic models of therapy, although awareness of self is valued. And although family therapy does not focus heavily on the past, the importance of history is recognized. Family history is explored to establish patterns of experience or behavior and elucidate family rules or legacies. Otherwise, the therapy tends to focus on the here and now and is not concerned with what caused a problem, but with what seems to maintain it. Many family therapy interventions are designed to create the experience of different behavior for family members, who can then support one another's efforts to change.

Common family therapy techniques include reframing, which means relabeling or otherwise redefining behaviors or situations and/or changing the context presented. For example, if a mother describes her teenage son's behavior as "running out on me" and "running off to his father's house when I get angry," the therapist might reframe the behavior by saying, "So this is a boy who takes a break when the tension gets high." This allows the mother to conceive of the son's behavior as something other than a rejection of her and provides a starting place for figuring out how the son could take a break without "running off."

Reframes are generally used to expand the family members' views or to reorient them in relation to their own or one another's behaviors or motives. Usually, a more positive, benevolent view is introduced, although there are occasions when the severity of a situation has to be punctuated with a reframe to a more negative view. An example of this might be when a parent is inadequately concerned about the depressed affect of a suicidal adolescent and calls it "pouting." The therapist might relabel the youngster as being "in tremendous pain" and the situation as "urgent."

Other typical family therapy interventions involve teaching communication skills or changing the patterns of family communications in the sessions by blocking certain interactions and encouraging others. Often, the therapist will combine these approaches and then explore with the family what it was like for them to be different with one another in this way. For example, if Dad always interrupts when Mom speaks to their teenage daughter critically, the therapist might point this out and block the pattern by stopping Dad from interrupting, allowing Mom and Daughter to finish their dialogue, and then discussing what it was like for all of them to have done this sequence differently.

In many family therapy approaches, the benefits as well as the costs of problem behaviors are explored, and the benefits of one person's behavior for others are especially emphasized. To continue with the previous example, the therapist might inquire about what the behavior sequence "gets for each of you." She or he might speculate whether Dad prevents Mom and Daughter from fighting to keep the tension down, which also keeps them from ever really resolving their issues. Does Mom get attention from Dad but feel unsatisfied because it is unpleasant attention? Does Daughter get some highly desired adolescent distance from Mom and Dad but also feel insecure about their tension and the threat to their relationship? Daughter's behavior may serve to engage Mom and Dad with each other and provide them with someone else to focus on so they avoid tension over their own relationship issues. These ways of exploring behaviors and their benefits and costs allow the family to recognize that many possible explanations and motivations exist for each member's actions. This is often more important than whether a particular explanation fits.

The use of metaphor is also a common technique in family therapy practice. Metaphors can help family members grasp the meaning of something, understand a problem, and/or envision alternative outcomes. In some cases, a metaphor or story may be complex and its relevance to the family's situation is overtly made clear; the metaphor is used to plant ideas. In other cases, a metaphor creates an analogy that is shared with the family and that may evolve into an ongoing theme in the therapy. For example, a teenage girl who is withdrawn and self-conscious might be likened to a butterfly in the chrysallis stage, hidden away in a cocoon, developing her inner and outer beauty and her strength. The story might continue to say that one day she will emerge and live happily in a lovely garden.

Family therapists also create change within the therapy sessions through very active, symbolic interventions, such as moving the family's chairs around or asking family members to change seats with one another in order to change images of relationships. For instance, when it emerges in a session that one parent perceives himself or herself to be "in the middle" between the other parent and a child, it is very common to notice that, indeed, that parent has unconsciously placed his or her chair between the other two. The family members might then be asked to switch chairs so that the parents are together to one side of the child. Sometimes the therapist will ask the family members to arrange themselves physically in ways that illustrate how they perceive themselves in relation to one another. This technique is called family sculpting and can create very powerful images that allow family members to gain new understanding of how others experience them.

Family therapists may also direct activities, such as parents playing with children or spouses touching each other in expressions of support or affection. Sometimes they assist the family to perform a task, such as working out a rule or a consequence for an adolescent child, perhaps developing a whole "contract" or set of agreements about rules and consequences. Parents might be helped to develop a plan for enforcing their authority and for monitoring the adolescent's compliance with rules. Family therapists also give "homework assignments," which might ask the family to accomplish similar tasks or to try out new behaviors outside the session.

The variety of family therapy interventions is enormous, and even standard interventions are often used very creatively in particular situations. Many of the publications in the reference list describe family therapy interventions in more detail and variety (see, for example, Falloon, 1988; Fisch, Weakland, and Segal, 1982; Fishman, Rotgers, and Franks, 1988; Haley, 1976; Hecker and Deacon, 1998; Imber-

Black, 1988; Madanes, 1981, 1984; Minuchin and Fishman, 1981; Nelson and Trepper, 1994, 1998; Nichols, 1984).

To summarize, although they may differ in emphasis, the schools of family therapy share a theoretical basis and many of the same techniques and interventions. All view the family as a system developing over an intergenerational life cycle. All recognize the existence of many systems in the context of the individual and the family and share the perception of the family as the most important system in the context of the developing child or adolescent. And all concentrate on changing the patterns of interaction in the family as a way to solve the problem that has brought the family to treatment.

FAMILY THERAPY MISUNDERSTOOD: THE ISSUES OF PARENT BLAME, BIOLOGICALLY BASED DISORDERS, AND THE DISEASE MODEL OF ADDICTION

Because the systems view is radically different from the usual assumptions about human behavior and causality, family systems theory is not widely understood by the general public or by some non-systems-oriented mental health professionals, giving rise to misconceptions about its purpose and ideas.

Parent Blame

Advocates for troubled adolescents and children and their families have been suspicious or skeptical of mental health professionals in general, fearing that parents will be blamed for the problems of their offspring. This legitimate fear grows out of the history of parent blaming in the field of mental health and the child guidance movement in the 1920s and 1930s. Also, parent blaming was blatant in the early research on families and schizophrenia. That legacy of blame continues to make people skeptical of those who want to address the family in treatment. As already noted, though, family systems theory eschews the very notion of linear cause and effect in human behavior and is thus inherently nonblaming. Indeed, the focus in family therapy is less on who or what caused the problem and more on what must change for the problem to be solved. In this sense, the issue of blame is a moot point, and families often feel empowered when they are given a direct role in helping one of their members to change.

Biologically Based Disorders

Another controversy arises out of the limited understanding of systems theory combined with the history of early family research on schizophrenia, which ignored possible biological factors. Some parents and health professionals believe that family systems theory is not compatible with the concept of biologically based mental disorders.

In fact, however, family systems theory is not inherently in conflict with the concept of biologically based disorders that reside within an individual patient. Systems theory acknowledges the importance of biological and psychological processes as well as family interaction and other social experience in all human behavior.

The Disease Model of Addiction

In a similar controversy, some professionals think that family systems theory is incompatible with the disease or medical model of addiction. Actually, this is not true. Unlike the medical model, the family systems model does not purport to explain the cause of drug abuse or addiction, but only to explain an important part of what sustains the pattern and could help to change it. There can be little doubt that biochemical and family relationship factors—and many others—influence continuing drug use. Thus, treatment professionals must recognize the biological factors in drug use—including the effects of the drugs themselves—and recognize that parents are an important resource for teenagers in the effort to stop use of alcohol and other drugs and to avoid relapse.

Family members offer the possibility of much-needed support for an individual's ongoing program of recovery, even though they may be struggling with their own issues. These issues sometimes include their own abuse of alcohol and other drugs. Substance abuse in the family affects all family members' lives and must be addressed. Its impact on individual family members is most effectively addressed when those members are involved in the treatment.

It is clear that the key to reliable treatment of alcohol and other drug abuse is not yet known. Successful treatment for these difficulties, however, must surely be informed by all relevant research and treatment experience. The disease model and the family systems model are not mutually exclusive. Instead, they represent different pieces of the same reality and together inform professional work with a richness neither framework alone can offer.

That richness is evident in the concept of codependency, which arose in the addictions treatment literature and is at the same time inherently systemic in nature. That is, codependency focuses on how a person behaves *in relation to others.* Codependency is related to boundary definition and the regulation of closeness and distance in relationships. These concepts are fundamental to family systems theory.

Therapy with these codependent clients often focuses simultaneously on the futility and costs of overinvolvement with the abuser and on the appropriateness and value of loving support for him or her. Al-Anon, Alateen, and Families Anonymous can be important sources of personal support for these ideas. Thus, the addictions treatment community and the family systems community share an understanding that can be a springboard for collaboration.

Differences in Terminology

The differences in terminology employed by family therapists and other disciplines may have contributed to the misunderstandings discussed here. The terms *disease* and *mental illness* have been controversial in the field of family therapy. The reluctance to use these terms, which are widely applied in the medical community and in substance abuse treatment, has sometimes led to alienation between family treatment professionals and others. In many instances, the use of alternative terms by family therapists is a therapeutic technique and does not imply denial of a biological basis for disordered behavior or affect. For instance, family systems therapists have historically used the term *problem* rather than *disease* to refer to the situations and behaviors presented by clients as the focus of treatment. Family systems literature refers to the "identified patient," leading some to believe that the patient is not really seen as the patient at all. Critics think the implication is that there is no disease or illness, only a problem, perhaps caused by the "unidentified patients" in the family.

Indeed, it is true that family therapists do not limit their attention to one member of the family—the identified patient. The very nature of family systems work dictates that the focus be on the whole family system. In addition, many family therapists resist the term *illness* because the sick role often includes helplessness, leading individuals or families to see themselves as helpless to change even those behaviors which are under their own control. Referring to a "problem" is often a way of classifying the behavior as manageable in order to help families exercise their competence.

Throughout this book, reference is made to problems and solutions. It is understood that, in some cases, a family member may indeed suffer from biologically based disorders that cannot currently be cured, but that can be coped with or handled. These include not only those conditions which we assume to have an organic component, although that component is yet to be identified, but those which are clearly biological, such as an adolescent with diabetes. In this instance, the problem referred to might be the stress perceived by the family and those aspects of behavior—both the adolescent patient's and his or her family's—that can be changed to some extent to bring relief to all family members. Such changes might require the use of medication, education, family therapy, self-help groups, or all of these. The changes effected and the family's relief would constitute the solution. In other cases, the meaning of the terms *problem* and *solution* are obvious.

Finally, the term *dysfunctional family* has been used in both the addictions and family therapy fields. Although many people have found relief and help by recognizing that problems in their families profoundly affected them, labeling families as dysfunctional can be a harmful and offensive practice. In fact, behaviors, not persons, are dysfunctional. That is, certain behaviors do not accomplish their intended goals (their functions) and/or result in unintended detrimental effects. The label dysfunctional reduces the family to a simple, negative force. In reality, families are complex systems and have strengths as well as weaknesses.

FAMILY-CENTERED TREATMENT IN A VARIETY OF SETTINGS

Whatever approach they use, the aim of family therapists is to help families as they struggle to meet the variety of challenges that confront them. Currently, family therapy is practiced in a variety of inpatient and outpatient, public and private, substance abuse and mental health treatment settings. The variety of settings in which family therapy approaches are practiced is reviewed here in order to emphasize that this approach can be an important part of treatment in many different settings.

Family-centered treatment is offered in many outpatient settings in both the mental health and drug abuse treatment fields. Settings include private practices and privately run programs, community mental health centers, and public substance abuse treatment programs. Many outpatient settings represent public-private partnerships, with private programs delivering services under grants or contracts from federal, state, or local governments. In these outpatient settings, families are often included in educational programs and individual and multifamily group therapy.

Under some circumstances, outpatient services are delivered in the family's home, especially when a child or adolescent is the focus of concern. Although home-based and crisis intervention services have a long history, the family preservation movement spawned a new interest in these programs, which typically offer crisis services to adolescents in danger of hospitalization or other out-of-home placement. They represent a community effort toward family preservation in most cases, though private insurers and managed mental health care companies are also becoming interested in these models because of their potential for cost-saving reductions in hospitalizations. Some of these programs are based on a family systems model and emphasize ongoing work with the families. Others are based on crisis intervention theory and assist the family through the crisis but do not provide long-term assistance. Such programs may refer families to outpatient family-centered treatment when the crisis has been resolved.

In inpatient settings, both public and private, substance abuse patients have historically been isolated from their families, often only being allowed to see them during brief visiting hours. Increasingly, though, families are involved in the inpatient care of their family member in both hospitals and residential substance abuse treatment programs. Once an individual is admitted to an inpatient facility, the family is involved in many treatment activities similar to those which take place in outpatient settings, including educational presentations and individual and multifamily group therapy. Some residential programs are exploring more innovative ways to involve families. In adolescent residential programs, for instance, parents are consulted when their adolescent acts out, and they are asked to recommend disciplinary tactics that the treatment staff will then employ. Other programs are making arrangements for families to stay on the grounds for several days at a time while they participate in their family members' treatment. A family focus in the treatment helps maintain an ongoing sense of involvement and prepares both the patient and the family for living together again.

Increasingly, inpatient facilities refer patients to aftercare programs following discharge. Many of these programs include the family in their activities in an attempt to facilitate the transition of the patient back into daily life. Their very existence acknowledges the systemic notion that the environment is a powerful influence in recovery and, similarly, that the returning patient is a powerful influence in the family's behavior.

Another setting in which family-centered treatment is taking place represents a relatively new concept in the treatment of substance abuse—day treatment or partial hospitalization programs. An even stronger family link can be maintained in these programs than in residential (overnight) programs because the patient sleeps at home and thus continues to live with his or her family. In addition, these programs can offer virtually the same treatment modalities as full hospitalization, but at greatly reduced costs.

The community itself is also a setting in which a family-centered approach to substance abuse problems has emerged. An increasing variety of community-based self-help groups target substance-abusing individuals and their families. These groups are familiar to all substance abuse counselors and include Alcoholics Anonymous, Narcotics Anonymous, Al-Anon, and Alateen. Alateen and Al-Anon, the self-help groups for families of alcoholics, reflect a systemic view of the interplay between the alcoholic and the family. Families Anonymous, a more recent addition to the list of twelve-step programs, targets the families of adolescents specifically. There are also numerous other self-help groups not based on the twelve-step model. These target a variety of specific problem situations. Through the Toughlove program, for instance, parents of adolescents who are acting out or severely misbehaving give one another both emotional support and practical help in dealing with their youngsters.

The very notion of self-help reflects the systemic, ecological understanding of human experience—that is, through interaction with others, meaning is created, needs are met, and behavior is influenced. The increasing development of self-help groups for the families of adolescents reflects a recognition of the interdependence and mutual influence among family members.

Families are increasingly afforded a central role in the treatment of substance abuse in many settings. Efforts are under way in both public and private settings to involve families in ways that hold promise for keeping them together. Even in the presence of enthusiasm and hard work, however, a number of factors constitute barriers to the full realization of the goal of community-based, family-centered care.

Barriers to Family-Centered Treatment

The organization of substance abuse and mental health services has long been based on the individualistic view of human experience. When it was believed that patients needed to break away from their parents to complete their development, treatment attempted to facilitate the patients' emancipation, and service organizations that furthered the rift between families and individuals in treatment were not seen as dysfunctional or counterproductive. Because of this history, a philosophy of individualism underpins the established services available. The need to reorient the philosophies of a large number of people involved in the treatment community presents a barrier to the implementation of a family-centered approach to treatment.

The categorical organization of treatment services also presents an impediment to a family focus. For example, substance abuse services may be separate (both geographically and administratively) from mental health services, creating difficulty for patients who need both. In addition, services that treat only one aspect of an individual's behavior miss the interrelationship of the biological, cognitive, social, emotional, and contextual factors that create the behavior. This lack of coordination among services represents a barrier to successful treatment, since some services may be duplicated while others are lacking. It is unrealistic to expect that a family can participate in a patchwork of uncoordinated services and programs.

Financial and practical issues also constitute a barrier. The financing rules, program policies and procedures, record-keeping practices, staffing patterns, and many aspects of service delivery are organized to serve individual patients or clients with specific diagnoses, rather than families in trouble. Treatment services for other family members and social services that might be helpful in coordinated combinations are offered in isolation from one another and sometimes even work at cross-purposes.

Financing presents both ethical and practical problems, in that reimbursement for treatment services is most often dependent on an individual being diagnosed with a mental disorder. This focuses attention on individuals and presents problems regarding whose health insurance benefits are to be used when a whole family is seen in treatment. Many other issues are related to the traditional structure of insurance benefits and the limitations of other sources of funding for family involvement in treatment as well.

Administrative concerns include the need for coordination both within programs and across service divisions. For example, the juvenile justice system is intimately involved with many of the same young people who are involved in substance abuse and mental health treatment services, but collaboration or coordination of treatment is often left to conscientious individual professionals who must negotiate through obstacles present in the existing systems.

Alcohol and other drug abuse and mental health treatment services themselves are often not coordinated, even though they are closely related and serve many of the same clientele. The administration of these services is separate in most states and localities. Even when they reside within the same department or agency, the coordination effort is challenging. The effort to cooperate, however, can be facilitated by a shared commitment to "family-centeredness" as the organizing principle among intake, referral, and treatment services.

Some individually focused professionals are concerned that family-centered treatment violates client confidentiality, and this belief constitutes yet another barrier. Family therapists are keenly aware of the potential problems related to confidentiality among family members but have developed approaches that prevent its standing in the way of effective treatment of the family.

Despite these obstacles on the road toward family-centered treatment services, a growing number of service providers have begun to work toward this goal. A final barrier that many programs face is the lack of clear, effective models for working with families in substance abuse treatment. This book is an attempt to provide substance abuse counselors with such a model. Although the challenges of working with families in treatment are many, the rewards make facing those challenges worthwhile. It is hoped that the model developed in this book will help guide substance abuse counselors through the challenges of including families in treatment.

Chapter 3

What Makes a Difference
in Treatment?

To work well with substance-abusing adults or adolescents and their families, it is important to know what factors help people make changes in their lives. Much of our training in the mental health and substance abuse fields concentrates on learning various models of treatment. Most substance abuse counseling programs, for instance, train students to use such things as twelve-step approaches, psycho-educational group treatment, cognitive-behavioral treatment, and relapse prevention strategies as the basis for their work with clients. The implication of such training is that using these models will lead to change. Surprisingly, however, a review of the research on psychotherapy outcome (Lambert and Bergin, 1994) suggests that the counselor's theoretical model accounts for only about 15 percent of treatment outcome. In other words, 85 percent of what helps people change in treatment has nothing to do with the models we spend most of our time studying and teaching in school.

Initially, this finding seems very discouraging and suggests that we do not know much about how to help our clients overcome their abuse of alcohol and drugs. We should not give up our efforts to be helpful too quickly, however. Rather, we should shift our focus to the other factors that contribute to positive outcomes in treatment and determine how we can use them in the counseling process.

What are those other factors? Miller, Duncan, and Hubble (1997) reviewed the psychotherapy outcome literature and found three other significant contributors to the changes people make in therapy. We think that any approach to treatment must address these factors if it is to have credibility and usefulness. The rest of this chapter will examine these common factors (common because they seem to cut across many diverse treatment models) and lay out the principles of treatment that we think flow from them. Subsequent chapters will describe the ways we have found to put these principles into action in our work with families.

CLIENT CONTRIBUTIONS

Unfortunately, we have to start on another seemingly discouraging note. By far, the largest contributors to therapeutic change are things that the counselor has little or no direct control over. Client contributions and chance events account for fully 40 percent of treatment outcome. In other words, clients' motivation and strengths, actions they decide to take on their own, and things that "just happen" outside of formal treatment sessions play a much greater role in determining treatment outcome than we have traditionally admitted.

What does this mean for counselors? Are we left simply to sit back and wait patiently for our clients to figure out how to change on their own? Although the picture is not quite that grim, the research findings do suggest that we should make some changes in how we work with clients and their families.

Focusing on Client Strengths

Counselors should find ways to recognize the strengths and abilities that clients bring with them to treatment and not just focus on their liabilities. This constitutes a major conceptual shift in a field accustomed to diagnosing client pathology and then formulating plans to ameliorate it. Such a patholo-focused model, based on the paradigm of medical treatment, has historically led us to examine our clients' behavior for evidence of problems. The research literature suggests, however, that we miss too many important resources for change when problems are our sole focus. But if we do not focus on problems, what *do* we focus on? The answer is deceptively simple. We focus on strengths.

Finding What Works for Clients

Primary among our beliefs about treatment is that all clients and families have areas of competence and strength, no matter how hidden they may be by the myriad problems that usually bring substance-abusing families to treatment. Given this, it is more important that we try to find out what is going well for clients than what is not going well. This does not mean that we wish to ignore or minimize problems, only that we want to give strengths and successes top billing.

This stance has several advantages. First, clients whose counselor is interested in what's going well for them are more likely to have hope that they can change and are therefore more likely to remain in therapy. Second, the therapist's job is easier if he or she is guided by the assumption that functional patterns already exist in the clients' lives, and that these need only be capitalized upon for clients to make a change. Often, clients are unaware of healthy or functional patterns in their lives and thus are not able to use them as the basis for change. The counselor, however, by searching for healthy functioning, can orient clients toward what is going well and thereby help them expand the influence of those functional parts of their lives.

A Client Strengths View versus a Problem-Focused View

Because, as mentioned earlier, substance abuse treatment has been largely based on a medical model of diagnosing and treating pathology, a focus on strengths seems suspect at first glance. How can change occur unless problems are focused on and understood? This is an important question, and one that gets to the heart of the differences between solution-focused approaches and traditional treatment. The goal of solution-focused treatment is to solve problems by expanding the strengths and solutions clients already have in their behavioral repertoire, thus squeezing out dysfunctional patterns.

Traditional approaches try to decrease dysfunctional patterns to create room in clients' lives for functional behavior. Since devoting time and attention to various aspects of clients' lives in counseling tends to expand the influence of those aspects, solution-focused therapists target the functional aspects of their clients' lives to expand and foster those helpful actions. In other words, you get what you focus on.

For example, most families come to treatment able to describe in great detail the problems they are having (especially the problems that are caused by one member of the family) but have a hard time talking about areas of competence or strength. To counter this focus on failures and inadequacies, strengths-focused therapists often ask families to pay attention to what goes well between sessions and to report their findings at the next meeting. Since experiences of supposed failure usually bring families to treatment, our request to look at strengths often surprises them, but most return to the next session eager to describe in depth the parts of their families that they are proud of and some of the things that are going right.

The comment we most often hear from families when we assign this task is, "No counselor ever asked us about what's going well before." The counselor's sincere interest in a family's strengths subtly begins to change the way these family members think of themselves—not just as people who have failed in important areas of life, but as people who have *both* strengths and weaknesses. Not only is this a more realistic view, it also points the way to change.

Client Strengths View and Denial

Another worry that substance abuse counselors have is that a focus on strengths is simply siding with clients' denial of their problems. In fact, we had some concern about this when we first began to work with families in which substance abuse was occurring. Would not a competency approach allow everyone in the family to pretend there was no problem when one actually existed? Somewhat to our surprise, we found this was not true.

Two factors seemed to make the difference. First, a focus on *strengths* does not mean that we never discuss *problems*. If people were not having problems, after all, they would not be coming to see us. So we have to talk about what is not going well. However, we want to make sure successes get enough attention so that they can be used to develop stronger and stronger solutions.

The second discovery we made came from our work with adolescents who were being seen in outpatient treatment. Usually they came to treatment with their families after having been arrested or suspended from school for drug use. The arrest or suspension typically created a crisis that made parents more vigilant about their children's drug use and led the adolescents to abstain or use less.

The first couple of family sessions were filled with descriptions of how well things were going. "It's like we have the old Steve back," one mother told us, "the one who talks to me and stays home on school nights and seems so much happier." We spent a lot of time with these families getting a detailed description of what was going differently and complimenting each family member on his or her contribution to the change. Since drug problems rarely go away so easily, however, we also worried that maybe we were ignoring problems lurking just over the horizon.

And we were right, at least in part. Although a few adolescents made a decision to stop using and stuck to it without a hitch, most parents soon came to a session reporting that their adolescent son or daughter had again gotten high or drunk. Although parents were angry or frustrated with this situation, and adolescents were defensive, our earlier focus on strengths and successes made it easier for both adults and adolescents to talk about what had happened and to begin to think through how to make a lasting change. Their firsthand experience that we wanted to know *both* the good and the bad in their family as well as the fact that we had refrained from predicting a relapse and had focused on successes while they were occurring made therapy a safe place; they had less fear that admitting to problems would be met with a face-losing "I told you so" attitude. Thus, an initial focus on strengths did not conceal problems, but it did set the stage for talking about them in a different way when they did arise.

Self-Efficacy

A focus on strengths has another advantage in drug treatment. A growing body of research indicates that self-efficacy, or a realistic belief in one's ability to resist the urge to drink or use, even in high-temptation situations, serves to decrease relapse after treatment. Not only do drug-using adults benefit from a strong sense of self-efficacy (Burling et al., 1989; Goldbeck, Myatt, and Aitchison, 1997; Kavanagh, Sitharthan, and Sayer, 1996; McKay, Maisto, and O'Farrell, 1993; Rounds-Bryant, Flynn, and Craighead, 1997; Sadowski, Long, and Jenkins, 1993; Solomon and Annis, 1990; Stephens, Wertz, and Roffman, 1993), adolescents do as well (Myers and Brown, 1990; Myers, Brown, and Mott, 1993; Robinson and Walsh, 1994). In fact, self-efficacy in general leads people to have more success with a wide variety of health problems whose management depends on making behavioral changes, such as weight loss, smoking cessation, and exercise (Holden, 1991; Kores et al., 1990; Yates and Thain, 1985). When the counselor helps family members look at their strengths and abilities, he or she also helps them feel more able to deal with the difficulties that bring them to treatment, increasing their sense of self-efficacy. Other aspects of solution-focused treatment also instill a sense of self-efficacy in clients, and we will discuss those later. For now, suffice to say that people tend to do better when they feel more able to deal with the problems they face. One goal in our work with families is to realistically increase that sense of ability to cope by pointing out areas where family members are doing well and ways in which they have solved problems in the past.

Many Ways to Solve a Problem

Another implication of the importance of clients' unique strengths and abilities to successful outcome is that it is impossible to predict the best way for any given client to solve a given problem. In fact, there is usually more than one solution to most problems, and problems are solved in many unique ways by the families who struggle with them. Some adolescents, for example, find going to Alcoholics Anonymous (AA) or Narcotics Anonymous (NA) is a way to end drug use. Others change their peer group and begin hanging out with kids who do not use to help themselves stop. Others might be helped by their parents' restricting their access to the car until they prove they are again trustworthy. Some even end drug use by learning to meditate or use biofeedback.

Because we believe many paths and many potential solutions exist, we do not begin therapy with a vision of what the client must do to get better. Instead, we work with the client to identify what pieces of a solution are already in place ("Well, I don't get high when I hang out with kids from my church group") and how those pieces can be joined to help the client solve the problem ("Maybe I could hang out with the church group more"). Thus, the solution to the same problem may be very different for one client than for another; therapy does not take a one-size-fits-all approach.

This assumption can be controversial in the field of substance abuse where so many people have been helped by twelve-step programs and other approaches to drug treatment that propose an invariable process that everyone must go through in order to recover. We want to be clear that we are not suggesting that twelve-step approaches should be abandoned or that they do not work for many people. We do believe, however, that the more families and individuals feel that they have contributed to the design of the treatment they are participating in, the more ownership they will feel in it, and the more likely they are to stick it out when the going gets tough.

An increasing body of research supports this view. Morgenstern and her colleagues (1997) found that the most motivated clients in alcoholism treatment were the ones most likely to become seriously involved in AA, and to continue that involvement. Further, AA participation was associated with better abstinence outcomes, at least in the short run. Therefore, it appears that *motivation* is the underlying curative factor expressed in continuing treatment. Anything that counselors can do to increase client motivation (such as promoting a collaborative sense of ownership in treatment) will work in favor of success.

With families, we try to increase their motivation by giving them a say in their treatment. We ask families what they think will be helpful in solving their problem, and what they envision a solution will look like. Many people find twelve-step groups a valuable part of their recovery, and we support them wholeheartedly. However, we do not rush to prescribe any approach to treatment before we have a clear picture of what the family thinks will be helpful. We also think that discovering what will be helpful is more a process than an event. In other words, it takes time for family members to determine the best way to work on their problem. Initial ideas about what will be helpful may not work as well as they hoped, and they may need to try something else.˙

The Role of the Counselor

If the family becomes the expert on figuring out how to solve its own problems, what is left for the counselor to do? Based on the traditional model of counselor as expert problem solver, that is an obvious question to ask. However, the role of the counselor in our approach is different. Rather than being the one who solves the problem through telling family members what to do, the counselor creates the circumstances under which they can develop their own solutions. One of our students described it this way:

> Penicillin is capable of effectively treating a wide range of maladies. However, penicillin is not a magic bullet. By itself, it is just mold. In fact, penicillin does not really do anything to the different germs for which it is prescribed. Instead, penicillin bolsters the human immune system so that it can successfully eliminate infection. Rarely are people forced to take penicillin, unless of course you are a child. If you choose not to take it you may not get better, you may become sicker, or you may get

better on your own. On the other hand, taking penicillin doesn't guarantee that you will get better. It has to be taken in the right dose, for the proper length of time. You might even be allergic to penicillin and need to take something else. Unfortunately, some problems may be too entrenched or developed to succumb to even the most aggressive medication.

Therapists are like penicillin. At our best, we can be helpful in a broad range of circumstances, but we must also recognize that there are situations that are beyond our capabilities. For the most part, people will choose to enter therapy. It is hard to say for sure what happens to those who do not. We might guess, however, that some families get worse, some manage to continue on, and some figure out how to take care of their problems on their own. The same is true of families who choose therapy. Hopefully, their chances are improved. But, the act of coming to therapy does not guarantee a cure. Instead, it is the therapist's job to help the family activate their resources so they can solve their own problems. (Smith, 1997, p. 1)

This role still calls for much expertise, although of a different kind than we typically associate with being an expert. The counselor is an expert at guiding sessions toward the discussion of strengths and how they might be used in the present circumstances. He or she is also an expert at asking questions that bring to light previously ignored aspects of a family's experience. And the counselor is an expert at patience and acceptance, knowing when to push ahead and when not to. At times, the counselor also shares his or her ideas of what might work with clients. However, he or she makes suggestions, not as the one right way to do things, but tentatively, as "something you might find helpful." The family members can decide if they want to give it a try and then can evaluate the outcome along with the counselor. In short, the counselor functions less like a physics teacher who tells students what the "truth" is, and more like a Zen master who poses questions that lead families to think in different ways and thereby find their own truth.

Emphasizing the Client's Own Change

Another aspect of using client characteristics in treatment involves looking for changes that are already happening in clients' lives. It is our belief that change is a constant and continuous feature of life. The counselor's job is not to create change; it is instead to help clients see the changes already happening in their lives. Once naturally occurring changes have been identified, the influence of those which are desirable can be expanded.

If change is always going on, however, why do clients come to therapy feeling stuck? One answer is that they do not see the changing aspects of their lives because they have a culturally defined view of themselves as constant. Consider, for example, a client who has been told repeatedly that he is a "bad kid." Since our cultural view of personality is that it is a fixed entity that changes only through great effort, any evidence the client encounters that suggests he is not a bad kid will seem irrelevant or incongruent to him. It will not fit his story of who he is, and he will simply dismiss it. If he has a good day at school, he is likely to say it happened only because "my math teacher didn't give me shit like he usually does." If he gets along with his parents for a few days, the explanation may be that "I stayed in my room so they couldn't hassle me."

Part of the therapist's job is to search out those incongruities and highlight them so that new data can enter the client's view of himself. Once these incongruities are found, the counselor then helps the client accept them as part of himself and not an anomaly. A "bad kid" who is very conscientious about taking care of his pet dog, for example, is now not so one-dimensional. He is both a "bad kid" and a "good kid" at the same time, and the therapist has a crack in the "bad kid" story to work with.

Therapists must be sure that they do not help clients trap themselves in a vision of constancy that ignores useful functioning and makes change harder. To do this, solution-focused counselors ask, "When *does* the problem *not* occur?" more often then they ask, "When does it?"

While the 40 percent contribution to change made by client factors and characteristics is something that counselors cannot influence directly, we can do a variety of things to take advantage of these factors and to give them the attention they deserve in therapy. We can search out client strengths, help families formulate their own plans for change, and be constantly on the lookout for evidence of change, no matter what its source. Doing so helps families begin to see their lives as full of flux and change, and themselves as people with a mix of strengths and problems who can likely find a way out of their current dilemmas.

THE THERAPEUTIC RELATIONSHIP

After client characteristics, what contributes most to treatment outcome? Here we move to more familiar ground for counselors, since the next most influential factor is the therapeutic relationship. Clients who give their relationship with their counselor a satisfactory or excellent rating are more likely to achieve their goals in treatment compared to those who do not. Both quantitative and qualitative data support this view. When couples in marital counseling as part of their drug treatment were asked what about therapy was most helpful, one common theme that emerged was their perceived relationship with their counselor (McCollum and Trepper, 1995). In a quantitative study, Connors and colleagues (1997) found that ratings of the therapy relationship were significant predictors of outcome for adult alcoholics in both outpatient and aftercare programs. In fact, 30 percent of outcome in therapy in general can be explained by this factor alone (Lambert and Bergin, 1994).

What are the ingredients of a helpful counselor-client relationship? According to Miller, Duncan, and Hubble (1997), three things emerge from the research. First, it is important for the counselor to accommodate treatment to the clients' level of motivation. A strong body of research in the substance abuse field supports this factor (for a review, see Prochaska, DiClemente, and Norcross, 1992). It is generally not helpful to push clients or families to make dramatic changes when they have yet to acknowledge a problem or the need for change. To do so will likely strain the therapeutic relationship and eventually cause the clients to drop out of treatment. This goes against the grain of more traditional approaches to drug treatment that emphasize a strong confrontational stance on the part of the counselor. However, in working with families, such a stance is not generally useful. Stanton and Shadish (1997), in reviewing the controlled-outcome studies of family and couples therapy for treating drug abuse, note that the involvement of family members significantly reduces treatment dropout rates. One explanation of this is that "unlike therapeutic approaches that use a confrontational approach to drug abuse, just the opposite appears to be the case with family-oriented therapies. Such families are often skittish and ashamed, and a gentle, supportive, positive track is suggested to keep them from abandoning treatment" (p. 186).

A second part of building a strong therapeutic relationship is accommodating clients' goals for therapy and their ideas about intervention. This means that we need to ask families what they want to get from treatment, and what they think can happen in treatment that will be helpful. It is not enough, however, to ask about global goals such as "being happy" or "succeeding in recovery." Goal setting works best when clients and counselors negotiate specific, concrete goals that the clients believe are possible to reach and will make a difference for them. Thus, an adolescent's global goal of "succeeding in recovery" would be broken down into specific actions to be taken to move toward that goal, such as attending two AA meetings a week, spending time with friends who do not use, and getting grades back up to a B average. However, the critical issue is that *the client,* not the counselor, defines the specific steps toward reaching a global goal.

Carl Rogers (1951) began to articulate the third aspect of a successful therapeutic relationship almost fifty years ago when he described the "core conditions" for helping—accurate empathy, respect, and genuineness. These counseling skills are widely taught to new counselors, but attention has been paid mostly to the counselor's and teacher's perceptions of how they are being delivered, and they are often taught in a mechanical manner that has become almost a parody of counseling interactions (remember the old joke—Q: What does Carl Rogers do when you knock on his door? A: He knocks back from the inside). Research suggests (Bachelor, 1991), however, that what is more important than the counselor's perception is the *client's* perception of how empathic, respectful, and genuine the counselor is. We cannot, in other words, rely on our own judgment alone in deciding whether we have formed a helpful alliance with substance abusers and their families. We must solicit their advice about how best to help them.

Clearly, the aspects of a helpful therapeutic relationship that we have just described demand a different stance from the counselor than do more traditional approaches. In order to accommodate the client's view of things—whether that be the family members' readiness for change, their goals for therapy, or their perception of what constitutes a helpful therapeutic relationship—we have to give up the traditional expert role in favor of a more collaborative one in which counselor and clients work together in deciding what treatment will be like. Of course, the counselor contributes his or her opinion to the counseling conversation, but this is done as a potentially helpful suggestion for the family to try, rather than as an expert's prescription of the right way to do things. The final judgment about what is helpful and what is not rests with the family.

We will talk at length later in the book about specific ways counselors can help clients set reachable goals and solicit clients' input about what will be most helpful in therapy.

HOPE AND EXPECTANCY

The third factor that contributes to successful therapy outcome—accounting for about 15 percent of treatment outcome variance—is *hope and expectancy.* Most families and adolescents come to treatment convinced that there are few, if any, alternatives to the troublesome path they are traveling. They have lost hope and have little expectancy for change. For treatment to be successful, the family must find in it the hope that things can be different. The counselor plays a key role in this process through taking several actions. Primary is the counselor's own conviction that solutions can be found and drug abuse and other problems can be left behind. Without this core belief, even the most elaborate attempts to provide hope will fall short and be perceived as only half-hearted by clients and their families.

Given a belief in their clients, counselors can take some specific actions to increase hope and expectancy. First, as we noted in the section on Client Contributions, we can find and highlight changes already happening and strengths already in evidence. What better way to begin to provide hope than to help clients see the areas in which they are already being successful? Creating a new solution to a problem from scratch can seem an overwhelming task if you have little sense of hope to energize you. However, using a strength already in evidence in one area of your life to solve a problem in a different area may seem more achievable because it requires only the use of existing strengths and not the development of brand-new ones.

Another way that the counselor can increase hope is to "separate the problem from the person." The disease metaphor for addiction is one way in which this can be accomplished with substance abuse problems. According to this approach, the person is not a moral failure or a weak person for being addicted. Rather, that person is viewed as having an addictive disease that he or she is not personally responsible for having. Of course, the person is entirely responsible for dealing with this disease, but the problem is seen as separate from the totality of who the person is. Narrative therapists call this process "externalizing the problem" (White and Epston, 1990).

We found a clear example of this when we visited a Native American treatment center in Washington State. One of the topics that was regularly raised in group meetings was the question, "How did alcohol come to Indian country?" The answer, of course, is that Europeans first brought it and often used it against Native Americans, who could be more easily taken advantage of when intoxicated. However, asking this question in treatment groups began to change the problem from one of personal failure to one of cultural oppression. Seeing their addiction in this light often inspired Native American clients to fight hard against this lingering expression of European oppression.

A final, yet very important way that counselors can foster hope in their clients is through shifting the focus of treatment from past failures to future possibilities. Rather than trying to figure out what happened in the past to cause the current problem, solution-focused therapists try to see what is going on in the present that might be used to solve it. They also help clients develop a clear picture of where they want to be in the future so that therapy is always working toward a goal. We will describe the process of negotiating clear goals later, but suffice to say for now that one of the most beneficial things a therapist can do for a client is to help him or her develop a clear vision of where he or she wants to go. Without that, therapy becomes a process of trying to get away from something negative, not of moving toward something positive.

A client whose goal in therapy is to stay away from drugs will have a harder path than a client whose goal is to develop a drug-free life that includes solid relationships, a satisfying job, education, or other pursuits that are incompatible with continued drug use. At least one research study bears this out (Iguchi et al., 1997). The researchers looked at the effect of urine testing, traditional drug treatment, and reinforcing prosocial, non-drug-abuse-related changes on drug use. Only the reinforcement of life changes resulted in a reduction of illicit drug use. Not only was this reduction maintained throughout the follow-up period of the study, it endured even after the reinforcement program was discontinued. So, while working on positive goals may seem to be avoiding the hard issues behind drug and alcohol use, it is an essential ingredient in helping clients reach their goals of abstinence and recovery.

THERAPY MODELS

The final 15 percent of change in treatment is associated with the model-specific actions that counselors take when they interact with clients, such as making psychoanalytic interpretations, constructing behavioral contracts, realigning interpersonal boundaries, and so forth. Miller, Duncan, and Hubble (1997) suggest that models primarily serve us by providing ideas about different ways to act in order to better match client needs and expectations. For instance, biofeedback therapy or behavioral approaches are often a good place to begin with a male client who prefers an active, hands-on approach to problem resolution. Such approaches accommodate the client's views of how problems are solved and progress is made. Using such an approach, however, with a female client who wants to feel understood before she can take action to change will likely fail, since it does not fit her view of what will be helpful. Treatment models, then, are like the tools in a carpenter's toolbox. Different tools fit different jobs, and in the case of working with families, a thoughtful counselor will pick the tool that seems to best fit the situation he or she is faced with and will try another tool if that one does not work.

A FINAL WORD

The assumptions of our model lie at the heart of our work with families. Throughout the rest of this book, we will present a set of techniques that can be used to translate these assumptions into practice. However, we want to be quite clear that it is a *belief in these assumptions* that is fundamental and not the particular interventions we will describe. It is possible to use all of the techniques described and still not believe in the assumptions presented. In doing so, a counselor will appear to be working in a collaborative, solution-focused way but will not truly be doing so. Conversely, it is possible not to use any of the interventions exactly as they appear in the book and still operate from the assumptions we have just described. It is what we assume about our clients and our roles as counselors that makes the difference.

So we ask you to consider carefully your stand on each of the assumptions we have presented. Do you really believe that people who are struggling with addictions have areas of strength and ability in their lives that can be useful in treatment? Are you willing to help clients explore their own thoughts about what will be helpful to them? Are you willing to share both the power and the responsibility for change with your clients in a collaborative relationship? Holding these assumptions is not as simple as it seems, since they challenge many of the things we have all been taught about being counselors, in general, and working with substance abusers and their families, in particular. However, we have found them to be useful in our work and invite you to see if they can be useful in yours as well (see Table 3.1).

TABLE 3.1. Summary: What Makes a Difference in Treatment?

Client Factors	40%	• Existing strengths and competencies • Past and partial solutions
Therapy Relationship	30%	• Matching client motivation • Letting clients set the goals • Empathy, respect, and being genuine
Hope and Expectancy	15%	• Separating the problem from the person • Highlighting competencies • Counselor's belief in change
Therapy Model	15%	• Different tools for different client needs

Source: Adapted from Miller, Duncan, and Hubble, 1997.

Chapter 4

Working with Families:
Basic Skills

"I couldn't believe it," Rhonda said in her supervision session. "I've been working individually with David for six weeks now, but he seemed like a different kid when I finally got his mother to come to a session. When we're alone, he usually tells me what's going on and how he's working on staying straight and about school and things like that. But when his mother came in, he wouldn't look at either of us, he wouldn't talk, he wouldn't do anything. When his mother started to talk about how worried she was about his grades, he said he was tired of listening to her bitch, and he got up and walked right out of the session. He'd never acted like that when I met with him alone. I tried to tell his mother how much better I thought he was doing, but she just said he was lying to me and that nothing had changed. And they're coming back next week. What am I going to do?"

Substance abuse counselors already have many of the skills they need to work with families. These skills—such as developing a good relationship, asking clear questions, gathering useful data, and so forth—come from their training and experience in working with individuals and groups. However, as Rhonda's story illustrates, counselors need to use their skills in somewhat different ways to work adeptly with families. Two things make family counseling different from individual or group counseling: *the power dynamics when more people are in the therapy room* and *the emotional intensity brought into sessions by a family.*

POWER DYNAMICS IN FAMILY THERAPY

The presence of more than one client in the room changes the power dynamics between the counselor and clients. When seeing an individual, the counselor, by virtue of his or her professional role, tends to have more power than the client and can confidently act from a position of authority. When a client is ordered to come to treatment by the court, or coerced by family members through the threat of divorce or other legal action, the counselor's power is increased. Having power does not mean that the counselor acts like a tyrant, only that he or she has a certain ability, for example, to set the agenda, limit the behavior of the client in the office, moderate the level of interaction, and ask questions with the expectation that they will be answered.

When family members come to treatment together, however, some aspects of this power arrangement change. The most obvious difference is that the family members outnumber the counselor. The counselor's job of developing a solid relationship with clients is made more complex when more than one person is in the room, especially when those people do not agree with one another about such basic things as the need to be in counseling, the goals of counseling, and whether a problem even exists.

It is tricky, for example, to help adolescents believe that you will not use family counseling to make them more dependent on their families, while convincing their parents that you will help them gain appropriate control over their drug-using children. Operating from an individual therapy perspective can cause counselors to try to solve this dilemma by labeling one part of the family as "right" and the other as "wrong." The task then becomes to convince the wrong part to become right. Unfortunately, this often backfires.

> Denise's mother brought her to outpatient treatment after Denise was busted with a joint at school. In an individual session, Denise let the counselor know that she had smoked marijuana a few times but that her main concern was that her mother was always trying to tell her what to do. When the counselor met with Denise's mother, a different picture emerged. "I'm worried about Denise's friends. I know she isn't heavily into drugs yet, but you should see the kids she hangs out with. Her teachers tell me they're all users. You've got to do something to help her before she becomes an addict."

In this case, the counselor decided that Denise's mother was being overprotective and anxious and began a campaign to convince her that she did not need to worry so much about her daughter. She enouraged Denise's mother to back off a little and let Denise work on her drug use in the group she was attending as part of her treatment. Although the counselor's position certainly had validity, Denise's mother believed that the counselor did not understand the depth of her concerns and therefore saw the counselor's suggestion that she not worry as an attack. She soon removed Denise from treatment, without either of them being able to discuss and resolve the differences in their relationship, and without Denise being able to benefit from being in group. If they intend to work with family members together, counselors must develop the ability to stay connected to people with different viewpoints about the problem.

EMOTIONAL INTENSITY IN FAMILY THERAPY

A second difference between working with families and working with individuals and groups is that a family system, especially a family system in crisis, can quickly generate a good deal of conflict and emotional intensity when the topic of drug use or other "hot-button" issues come up. Unlike a therapy group of strangers formed for treatment, which develops under the direction of the counselor, families bring with them a history that predates their association with the counselor, and that has many past hurts and emotional currents that are not immediately obvious to outsiders.

> One of our supervisees, Ray, said his first sessions with families felt like walking through a minefield blindfolded. Several times he brought up what he felt was a neutral topic, only to find that underneath it lurked an issue full of explosive emotion. "One day I complimented Sara on her new earrings. Her parents blew up at each other. Mom had let her get her ears pierced without telling Dad, and he started yelling about that right in the session. It took me ten minutes to get things calmed down again, and Dad was mad for the rest of the session."

Since emotional intensity is often present when working with drug-abusing adolescents and their families, counselors must have the ability to anticipate and deal with it.

LEARNING TO JOIN WITH FAMILIES

Carl Whitaker, a pioneering family therapist, once said, "If family therapy is like surgery, the relationship with the therapist is the anesthetic." There has probably never been a more succinct statement of the importance of the relationship between clients and therapist in working with families. Recall, too, that 30 percent of the outcome of any treatment is accounted for by the quality of the relationship between client and therapist (Lambert and Bergin, 1994). Thus, forming a strong relationship, or joining with the client, is vitally important.

Substance abuse professionals are already skilled at joining with clients individually and in groups. The skills that Carl Rogers (1951) described many years ago—accurate empathy, unconditional positive regard, and genuineness—still form the basis for training in most of the mental health professions. There is no substitute for letting clients know that you are taking them seriously, trying to understand their situation as best you can, and trying to be straight with them. However, when working with families, some other skills are also needed in order to join well.

We will discuss joining as if it is a discrete task that is accomplished at the beginning of therapy, but that is not truly the way it is. Joining with clients and attending to the state of your relationship with them is important from the first meeting until the last. In fact, when you find yourself stuck with a client or a family, one of the two most useful questions you can ask yourself is, "How well have I joined with this client?" (We discuss the other useful question—"Do we agree on the goals for therapy?"—later in the book.) In the absence of a well-developed relationship, your efforts to be helpful run the risk of being seen as misguided, naive, or attacking. Denise's counselor certainly experienced this when she tried to convince Denise's mother to worry less before she had joined well.

Establishing Leadership

The primary skill that counselors must have to join well with families is the ability to establish leadership in the session. Doing so demands that therapists take an active and directive stance in their interaction with family members. This stance is often at odds with the more passive stance counselors take when working with individuals and reflects the power differential between counselors and family members that we discussed earlier. Counselors must be active and directive enough from the start to establish control of the therapy. If they are not in control, the families will experience therapy as an unhelpful or unsafe place to talk about their problems and may not return. Without leadership, therapy sessions are destined to turn into a continuation of the repetitive, fruitless conflicts that family members find themselves mired in at home, leaving everyone feeling hopeless and discouraged. Rhonda saw how easily this could happen, as illustrated in the vignette at the beginning of the chapter. Without adequate leadership on Rhonda's part, David and his mother had pretty much the same experience they have at home: when they tried to discuss difficult issues, David got mad and left, effectively preventing them from doing anything that would lead to a different outcome.

What does effective leadership look like? Eric's (McCollum) first clinical supervisor used the metaphor of "directing traffic" to describe how the counselor effectively leads the session. Think for a moment of the last time you saw a police officer directing traffic on a busy road. By carefully and clearly signaling who is to do what and when they are to do it, the officer is able to create a safe environment in which traffic can proceed. However, the officer must be active and directive in order to function effectively. Imagine what would happen if a traffic officer had taken a course in nondirective counseling and decided to use that as a model for directing traffic! The same sort of collisions can occur in families when the counselor is not active enough.

Two caveats about leadership. First, the counselor must attend to leadership right from the beginning of the session. It is much easier to take charge from the beginning and guide the family members to a different experience than it is to try to establish control in the session once they have gotten "past the point of no return" in their familiar conflict cycle. The second caveat is that leadership is not the same as tyranny! Therapeutic leadership is designed not to impose the wishes of the therapist on family members but to promote harmony and balance in their interaction during the session. Counselors accomplish this task by being firm in enforcing the necessary structure of the session as well as by being encouraging, fair, and flexible. Not only does this stance provide a feeling of safety for family members during counseling, it also models the ingredients of effective leadership that the family can use when treatment is over. Breunlin, Schwartz, and

MacKune-Karrer (1992) provide a more extensive discussion of leadership in families.

In addition to leadership, family joining skills are composed of three broad actions: *making contact, balancing interaction,* and *moderating intensity.*

Making Contact

The first step in creating a strong relationship with a family is to make contact with each member. If family members think you have neglected them, or that you are not interested in their views about the problem, their continued participation in therapy is in jeopardy. In addition, they will watch you closely to see how you join with each of them. If you do a poor job of relating to anyone, it will decrease the family's confidence in your ability to be of help.

This applies even to children. When asked what they found most unpleasant about coming to family therapy, children ages nine to twelve said that being left out of the process was the most unsatisfying thing for them (Stith et al., 1996). Younger children feel left out both when they are physically excluded from sessions (e.g., made to stay in the waiting room for most or all of the session after you have asked that everyone in the family attend) and when the session involves only "adult talk" to which the children cannot contribute. If children are to be included, the session must involve activities in which they can participate (e.g., the family making a drawing together).

The counselor can make contact with family members in a number of ways. Begin by introducing yourself to each person who has come to the session. Ask their names and then use their names as you speak to them. It is usually helpful to begin the first session with a period of "small talk" to let the family get to know you and to become comfortable in your office, or wherever else you are meeting with them (e.g., you can ask if they had trouble finding the agency). Since you typically only have information about the family from one member, or maybe just from a referring professional, it is also important to let the family know what you know about them. This serves a number of purposes. First, it gives all family members access to what you know about them and suggests to the family that you do not intend to keep information secret from them. Second, it gives the family a chance to correct any misinformation you might have, and each individual can offer his or her opinion if it differs from what you have heard. Finally, it shows that you intend to listen carefully to all family members' views and not rely solely on information from only one family member or an outside source.

Balancing Interaction

The second skill that counselors use to join effectively with families is the ability to balance interaction in the session. Unlike working with individuals, where the counselor and the client are the only two participants in the session, family members meeting together vie for the attention of the counselor and for the "floor" in sessions. An important part of the counselor's job, then, is to make sure that everyone gets a chance to have a say about the situation that brings them to treatment, that no one dominates the discussion, and that no one fades into the background. If the counselor is unable to effectively balance interaction, the likelihood of all members really participating in the session diminishes. Some may simply not return to family meetings; others may come but not become truly involved in the sessions. Why should they risk involvement, after all, if the counselor has not shown the ability to make space for the views of everyone?

Balancing interaction is not as easy as it sounds. At times the counselor must act in a way that would seem rude in any other circumstances (and may, at first, seem rude to the family) in order to achieve some balance. The counselor can begin the session by setting some ground rules that will help with balance. One useful ground rule is that only one person in the family talks at a time. Especially in anxious or chaotic families, a great deal of confusion can be generated very quickly as family members compete to tell their stories, argue with one another, correct what the others have said, and so on. The counselor will likely not get much useful information if he or she is not successful at having family members talk one at a time.

A second useful ground rule is asking that family members speak for themselves. This involves not letting one family member answer for another, or "mind read" and tell you what the other person really means, or tell the other person that he or she has not given the right answer. Part of what may need to be sorted out in counseling are the varying perceptions that family members have of the situation in which they find themselves. Without being able to hear each person's views, the counselor will not be able to help the family with this task.

Ground rules may set the stage for balancing interaction, but counselors must actively guide the session to make sure that the rules are followed. Such guidance will take the form of "directing traffic," as we described earlier. When it comes to balancing interaction, counselors need to do several things. First, they must do their best not to get drawn into talking to just one person at a time. We both watch many hours of videotape of client sessions conducted by our students as part of supervising them. Nothing is more telling than the looks of boredom or frustration on the faces of family members when the counselor and one member of the family engage in a lengthy conversation that includes no one else. It is as if the counselor is doing individual therapy in front of an audience. Counselors must make every effort to engage all members of the family in interactions with them. How does this work? Consider the following vignette:

> **Counselor:** Okay, let's get started by each of you giving me an idea of why you're here today.

> **Mother:** I'm just at my wit's end with Jerome. He's got four unexcused absences from school already this semester, and then the principal called to tell me that they found marijuana in Jerome's locker. He's got to go to court next week, and he doesn't seem at all concerned about it. I keep trying to tell him that this means he's in big trouble, but all he says is, "'Whatever.'" He's just like his father . . .

> **Counselor:** Wait just a second, Mrs. James. I know there's a lot of background information I need, but you just told me some really important information there, and I want to get Jerome's view before we move on. Jerome, what do you think the reason is that you're here?

In this example, the counselor firmly but politely interrupts Mrs. James and allows Jerome to have a turn at speaking. This prevents the situation of an extended conversation between Mrs. James and the counselor while Jerome sits silently listening to them talk about him as if he were not there.

Another skill that counselors must use during the session is to curtail monologues. Sometimes a family member will talk on and on, preventing even the counselor from having a chance to ask questions or make comments. Frequently, this is part of the family process that is a source of conflict. The longer that the counselor lets it continue, the more dispirited the other family members will become, fearing that even the counselor cannot help them change the habitual but frustrating pattern. Interrupting a monologue is often difficult because it represents a way for the person talking to control the session and thereby keep his or her anxiety at bay. We find it less useful to think of a monologuer as controlling than we do to think of him or her as anxious. Counselors must work to continually insert themselves into the conversation by asking questions, making comments, and even pointing out the process. As a last resort, counselors can simply tell the person talking to stop because no one else is getting a chance to contribute to the session.

A final skill that counselors must use to achieve balance in the session is the ability to draw out quiet or silent family members, if possible. Sometimes people are silent because their style is to remain on the edges of an interaction until they feel safe, or invited, to join in. When this is the case, counselors should use direct questions to elicit an appropriate and detailed response. For example, consider the following situation in which Jeannine has been quiet for several minutes while her husband talks about his drinking problem with the counselor:

> **Counselor:** Jeannine, what have you been thinking while Herb has been talking about his efforts to stop drinking?
>
> **Jeannine:** It's hard for me to listen to him because I really want to believe he's involved in treatment this time, but I've been disappointed so many times in the past. Before, he'd swear to me that this was the time he was going to make it, that he wasn't going to drink at all anymore, and then he'd start coming home later and later, and I knew he was hanging out with his drinking buddies. Pretty soon he was back drinking as much as ever.

Jeannine's answer suggests that she is actively involved in the counseling session even though she has not been talking. This serves as a cue to the therapist to periodically ask her a direct question to make sure that her views are included.

More problematic than a family member such as Jeannine is the one whose silence indicates a wish not to be in counseling at all. Adolescents often adopt this role when they are forced to come to therapy by their parents or their probation officer. Efforts to draw them out in the session usually result in either a continuing stony silence, one-word answers ("Whatever"), or that infamous verbal mark of adolescence—"I don't know." In a later chapter, we describe ways to deal with clients who are forced to come to therapy. Suffice it to say for now that it is best to invite them to participate periodically but not to get drawn into a power struggle with them in an effort to make them participate. Working with families simplifies this task because there are other people in the room with whom the counselor can interact.

MODERATING INTENSITY

Managing emotional intensity is one of the key ingredients of working with families. Intensity is the amount of emotional investment the family has in counseling. Family members manifest their level of intensity by their emotional reactions to one another during sessions; the pace, volume, and tone of their speech; the level of overt conflict they allow to surface during sessions; and such impulsive actions as stomping out of sessions, shouting down the counselor, and name-calling. The counselor's job is to keep the level of emotional intensity in the session within reasonable bounds.

What are reasonable bounds? Although a great deal of emotional intensity may make for a dramatic meeting, and the illusion that a lot of work is being done, the usual outcome of an overly intense session is that the family members become so involved in the intensity of their interaction that they are unable to step back and think about what is being said. Reacting to one another without thinking means that whatever might have been learned in the session is lost and cannot be used in other situations where it might help. Thus, counselors should not think that the absence of tears, anger, emotional outbursts, or other manifestations of intensity mean that nothing is happening in counseling.

On the other hand, too little intensity can lead to flat, listless sessions that do not really involve family members in change. Whereas an overly intense session leaves the family mired in emotionality, a lack of intensity results in family members not engaging one another or the counselor. As a result, no movement toward change occurs.

Lowering Intensity

In working with families, most of the time counselors will be attempting to lower the level of intensity. Families in which drugs or alcohol are used often have high levels of emotional intensity relating to, or as a result of, drug use. Substance abuse counselors are already familiar with the level of intensity that can arise in group treatment of drug and alcohol abusers. Families generate even more intensity concerning drug and alcohol issues because all members have been subjected to the anxiety and chaos of having a family member who is using. Thus, the primary skill counselors need to develop is the ability to reduce intensity.

Techniques to Reduce Emotional Intensity

Several techniques can reduce the emotional intensity in a family session. Some of the ground rules discussed earlier, such as speaking for oneself and talking one at a time, can be helpful. If the counselor senses that tension is rising, he or she should slow down the pace of the interaction. It often helps just to ask the family to slow down. The counselor can ask family members to explain what they are talking about so that they are not left simply to react to one another. The counselor can also model a slower pace in his or her own speech. If slowing down is not effective in easing the intensity, the counselor can ask that family members speak only to him or her and not to each other. When difficult topics arise, family members may be tempted to become involved in heated debates with one another about what happened, who is right, whose memory is accurate, and so on. This leads to more and more intensity in the room as each person fights to have his or her say. Asking that everyone speak only to the counselor puts the other family members in the position of having to listen to what is being said, if only so that they can respond or disagree. The counselor must take leadership in enforcing this rule once it is instituted. Not doing so leaves the family still engaging in the same old conflict cycle and less sure of the counselor's ability to help them do something different in the session.

Sometimes families generate so much emotional intensity that neither they nor the counselor can control it when they are all together. In this case, it is usually best for the counselor to meet individually, or in smaller groups, with family members. For example, when an adolescent becomes so angry that the youth swears at his or her parents, acts provocatively, or refuses to speak, the counselor should meet individually with the parents and the adolescent. This can be done either by scheduling separate appointments or by splitting the appointment time between the parents and the adolescent. Both parties will likely need some time to vent their feelings about the other, but the counselor should try to steer them in the direction of considering what *they* could do to improve the situation in the family. The goal is to help both parties reach the point at which they can come back together and listen to what the other is saying. Some of the solution-focused techniques discussed later in the book will work well in achieving this change in viewpoint.

Finally, at times, emotional intensity that is not manageable may erupt in the session without the counselor anticipating it. Rarely does a counselor know all the "hot topics" in a family, and it is possible to stumble into such an area without meaning to. When this happens, and when the intensity is extreme, it is usually best to separate the family members who are in conflict and meet with each individually to calm the situation. Usually physical separation is enough to bring some calm to both parties, since the intensity is fed by their interaction as much as by the issue they are discussing. Ask whoever appears to be calmer to leave the room and meet with the other partner or family members. Use a calm voice and factual questions to settle the person with whom you are meeting. Empathize with what a difficult situation it is to meet together when tension is so high. If need be, help the family arrange to take a longer cooling-off period by leaving the agency separately or even spending the night apart. Always assess for the likelihood of a violent confrontation in situations such as these.

THE REM APPROACH
TO WORKING WITH CONFLICT

Hecker and Trepper (2000) describe a three-step approach to working with conflict in counseling. This approach is designed to reduce the level of conflict while still allowing the *meaning* of the conflict to be understood and used to effect change. REM is an acronym that stands for the three steps in the approach: (1) **R**eframe angry positions. (2) **E**mpathize with each partner's positions. (3) **E**stablish **M**utual goals. We will describe each of these steps in turn.

Reframe Angry Positions

Reframing is an intervention in which the therapist reinterprets, redefines, and replaces one view with another. First described by

Watzlawick, Weakland, and Fisch (1974), reframing means to "change the conceptual and/or emotional setting or viewpoint in relation to which a situation is experienced and to place it in another frame which fits the 'facts' of the same concrete situation equally well or even better, and thereby changes its entire meaning" (p. 95). This is a simple, yet powerful technique. Multiple meanings can be applied to any given behavior, statement, or feeling. For many reasons, however, some families, especially those with a substance-abusing member, attend to the negative meanings more than the positive ones. This often becomes reciprocal among family members and leads them to assign the most negative meaning to other family members' actions.

For example, an adolescent who does not speak at all during a counseling session could be viewed as *angry* or *thoughtful.* Obviously, if his parents or the therapist use the first meaning, the adolescent will be seen far more negatively than if they use the second. That negativity can become compounded by the *parents* becoming angry that their son is angry, and so on. Also, a therapist may have fewer clinical choices to intervene with an "angry, silent" adolescent than with a "quiet, thoughtful" one. But most important, reframing the meaning to a more positive one allows the therapist to encourage the family members to take a more empathetic stance toward one another.

The therapist first listens attentively to what each partner or family member is saying, paying particular attention to the underlying *meaning* of what is being said. Then, the therapist gently offers a reframe, not in a confrontational or antagonistic way, but almost slips it in. For example, a therapist might use a statement similar to the following:

- It looks like Josh is the quiet, thoughtful one of the family.
- It sounds like you two are both strong individuals who get into passionate arguments.
- So it sounds like when you withdraw from your wife, you're trying to protect her from your temper.
- So when your husband hears you being "bitchy," it sounds like you are really worried about making things work between the two of you to the point where you are frantic.
- Couples who argue as much as you are usually quite invested in their relationship.
- It sounds like when you start yelling at your partner, you are really asking for a time-out and need some space from the argument.
- So you leave the house in order to think more clearly about the problem.

As you can see, none of the reframes are inaccurate or Pollyannaish. Also, because they are somewhat benign, they are not likely to offend the person holding the negative views about the other. For a reframe to be useful, it must be sincere. If the therapist does not believe the statement, he or she should not use that particular one but find another one that is possible to endorse. Finally, one should never attempt to positively reframe abuse because of the potentially devastating consequences that could have on a victimized family member.

Usually the result of the therapist maintaining positive reframes throughout the session is a reduction in the intensity of the conflict. Also, once a reframe has been offered, the therapist should continue the theme throughout the session. It is far better to stick with one reframe, develop it, and keep mentioning it whenever the opportunity arises than to offer two or three reframes scattered throughout the session.

Empathize with Each Partner's Position

. Once the therapist has reduced the initial conflict with the positive reframe, the natural flow is to encourage the other family members to accept the reframe as well. When they do accept the reframe and incorporate it into their own description of other family members, that is an indication of the beginning of empathy. When the husband accepts that his wife yelling at him is indicative of her fear (e.g., that he may get arrested for using drugs and end up in jail) rather than her anger at his lifestyle, he is demonstrating empathy and is more likely to think positively about his wife. It is also important to directly encourage family members to empathize with one another. Although seemingly easy, most members in conflictual families find it difficult to empathize with one another's positions in a conflict. This is essential, however, in reducing in-session conflict and follows logically from successful reframing.

One way the counselor can promote empathy on the part of family members is to model it. For example, the counselor might say the following:

> Bob, your wife, Alyssa, demanded that you come to marital therapy and stop drinking, and you agreed to do that since you

love her and want to save your marriage. At the same time, it sounds like you may feel trapped being here. Alyssa, what does it mean to you that he is able to come here in spite of feeling trapped and uncomfortable?

In addition to modeling empathy, the therapist is directly encouraging the partner to express it as well.

Establish Mutual Goals

Once the conflict has been positively reframed, and each partner's position has been empathized with, small mutual goals should be established. These goals should follow logically from the reframing and empathy positions and will most likely have to be suggested by the therapist. The goals should be attainable, observable, specific, and solution focused. We will discuss ways to arrive at such goals with clients in Chapter 6. (The REM model is summarized in Table 4.1.)

TABLE 4.1. The REM Model

Reframe Angry Positions	• Provide a positive interpretation of each partner's position
Empathize with Each Partner	• Model empathy • Encourage partners to empathize with each other
Establish Mutual Goals	• Set small, mutually agreeable goals to build cooperation

Source: Adapted from Hecker and Trepper, 2000, p. 49.

DOMESTIC VIOLENCE AND SAFETY

So far, we have discussed the issue of how to reduce emotional intensity in family counseling sessions. From our perspective, emotional intensity includes such things as expressing intense emotions, engaging in arguments, and spiraling patterns of conflict. Left out of our definition of emotional intensity are emotional, sexual, and physical abuse and violence. Sadly, anyone who works with couples and families in substance abuse treatment settings must be mindful of these issues because domestic violence and substance abuse problems often coexist. Between 60 and 70 percent of violent men commit assaults against their female partners while intoxicated, and 13 to 20 percent assault their partners while using other drugs (Lee and Weinstein, 1997). One study found that 83 percent of men in alcoholism treatment reported having been violent to an intimate partner at some point in the past, and 55 percent said they had been violent in the past year (Livingston, 1986). Brown and colleagues (1998) similarly found that 58 percent of men reported at least one violent episode in the past year, and 100 percent reported having engaged in an act that met the criteria of psychological or emotional abuse. Obviously, anyone working with families in substance abuse treatment must assess for domestic violence and be prepared to take measures that will ensure the safety of all family members. In addition, no relationship can flourish and become a vehicle for recovery from substance abuse if either or both of the partners feel devalued, or physically or emotionally unsafe.

What Is Abuse?

To assess carefully for the presence of domestic abuse, it is important for counselors to understand what it is. Although we typically think of abuse as physical assault that leads to injury, that is only part of the picture. We will discuss four types of abuse: physical violence, sexual violence, destruction of property and harming pets, and psychological violence.

Physical Violence

Although defining physical violence would seem fairly straightforward, in fact, we all have differing ideas about when a physical interaction becomes violence. In this book, we use a wide definition of physical violence, beginning with such actions as pushing, shoving, or grabbing and holding someone against his or her will, and ending with killing another person. In between are such acts as slapping, kicking, choking, scratching, punching, pulling hair, biting, pulling someone to force him or her to go somewhere, and hitting someone with an object or a weapon. In our view, none of these kinds of physical force is justified, except in the case of absolute self-defense. Even when one is threatened, it usually takes considerably less force to get away than to engage in a fight, retaliate, or try to teach the other person a lesson. Too often, self-defense is used as a way to justify retaliatory violence that need not have occurred.

Sexual Violence

Although rape is the act typically associated with this type of violence, sexual violence is not limited to forcing someone to have sexual intercourse. Anytime physical force or the threat of force is used to make someone perform a sexual act that he or she does not want to do *at that time* is an instance of sexual violence. Even if someone has willingly engaged in a sexual activity before, no one is justified in making that person do it when he or she does not want to. Furthermore, marriage does not give a man the right to force his wife to have sex with him. Most states have laws against spousal rape, and the fact of being married is never grounds for forcing someone to have sex.

Destruction of Property and Harming Pets

Acts do not have to result in injury to a person in order to be violent. Destroying property by throwing things against the wall, breaking windows, punching holes in doors, breaking furniture, and destroying objects that are precious to someone else are all violent acts meant to emotionally hurt and physically threaten another person. Similarly, abusing, neglecting, or killing a pet is also a violent act and should be treated as such. Both destroying property and hurting a pet can be very frightening for those forced to watch, who may imagine themselves in the place of the object or animal being hurt. In addition, of course, anytime that objects are thrown, someone can get hit by accident.

Psychological Violence

Psychological violence is a systematic attempt to control another person's thinking and actions. Sometimes threats of physical harm are used as the mechanism of control. At other times, the process is more subtle. Abusers may limit their partners' ability to spend money, leave the house, have contact with friends or family, use the telephone, or otherwise function as independent people. They may make demands about their partners' appearance and force them to account for their every action. They may also try to destroy their partners' self-esteem through name-calling, humiliation, and other forms of subjugation. The end result of psychological violence is intimidation and control. Victims of severe psychological abuse become almost like hostages in their own homes, terrified of their abusers yet afraid to leave because they have come to believe the abusers' claims that they are incapable of surviving without them. (Abuse criteria are listed in Table 4.2.)

All four types of violence have several things in common. First, they are all against the law. Second, they can each have serious psychological and/or physical consequences for the intended victim, the unintended victims, such as children who witness the violence, and the perpetrator. Third, all represent attempts to dominate, control, and intimidate another person. Finally, each type of violence eventually destroys any positive aspects of the relationship. For these reasons, substance abuse counselors need to be aware of, and assess for, the presence of violence in the families they treat.

TABLE 4.2. What Is Abuse?

Physical Violence	• Hitting, kicking, slapping, restraining, pushing, shoving, pulling hair, biting, killing
Sexual Violence	• Rape, using threats to get sex, making someone perform a sexual act against his or her will
Harming Property or Pets	• Throwing objects, hurting or killing pets, punching holes in walls, breaking windows or doors
Psychological Violence	• Controlling access to money, dictating a partner's appearance, keeping a partner from friends and family, humiliation, name-calling

Do Women Abuse Men?

Most studies on domestic physical violence have focused on men abusing women, even though women assault men about as often as men assault women (O'Leary et al., 1989; Steinmetz, 1977-1978; Straus and Gelles, 1990). The primary reason for the focus on violent men is that they cause much more serious injury to their partners than do women. Cascardi, Langhinrichsen, and Vivian (1992) found that women are more likely to suffer severe physical injuries and depressive symptoms as a result of couple violence than are men, a finding echoed by Stets and Straus (1989). Of women seen in emergency rooms, 35 percent are there for treatment of injuries caused by a male partner's abuse (American Medical Association, 1992). Gelles and Straus (1990) found that severely abused women had twice as many headaches, four times the rate of depression, nearly six times more suicide attempts, and nearly twice as many days in bed due to illness as women who were not abused. And in 1993, 31 percent of the nearly 5,000 female homicides that occurred in the United States were committed by husbands, ex-husbands, and boyfriends (Federal Bureau of Investigation, 1993). Clearly, the costs of men's violence against their female partners are high.

It is important for counselors to be aware of the possibility that both partners can engage in violence. Men can be hurt by their female partners. Still, a woman's assault on her partner is not an excuse or reason for him to retaliate and hurt her. No violence is acceptable. Furthermore, evidence suggests that women who assault their male partners are at much higher risk of being hurt themselves (Feld and Straus, 1989). Counselors must assess for both male and female violence when working with couples in substance abuse treatment.

How to Ask About Abuse

We suggest that counselors who work with couples and families in substance abuse treatment make it a practice to ask all of their clients about past or present violence in their relationships. However, even asking about violence must be done carefully to preserve the safety of a partner who is being abused. First, use an individual meeting with each member of the couple or family to ask about violence. If there is current violence or the threat of violence in the relationship, the victim may be unwilling to discuss it in front of his or her partner for fear of retaliation. Thus, the victim is faced with the choice of either lying to the counselor or putting himself or herself in greater danger by telling the truth. Asking about violence individually gives the victim a safe place to discuss what has happened and how safe he or she feels. It also gives the perpetrator of violence a chance to reveal what he or she has done, if the person so chooses, without being put in the position of being told on by his or her partner in front of the counselor.

The counselor's choice of language is also important when asking about violence. Each of us has our own ideas, based on our experience and values, about what constitutes abuse and violence. Using general terms such as *violence* and *abuse* when interviewing clients means that the counselor is getting only a partial picture of what is actually happening in the relationship—a picture based on the client's definition of violence. Although one could argue that if the client does not define an act as violent, then it is not, this approach is not satisfactory. The counselor needs specific data about what has happened in order to make the best decision about how to work with the couple or family. Thus, we recommend that counselors use specific language when asking about violence. Many people who have been slapped, kicked, threatened, or forced to have sex will say "no" when asked if their partners have ever been abusive toward them because they think abuse only involves broken bones or black eyes or other serious injuries. By the same token, only knowing that people feel abused does not give the counselor a picture of exactly what has happened and how much current danger exists. In the following vignette, Robert begins with a general question about violence and then follows up with specific questions to make sure that he understands Angelique's situation with her husband Tom:

> **Robert:** Let me ask you a question I ask everyone, Angelique. Have you or Tom ever done anything to each other that you consider to be violent or abusive?
>
> **Angelique:** No. We have fights sometimes, but I don't think they're violent.
>
> **Robert:** Let me make sure I'm clear. Has there ever been a time when you or Tom have pushed or shoved each other?
>
> **Angelique:** Oh, sure. That happens all the time. Sometimes he gets so mad he shoves me out of the way and leaves.
>
> **Robert:** Have you ever been hurt because of being shoved like that?
>
> **Angelique:** Last week, I tripped over the trash can and hit my head on the kitchen counter, but it was really my fault. I know I should let Tom just leave when he gets like that, but sometimes I just get scared he won't come back, so I try to make him stay.
>
> **Robert:** Did you go to the doctor because of hitting your head? How badly were you hurt?
>
> **Angelique:** It wasn't bad. I had a headache for a day or so, but that was about it.

Obviously, if Robert had not asked Angelique specifically about pushing and shoving, he would have been left with the mistaken idea that no violence was taking place in her relationship with Bob. As it is, his questions reveal that not only is there violence but that Angelique has been injured recently as a result of it.

Safety Planning

What should counselors do when they discover that violence has been occurring with a couple or family with whom they are working? The first step is to ensure the safety of the family members. The second step is to determine if family or couple counseling can continue.

Developing a Safety Plan

The first step in ensuring safety is to determine if the victims even feel safe leaving the session with their partners. If not, counselors can help them leave without their partners and may even direct them to a shelter or other safe place. Counselors should always take seriously victims' fears about their safety. It is always better to err on the side of too much caution, rather than not enough.

If the victims feel safe with their partners, the next step is to make certain that each partner has a safety plan. Victims should have a specific plan of what to do the next time any violence or threat of violence occurs, such as calling the police, leaving the house to go to a friend's or relative's house, or going to a shelter. Victims need detailed plans, not general ones. A vague idea about going to a shelter, for example, will not be helpful in the midst of a violent episode if a female victim has not thought through how she will get to the shelter, how she will get away from her partner, or what she will do about getting her children out of the house. Counselors should help victims anticipate what could happen and how they can prepare for it. For instance, the victim in the previous example may need to hide an extra set of car keys and some cash outside the house if her partner is especially controlling and she expects he will try to prevent her from leaving. Counselors should review the plans several times with the victims to make sure that they are clear on what they will do.

The safety plan for violent partners should involve preventing further acts of abuse. Not only will this ensure the safety of their partners, it will also protect them from doing something, such as injuring a loved one, that they may later regret, and it will keep them from facing criminal charges. A good safety plan protects all parties.

The best safety plan for perpetrators is for them to participate in a batterers' treatment program. Such programs are usually available through a variety of community agencies. Using a psychoeducational group format, batterers' groups help perpetrators understand the personal and societal roots of violence in relationships and learn to control their own violent efforts to control their partners.

Time-Out

The foundational technique taught in batterers' groups to increase safety is *time-out.* Time-out involves learning to recognize the precursors to violence and developing an alternative plan so that one does not become violent. Usually, the alternative plan involves leaving the situation until one is able to regain control over self and feelings. Matthews (1995) describes seven steps in a good time-out plan:

- Identify the signals that tell you that you need to take a time-out.
- Determine what you will do or say to leave in a positive way.
- Consider what you will say to yourself (positive self-talk) to help you leave.
- Develop three options for where you will go, what you will do, and how long you will be gone.
- Think of three people you can contact who will help you cool down. Be sure you have their phone numbers or other ways to contact them.
- (Reconnecting) Identify the signals within yourself that will tell you that you are ready to approach your partner in a respectful manner.
- Plan what you can do or say to reconnect in a way that is respectful of your partner and yourself.

Although a batterers' group provides the best intervention for violent partners, substance abuse counselors can help these perpetrators develop a time-out safety plan as a way of reducing some risk, at least. Remember, however, that developing such a plan in isolation from the rest of the material taught in a batterers' group is only a stop-gap measure. (See Table 4.3 for a summary of safety planning.)

TABLE 4.3. Safety Planning

Victim	Perpetrator
Safety Plan	Time-Out
• Plan where to go • Have money, keys, driver's license available • Plan how to get out of the house • Plan transportation • Know where shelter is • Have important phone numbers available • Be ready to call police if needed	• Recognize signs of rising anger • Agree with partner on a signal for time-out • Have three options of where to go • Have three people to call as calming resources • Recognize signs of readiness to reconnect • Plan how to reconnect respectfully

Can Couple or Family Counseling Continue?

Once safety plans are in place, the counselor must decide if it is appropriate to continue couple or family counseling when violence has been reported. At times, the intensity that arises from discussing difficult issues in counseling can lead to further violence or threats of violence. Since safety is always the primary concern, the counselor may decide to meet individually with family members, rather than risk a joint meeting. Individual meetings should continue to focus on safety and lowering intensity using techniques described earlier in this chapter.

We use two gauges to decide if it is appropriate to meet jointly with couples following the revelation of violence in the relationship. The first gauge is straightforward. Does the victim of the violence feel safe to meet jointly? If the victim does not, for whatever reason, the counselor should not force him or her to take part in joint meetings. Even if the counselor thinks that the victim is overestimating the risk involved, the victim will not be able to participate freely in a session with his or her partner if *he or she* does not feel safe.

When victims feel safe resuming joint counseling sessions, counselors must still make their own evaluation of the risk involved in resuming couples work. We believe that couples counseling can be considered if the following conditions are met:

- Neither partner reports current violence in the relationship.
- The violent partner (or both partners) is willing to sign a no-violence agreement.
- Both partners have well-developed, credible safety plans and are willing to act on them.
- The violent partner (or both partners) is clearly able to take responsi-bility for his or her own violent actions and realizes that the other person does not cause this violent behavior.

These, we believe, represent the minimum conditions for couples work. As stated earlier, it is better to err on the side of safety and delay resuming couples work than it is to rush into it and put one or both partners at risk. Once the counselor begins to see the couple together again, he or she must consistently monitor their level of intensity and their potential for violence. Individual meetings can always be used to assess risk and calm the situation, if need be.

Personal Reactions to Violence

Dealing with violence in couples and families is emotionally challenging for even the most experienced counselor, and it is not unusual for counselors to have personal reactions to these situations that may limit their effectiveness with the clients they serve. The following are some common emotional reactions:

- Anger at a woman who stays with an abusive partner despite all evidence that she is in danger
- Seeing the abusive partner as only a monster with no human side
- Feeling hopeless about a couple's ability to end violence
- Blaming the victim for the abuse ("If she wasn't such a nag, he probably wouldn't hit her.")
- Discounting the level of violence based on other clients or personal experience ("I don't know what she's complaining about. Lots of abused women would be happy to have a man who only calls them names once in a while. Doesn't she know how good she has it compared with what other women deal with?")

If such feelings are not dealt with, they can lead the counselor to underestimate the risk in a family, to alienate one or both partners through not understanding their experience (even though not agreeing with the rationalizations used to justify violence), or to give up, covertly convincing couples to drop out of treatment, because the counselor is frightened of (or does not know how to deal with) the violence in their relationship.

Strawderman, Rosen, and Coleman (1997) present a five-step approach to working with personal reactions to domestic violence:

- The first step is to recognize and acknowledge a personal reaction to a couple's violence. This involves a high level of self-awareness on the part of the counselor as well as a supportive supervision relationship that allows such feelings to be safely expressed. All counselors have personal reactions to some clients at some time. The biggest danger comes when those reactions are denied because the counselor is then likely to act on them unconsciously.
- The second step is for counselors to name their feelings. Counselors may feel angry, disgusted, frightened, or frustrated, among other things. Naming feelings makes it easier to talk about them.
- The third step is to accept the feelings, while being clear that they do not need to be acted upon. Some counselors are under the impression that having negative feelings about clients or their situation is a sign that they are not doing a good job. It is more helpful to recognize that the feelings exist for a reason, and that understanding that reason can both further counselors' personal growth and help the treatment. Maintain a curious and respectful attitude toward feelings about clients in order to discover what they have to teach.
- Step four is to examine the source of the personal reactions and their impact on both counselors and treatment. This step involves a shift in focus from trying to understand why clients are acting in ways that make the counselors uncomfortable to the counselors trying to understand their own responses. Questions to ask include the following: "Is this situation triggering something in my own experience?" "How does this feeling affect my work with this couple or family?" "Is it helpful to the client if I respond this way?" "Have I taken over the feelings the client should have—for example, being angry for her, or being scared for her?"
- Step five involves finding strategies to manage and use personal reactions in the treatment process. A supervisor's help is invaluable in this step to help counselors stand back and look for ways to prevent personal reactions from interfering with treatment. Some counselors find that supervision immediately prior to a session with a difficult couple can be helpful. Others

find that appropriately expressing their fears or anger directly is useful to clients. Because there are no "cookbook" strategies, each counselor must find his or her own way of dealing with personal reactions to couples.

Raising Intensity

In some cases, rare in our experience, the counselor will need to *raise* the intensity in family sessions to set the stage for change. Use caution in this area. As noted earlier, most families in which members are using drugs or alcohol have plenty of intensity already. The counselor's job will be to help contain it, not to create more.

What are the signs that indicate it may be important to raise intensity when working with a family? Raising intensity is most helpful when family members are stuck in an unhelpful pattern of interaction but are exerting little obvious effort to change.

> Ellen came to counseling with her eighteen-year-old son, Rob, who was using marijuana occasionally. Rob had dropped out of school, had no job, slept until noon most days, and kept Ellen awake at night playing his stereo. Ellen was working two jobs to support the family, which also included Rob's fourteen-year-old sister. Rob invited his nineteen-year-old friend Eddie to move into Ellen's home, and the two boys set up a semi-apartment in the basement. One day, Ellen came home to find Eddie and his girlfriend taking a shower together in her bathroom. In counseling, Ellen said she hated what was going on, felt Rob showed little respect for her, and worried about his future. While she agreed with the need to set some rules for Rob and Eddie, she was reluctant to do so, fearing that taking a stand would alienate Rob. After several stuck sessions in which Ellen complained about her situation but found it impossible to take action, the counselor began to think the situation was hopeless, so his supervisor suggested trying to raise the intensity.

Techniques to Raise Intensity

Counselors can employ several strategies for raising intensity. They can speed up the pace of interaction, using their own energy and activity level to stimulate the family members to interact more vigorously. They can ask family members to talk to one another directly, rather than mostly to them. It is harder to maintain a passive, detached stance when you are talking directly to the person with whom you are having a conflict. Since physical proximity often mediates intensity, asking family members to sit closer together as they talk can further raise the intensity of their interaction. Finally, counselors can direct family members to keep talking about a difficult issue past the point at which they usually would have thrown up their hands and given up. This raises intensity by preventing the family's typical cycle of withdrawal and avoidance.

We want to reiterate at this point our caveat that rarely will substance abuse counselors find themselves in the position of having to raise intensity with the families they see in treatment. And before they even consider doing so, they must be certain that the families do not have a history of violence or other destructive acting out. To raise intensity without carefully thinking through the potential consequences is to practice irresponsibly.

What about Ellen and Rob? Their counselor used a somewhat different technique. He met with Ellen alone and complimented her on her love for her son, love so strong that she was willing to sacrifice all her own goals and dreams for him. The counselor encouraged Ellen to consider what sacrifices she would have to make when Rob was twenty-five and still living with her. She would have to give up her dream of going back to school for a teaching degree, of course, and probably give up her dream of remarrying, since supporting Rob would take all of her time.

The counselor then asked Ellen to consider what she would have to do to support Rob when he was thirty-five and still living at home. She would not be able to put any money away for retirement, of course, nor would she have the chance to do the traveling she had always dreamed of doing. And what would it be like when Rob was *forty-five?* As the counselor extended Ellen's decision to care for her son at any cost to its (il)logical conclusion, she became more and more upset. She left the session, went home, kicked Eddie and his girlfriend out of the house, and told Rob he had to return to school or get a job or she would kick him out, too. To her surprise, Rob said, "I'm surprised it took you this long, Mom. You shouldn't let me get away with stuff like that."

USING GOALS TO FRAME COUNSELING

Another skill that counselors need to work well with families is the ability to use negotiated goals as the basis for counseling. One of the key words in this statement is *negotiated.* Goals are most useful when clients and counselors come to an agreement about what they are going to work on together. This does not mean that counselors have to accept any goal that clients suggest, but neither should they impose their own goals on the family members without their being able to participate in choosing which problems to work on.

In addition to agreeing on the goals of treatment, it is important that counselors and family members agree on what will have to happen for everyone involved to know that the goal has been reached. For example, family members may say that their goal is to work on the conflicts in the family. Their counselor may see the reduction of conflicts as a reasonable measure of success, while the family believes (unrealistically, perhaps) that ending conflict altogether indicates progress. Unless the criteria for success are discussed openly, the family and counselor may agree on where they are trying to go, but not on how they will know when they get there. Solution-focused therapy techniques offer a variety of ways to help clients define their goals and the mileposts they will use to measure progress toward them.

Goals, once set, serve as a framework for the rest of the treatment. Each session should work toward achievement of the goals the counselor has set with the family. If a couple's goal is to have better communication, then each session should focus in some way on improving communication. The counselor should consider how whatever is planned for a session will further the goal of improved communication. He or she should also involve the couple in evaluating the relevance of the session to the general goal. The counselor might ask, for example, "Is what we're doing today getting you closer to your goal of improving your communication?" If the couple thinks that it is not, then they and the counselor can negotiate a more relevant course of action.

Goals also frame the entire treatment process itself. The content of one session should build on past sessions to further the family reaching its goals. When counselor and family members agree that goals have been met, it is time either to consider termination or to negotiate new goals. Often, in the course of reaching a preliminary goal, other issues that the family wants to work on will arise. If the family decides to contract with the counselor to work on those issues, the process of goal setting, defining goal achievement, and monitoring progress begins again.

If goals are not set, or are not defined clearly, treatment can take on a drifting, unending quality and become a routine matter, with sessions being scheduled just because "we always meet Tuesdays at seven," rather than because the family and counselor are truly engaged in a change effort. Under these circumstances, all involved lose track of why the family is coming to treatment and how to judge success. In an age of managed care, limited treatment, and increased counselor accountability, no family can afford to waste valuable treatment sessions because the counselor has not helped members set clear goals. We will discuss goal setting in detail later in the book.

ATTENDING TO PROCESS

A final skill that substance abuse counselors need to develop as they work with families is the ability to attend to the *interpersonal process* in families as well as the content of the problems. Process refers to the pattern of interactions apart from their content. For example, attending to process means that the counselor tries to figure out how a client family solves (or does not solve) a conflict, rather than getting wrapped up in what the conflict is about.

> Judy and Bud came to therapy when Judy was in recovery. Bud also was in recovery and had been for a number of years. Having found AA very helpful to him, Bud decided that the best thing he could do to aid Judy was to point out to her all the ways she was failing to live up to the twelve-step philosophy. The more Bud tried to advise Judy, however, the more she felt compelled to disagree with him to show her independence and to convince him that what had worked for him wasn't necessarily the answer for her. In one argument, Bud told Judy that she had yet to truly admit she was powerless over alcohol and that she wouldn't get anywhere until she did. In response, Judy reminded him of all the changes she had made in her life, including not drinking for several months. Feeling hurt that his advice wasn't being taken, Bud tried even harder to convince Judy that she wasn't following the twelve steps as she should. A fight ensued that left both of them in stubborn silence for two days.

In another instance, Judy came home from work complaining about an unfair decision one of her bosses had made. Bud told Judy that she needed to "Let go and let God," since there was nothing she could do about it. Judy disagreed and said that she was thinking of writing a letter to her boss protesting the decision. Again Bud tried hard to convince her that she was not following the twelve steps correctly, and Judy argued just as hard that she was. In these two cases, although the content was different (powerlessness versus "Let go and let God"), the pattern of interaction (Bud advises, Judy resists, a fight develops) was the same.

Why is it important for the counselor to attend to process? Because that is where most families get stuck. Few families come to treatment with only one conflict to resolve. Most are unable to settle a variety of conflicts, not because the content makes them insolvable, but because the process families use to try to solve their problems is not working. Tracking process helps the counselor get a picture of the interpersonal patterns that create "stuckness."

Perhaps another analogy will help. Think of driving a car. The "content" of a drive in the car is the destination you want to reach and the route you will take to get there. The "process" is the act of driving—putting the car in gear, pushing on the gas, signaling turns, and so forth. If the process of driving is not clear and functional (e.g., you push hard on the gas but never put the car in gear), you will not reach *any* destination, regardless of what it is. A driving instructor who suggests that you choose another destination when the problem is in how you are trying to drive will not be of much help to you.

Likewise, a counselor who keeps suggesting ways to solve a problem without looking at the interpersonal process that supports that problem will not be of much help either. In Bud and Judy's case, the counselor might help them recognize the "advise-react" pattern and help each person figure out what part of that pattern he or she can change. This will ultimately give Bud and Judy the tools they need to work effectively on future conflicts.

Once the counselor uncovers the process going on in a family, he or she can help the family look at it. To do so, the counselor points out patterns *across* content areas. Again using Bud and Judy as an example, the counselor might say,

> I notice that whenever Bud gives you advice, Judy, you seem to feel that he's saying that you don't know how to manage your own life, and you point out to him all the ways his advice isn't

helpful. At the same time, Bud, when Judy tells you that she doesn't need your advice, it seems you feel she is rejecting you completely, and you try harder to be of help to her. Is this a pattern that happens a lot with the two of you?

Such a question helps the couple begin to look not only at *what* gets them into trouble but also at the *interactional pattern* this trouble takes. Recognizing this pattern in the present is the beginning of being able to change it.

SUMMARY

Working with families in substance abuse treatment uses many of the skills substance abuse counselors already have as well as calling on some family therapy skills. Counselors must become adept at the following:

Joining
• Ability to develop supportive relationships with more than one person, even when they are in conflict
Managing Intensity
• Ability to raise or lower the family's level of emotional intensity as needed   • Ability to assess for intrafamily violence and design safety plans
Goals
• Ability to negotiate mutually acceptable goals for treatment and use those goals to provide a framework for treatment
Process
• Ability to see the *patterns* of interaction in a family as well as follow the content

With these skills as a foundation, we will move on to looking in detail at how counselors can work with families using a strengths-focused approach.

Chapter 5

Assessing Motivation

James, a counselor-in-training, was seeing Rachel and Ed in couples therapy. Rachel arranged the couple's first appointment, telling James over the phone that she had been feeling depressed and that she also found herself angry at Ed much of the time. At their first session, Ed said that he didn't understand what was bothering Rachel, only that she "got bitchy" a lot and he thought it had to do with "her time of the month." He did say that he was interested in "getting Rachel off my back and getting things back to how they used to be when she wasn't so hard to get along with." As James asked more questions about Rachel's and Ed's views of their difficulties, Rachel mentioned that Ed's drinking bothered her.

"How much do you drink?" James asked Ed.

"Not much. Just a beer or two now and then."

"Tell the truth, Ed," Rachel chimed in. "You know you get a couple cases of beer every Saturday when we go grocery shopping, and they're finished by Friday night."

James did some quick math in his head. "It sounds to me like you have a pretty severe drinking problem, Ed."

"She's exaggerating," Ed replied, his neck beginning to turn red. "She just wants to blame all her problems on me. I don't have a drinking problem."

"Denying that you have a problem is one of the first signs of alcoholism," James said.

Ed began to shift around in his chair. "I'm not denying any-thing," he said. "There's nothing to deny. I came here to get Ra-chel to quit bitching at me all the time, not to have some junior counselor tell me I've got a drinking problem."

"There's no point trying to work on a relationship problem when one person is drinking too much," James told them. "Ed, what are you going to do about your problem?"

Ed sat silently for a moment, his whole face red now. Then he turned to Rachel. "I told you this was going to be a waste of time," he said. "You can stay around to listen to this bullshit if you want, but I'm not going to." With that, he got up and walked out of James's office. Despite Rachel's repeated efforts over the next few weeks to get him to come back, he never returned.

Where did James go wrong? He was probably accurate in his as-sessment that Ed had a drinking problem. And it was not unreason-able to suggest that Ed make some plans to deal with his problem. What James did not take into account, however, was Ed's *motivation to change*. Instead, he jumped right to making plans for treatment be-fore Ed even saw himself as having a problem. The more Ed fought to present his view that his drinking was not the issue, the more James confronted him. The result was Ed's decision to leave therapy and never return. Not only did this outcome lead to no treatment for his drinking problem, it also deprived Rachel of a chance to work with her husband to strengthen their marriage. In the end, Rachel decided to leave Ed, citing his refusal to come back to therapy as one of the reasons for her decision.

Few counselors would so blatantly make the mistake James made in his first session with Ed and Rachel. Many counselors, however, make a more subtle version of James's mistake every day when they ignore the issue of client motivation in their work.

WHAT IS MOTIVATION?

On the face of it, the definition of motivation seems simple enough. Traditionally, we think of it as an innate quality of individuals that re-flects their desire to change their behavior in order to improve some-thing in their lives. Thus, when Ed decides not to return to treatment, we assume that he does not possess adequate motivation to make changes in his life. However, there is another way to look at motivation in treatment, that is, to view motivation not solely as a quality that the client possesses but as a quality of the *relationship* between the client and counselor. What is the advantage to looking at motivation this way? For one thing, it gives counselors a part to play in enhancing clients' motivation. Counselors are not simply stuck with unmotivated clients; they can try to construct relationships that maximize the clients' desire to change. A second reason to adopt an interactional view of motivation is that it works.

Early studies in the field of substance abuse found that rates of treatment dropout varied widely between counselors, even within the same treatment agencies. Some counselors lost few of their clients, whereas others lost many. In fact, a relatively large number of dropouts were the clients of a relatively small number of counselors (Greenwald and Bartmeier, 1963; Raynes and Patch, 1971; Rosenberg et al., 1976; Rosenberg and Raynes, 1973). This fact led to further investigations of the qualities of counselors whose clients seemed to be more motivated to complete treatment. What are those qualities? We discussed many of them in Chapter 2 when we talked about joining. As noted there, our approach to working with couples and families emphasizes *cooperation* over *confrontation* as the best stance for the counselor to take. Cooperation begins with assessing the client's motivation to change and acting in ways that are consonant with his or her level of motivation. To understand a client's motivation, we must assess three things. First, we need to know what *stage of change* the client is in. Second, we must figure out *what* the client is motivated to change. Finally, we must know the client's views of *who* must change for the situation to improve.

We have found aspects of two models helpful to us in understanding clients' motivation: the solution-focused and "stages of change" models. Solution-focused therapists (e.g., Berg and Miller, 1992) have been exceptionally thoughtful about the type of counseling *relationship* a client wishes to have with the counselor. They focus on whether the client thinks there is a problem that needs a counselor's attention and who is in the best position to make a change in the problem if one exists. Before the reality of clinical practice sets in, beginning counselors often expect to be working with clients who see a problem and are convinced *they* must make a change to solve that problem. In the solution-focused model, these people are seen as wanting a *customer* relationship in therapy. Most of our training focuses on such people. We talk about getting the client's definition of the problem, helping the client formulate a plan for change, planning action steps, and so on. Disappointingly, however, many of the people who come to treatment are not customers. Some people do not believe a problem exists at all. They have been forced to come to treatment by a judge or by family members and wish to establish a *visitor* relationship with the counselor. They really see no need for a counselor's help and want to make the best of a bad situation by keeping their contact as superficial (and brief!) as possible—a visit to treatment. Finally, some clients see that a problem exists but are convinced that someone else must take steps to solve it. Counseling offers them an opportunity to explain in detail how the actions of another person are the true cause of the problem. These people wish to form a *complainant* relationship and think that it is important for the counselor to hear and appreciate their complaints about their situation. (Therapy relationship types are summarized in Table 5.1.)

Why does it matter what type of therapy relationship a client wishes to have when he or she comes to treatment? Basically, if the counselor tries to engage the client in a different type of relationship than the one he or she is looking for (e.g., treating a complainant as if she were a customer), the client is likely to feel misunderstood and begin to engage in actions we often label as "resistance" or "denial." The harder the counselor tries to engage the client in one kind of relationship, the more the client tries to make clear to the counselor that he or she wants a very different kind of relationship.

TABLE 5.1. Therapy Relationship Types

Customer	• Sees a problem • Wants counselor's help to take action to solve the problem
Complainant	• Sees a problem • Wants counselor's help to have someone else solve the problem
Visitor	• Does not see a problem • Does not want counselor's help

Source: Based on Berg and Miller, 1992.

Denise came to treatment convinced that if her husband, Robbie, would only quit drinking, their conflicts (which had gotten to the point of violence at times) would disappear. She gave Elaine, the couple's counselor, detailed descriptions of the ways in which Robbie's drinking made life difficult for her and resulted in conflict. Not realizing that Denise was seeking a cómplainant relationship, Elaine began to suggest that Denise herself could make some changes that would help the relationship.

"Have you tried talking calmly to Robbie about how upset you are?" Elaine asked Denise. "Maybe Robbie doesn't know how much his drinking worries you."

"I've talked to him until I'm blue in the face," Denise replied. "It doesn't do any good. Robbie has just made up his mind that he's not going to quit, and there's nothing I can do about it."

Had Elaine been more familiar with the solution-focused model, she might have realized that Elaine was seeking a complainant relationship. There was clear evidence that Denise saw a problem (Robbie's drinking and their marital conflict) but also that she didn't see herself as being the one able to make a change ("there's nothing I can do about it"). Elaine missed these cues, however, and continued to push Denise to do something about the problem.

"What do you really want to say to Robbie?" she asked. "Maybe you haven't been clear enough."

"I've been plenty clear. Robbie's just so thick-skulled that nothing gets through."

"Why don't we role-play how you talk to him," Elaine said. "Maybe I can help you communicate better."

"This is stupid," Denise said. "There's no talking to Robbie, period. Can't you understand that?"

The more that Elaine treated Denise as if she were seeking a customer relationship in counseling—in other words, a relationship that was based on Elaine helping Denise decide what she could change to improve things—the more Denise tried to tell Elaine that she saw all the power to change as being in Robbie's hands. When Elaine did not take this view into account, her interactions with Denise became more and more argumentative. It is not that Elaine's view is wrong. In fact, there are probably a number of things that Denise might do to help decrease the couple's conflict. However, until she sees herself as being able to make a change that matters, Elaine's suggestions will only seem irrelevant or misguided to Denise. The more Elaine pushes Denise to take a different view, the more rigid Denise is likely to become. If we take only an individual view, we might see Denise as a resistant client who is doing her best to fend off Elaine's efforts to help her. However, if we look at the interaction between Elaine and Denise, we see that each brings to their interaction a different understanding of how counseling can help. The more each tries to convince the other that her view is correct, the more rigid and adversarial their interaction becomes. Without a shift in perspective on either part, this pattern is likely to continue until Denise either decides not to come back to counseling or superficially gives in to Elaine's view that she must make a change but takes no meaningful steps to do so. The shift the counselor can make is to understand and accommodate to the client's view of what will be helpful and not treat a visitor or complainant as if he or she were a customer. Later in this chapter, we describe specific strategies for doing so.

· The second model that has been helpful to us in our efforts to understand client motivation is the "stages of change" model developed by Prochaska and DiClemente (1982, 1984, 1985, 1986). This model describes the various steps individuals go through as they move from not even realizing they have a problem to taking steps to solve that · problem. The model proposes six stages: precontemplation, contemplation, determination, action, maintenance, and relapse.

The *precontemplation* stage is characterized by clients being unaware that they have a problem. A man with three drunk-driving convictions, for example, may be convinced that none of them was his fault, and that he has no real reason to be concerned about his use of alcohol.

In *contemplation,* clients begin to weigh the pros and cons of their behavior, asking themselves if perhaps a change should be made. The hallmark of the contemplation stage is ambivalence. Many smokers, for example, become quite concerned about the effects of smoking on their health long before they actually stop smoking. While they do not deny the negative health effects of smoking, they also do not take action to quit.

Clients enter the *determination* phase when they decide to take action to change. Many people in recovery, for example, can pinpoint the exact time when they made a firm commitment to no longer using. In her memoir *Drinking: A Love Story,* journalist Caroline Knapp (1996) describes how, drunk one day, she stumbled and fell while recklessly swinging her friend's young daughter by the arms. The child's skull was nearly crushed, and Knapp knew at that point that she had to stop drinking. She had her last drink that day.

The *action* stage begins when clients take action to make a change. Sometimes determination and action accompany each other closely, as they did in Caroline Knapp's case. At other times, the decision to change may occur a while before any steps toward change are actually taken. And the action stage does not always go smoothly. For many clients, the process of change is two steps forward and one step back, rather than a steady upward trend. A teenage girl may refuse a friend's invitation to get high one day, for example, only to join in the next day at her boyfriend's urging. Putting a successful action plan in place often means learning new skills and coming up with effective coping strategies, a process that takes time.

As clients become more secure in the changes they are making, they enter the *maintenance* stage. In this stage, clients learn to maintain the change across a wide variety of situations. For example, clients may no longer need to avoid places where alcohol is being served to be secure in their resolve to not drink.

For many people who are struggling to end drug or alcohol abuse, the process of change involves one or more *relapses.* A relapse starts the change process over again as clients move from the maintenance stage back to an earlier stage in the model. Clients may, for example, gradually develop the conviction that a period of abstinence means that they can now control their drinking or drug use and can use again without losing control. This may signal a return to the precontemplation stage, with its denial of a problem, or to the contemplation stage, where ambivalence about change is characteristic. In either event, clients begin another cycle through the stages of change. Miller and colleagues (1994) represent the stages of change as circular in nature (see Figure 5.1), which emphasizes the fact that some clients will progress through several cycles before achieving stability in the changes they are making.

As with the solution-focused model discussed earlier, counselors can use the stages of change model to match their interventions to the clients' current state. It makes little sense, for example, to lecture clients in the action stage about the reasons they need to stop using drugs. Having already made a commitment to stop using, clients will

FAMILY SOLUTIONS FOR SUBSTANCE ABUSE

FIGURE 5.1. A Stage Model of the Process of Change

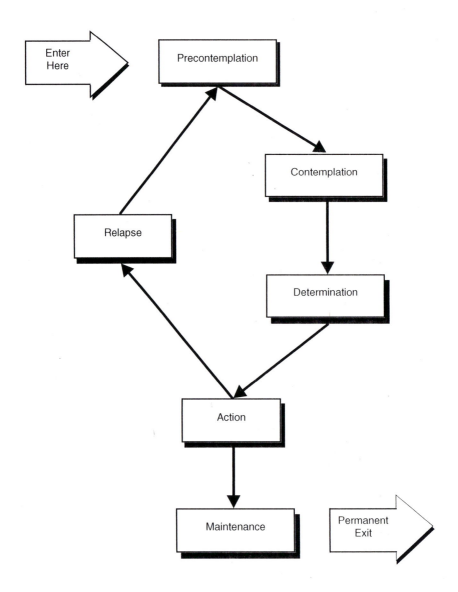

Source: Adapted from Miller et al., 1994.

find such information largely irrelevant. Instead, counselors can best help clients in the action stage plan and carry out strategies for change. We have combined aspects of both the stages of change model and the solution-focused therapy model in the following description of how we assess clients and family members' motivation. In the following sections, we discuss both the categories we use to understand clients' motivation and how to build a relationship with clients in each group. We then present our strategies for working with families and couples with members who are not in the same stage of change.

VISITORS

As noted earlier, clients who come to therapy wanting to have a visitor relationship typically do not see a problem about which they need to be concerned. Thus, the idea that they need to make changes in their lives does not make sense to them. Visitors are probably the most challenging group of clients for counselors to work with because they either explicitly or implicitly refuse the help that we would like to offer them, leaving us with no clear role. Although it is tempting to try to convince visitors that they do have a problem and that they need our help in solving it, such direct efforts rarely work. Instead, counselors' initial goal with visitors should be to treat them kindly enough to keep them at least minimally engaged in counseling. As long as counselors can keep the conversation going, they may be able to determine what help, if any, clients might be customers for.

Although easy to describe, this work takes a great deal of patience and skill. Often, we can clearly see the problems that such clients have and how their lives would be better were they to work on those problems. However, following the temptation to try to convince visitors to work on problems they do not believe they have is usually futile, in our experience. It is better to start by trying to understand and empathize with a client's view even if it does not make sense from the counselor's perspective. While in many cases such a stance by the counselor will result in helping a visitor move to being a customer, this does not always happen. Each counselor has to decide how long it is useful to see a client who adamantly denies that he or she is in need of any help.

In our experience, visitors take one of two stances when they come to drug and alcohol treatment. Some come as *opponents,* others come as *absentees.* Joining with each type requires a somewhat different stance on the part of counselors.

Opponents

Opponents come to counseling expecting to be blamed and lectured about their actions, their irresponsibility, their use of drugs and alcohol, or any number of other things. Often, other people in their lives react to them in this way, and they see no reason why counselors would be any different. Believing that the best defense is a good offense, opponents therefore come to counseling hoping to engage counselors in a struggle. If counselors take the bait and enter the struggle with clients, three things are likely to happen. First, whatever problems clients may have will be camouflaged as the fight consumes all the energy in the counseling session. Second, clients will have produced evidence that counselors are "just like everyone else" and therefore do not need to be listened to or taken seriously. Finally, the stage is set for counseling to become a series of adversarial, unproductive interactions.

> Jeff, a fifteen-year-old, was ordered to come to drug treatment by the juvenile court judge after being busted for dealing marijuana at his school. Jeff slouched in the chair farthest from the door and didn't say a word when he entered Pete's office for his intake appointment.
>
> "Your PO said you were dealing at school," Pete said.
>
> "Whatever," Jeff muttered under his breath.
>
> "Well, it must be kind of a problem for you. You've got to come here, report to your PO, and you got kicked out of school."
>
> Jeff looked disgusted. "This is all bullshit," he said. "It was stupid. I didn't do anything that lots of other kids aren't doing, and they don't have a fucking problem. Now I gotta waste my time talking to some stupid shrink. You're probably an ex-junkie yourself."

Adolescents are particularly skilled at initiating an opponent relationship with substance abuse counselors. With clients such as Jeff, it is very tempting to confront their denial, the seriousness of what they have done, their need for counseling, and so on. Take a minute to think about what the rest of the session might be like if Pete takes this approach with Jeff. What would Jeff be likely to say? If Pete persisted, how would the session end? What would the next session be like?

In our experience, directly confronting opponents only strengthens their opposition. In fact, at least one research study (Miller, Benefield, and Tonigan, 1993) suggests that confrontation in alcohol abuse treatment is associated with more drinking, not less, after treatment has ended. So what is a counselor to do? Pete proceeded this way:

"You know," he said to Jeff, "you're a pretty responsible kid, it seems to me."

Jeff didn't say anything, but he did glance at Pete with a somewhat surprised look on his face.

Pete continued, "You came here today, and kept your appointment, even though you don't really think you need counseling or any other kind of help. That tells me that you want to do the right thing."

"My PO made me come," Jeff said.

"Well, maybe. But I sure know lots of kids who don't keep their appointments, and who end up spending time in detention because of it. Seems to me you've decided to be responsible even though you don't agree."

"Yeah . . . so?" Jeff said.

"I just wanted you to know that I see that you're trying," Pete told him. "That's all."

Pete's compliment, and highlighting of a strength, caught Jeff off guard. It also kept Pete from participating in building an opponent-style relationship with Jeff. Two important aspects of Pete's responses to Jeff illustrate good places to start when working with opponents. First, he *empathized* with Jeff's understanding of the situation. Jeff felt unfairly treated, even though an outsider might see Jeff himself as responsible for his predicament. Second, Pete found something to *compliment* Jeff about. Jeff was complying with the requirement of his PO, even though reluctantly. Having his counselor compliment him was clearly not what Jeff expected. Through these two strategies, Pete was able to head off, at least for the time being, getting involved in a struggle with Jeff. His unexpected actions also captured Jeff's attention because they were not what Jeff had anticipated. Thus, he was able to meet the first goal of working with an opponent, and that is to keep the conversation going.

Absentees

Absentees require a similar strategy. Whereas opponents actively work to set up a struggle in counseling, absentees do so passively. They miss appointments, come late, "forget" to do homework assignments between sessions, fail to recall whát they discussed the last time they saw the counselor, and are generally absent from the process, either physically or emotionally. In some ways, absentees are more difficult to deal with than opponents because they try not to engage with the counselor at all.

> Although not identified as a drug or alcohol user, Derrick presented as a perfect example of an absentee. He typically came to sessions a little late, complaining of traffic problems or difficulty getting off work, but he was genial and talkative. Despite the fact that he had been part of two incidents involving a handgun—one that almost resulted in his being shot by the police when he brandished his weapon at them—he said that his problems were now resolved and that the whole incident had been a misunderstanding. When his counselor asked him to help her understand the sequence of events that had led to his arrest by drawing a time line, Derrick politely refused, saying he preferred to put the past behind him. He talked at length in sessions about his many efforts to be helpful to other people and his concern for his family. Although always polite and physically present, Derrick deflected all efforts on the part of his counselor to really engage him in the process.

As with opponents, the first step with absentees is to *empathize* with their viewpoint and find something to *compliment* them on.

> "It must be hard to come here week after week and keep these appointments when you're sure you've already moved beyond

the problems that brought you here," Derrick's counselor told him finally. And then, using information Derrick had given in earlier sessions, she said, "It must take a lot of patience to put up with your pastor and your girlfriend and your PO hassling you about those old problems all the time."

"No shit," Derrick said, brightening up a little bit for the first time. "I'm getting really tired of it."

Visitor to Customer

In working with both opponents and absentees, the goal is to change the type of relationship the client is seeking from a visitor relationship to a customer relationship. As noted earlier, this is not always possible, and the counselor must be thoughtful about how much effort to expend on any one client who is insistent about not wanting treatment. However, it is also a mistake to give up too easily on a client who presents in visitor mode. Often, it is possible to change someone seeking a visitor relationship to someone seeking a customer relationship. The key to doing this is to find what the client might be a customer for. There are two steps in this process.

"We Are Stuck with Each Other"

This strategy, also known as forming a benign triangle, is useful when clients want to blame counselors for their being in counseling. It is as if clients believe counselors have made the decision to force them to attend treatment sessions. Of course, that is not the case. A third party—parent, judge, PO, child protective worker—is usually the force behind a visitor's entry into treatment. With many visitors, this person can play the "heavy," requiring them to attend a certain number of sessions. In essence, counselors can say that the decision for clients to come to treatment is out of their hands. They can then make the case that, "Since we're stuck with each other for ten sessions, maybe we should see if there's something you need help with. Maybe it isn't what your PO thinks you need help with. I'm interested in what you think would help your life go better." Remember that this happens *after* the counselors have done their best to join with clients through empathy and compliments, so the clients feel less need to present a case for why they should not be required to come at all.

Finding Meaningful Goals

This strategy follows from the previous one, and we hinted at it at the end of the previous section. Clients may wish to create a visitor relationship with counselors concerning the goals that everyone else is worried about, but that does not mean they might not want to create a customer relationship to work on something else, a goal that is meaningful to them. Finding such a goal begins the process of moving the counseling relationship from a visitor-based relationship to a customer-based one.

> Shannon, a fourteen-year-old with a history of alcohol and marijuana use and of running away, flatly denied that her drug use was any kind of problem.
>
> "I can take it or leave it," she said. "It's not my problem that everyone gets so upset just because I smoke a little pot and have a beer now and then. Shit, half the kids at my school use more than I do. They're the ones who need treatment, not me."
>
> "It must be a hassle seeing everyone else doing drugs and not having to go to treatment," her counselor told her. "But, you know, your PO says you gotta come here for six weeks at least. Is there anything we could work on that might make things easier for you?"
>
> "I wish my mom wasn't on my case all the time," Shannon said.
>
> "Do you want to try to do something about that?" the counselor asked.
>
> "She'll never change," Shannon said. "She's always been this way."
>
> "Maybe not," her counselor said, "but it's going to be pretty boring for the next six weeks if we don't have anything to talk about. How would you like to see things between you and your mom change?"

Clearly, it will take more than one simple question to help Shannon move from being an opponent visitor to an enthusiastic customer. However, as this short vignette illustrates, asking a simple question helps Shannon begin to consider what *she* wants to get from her meetings with her counselor. The process of moving from visitor to customer is often a "two steps forward, one step back" process, as clients vacillate between fighting against treatment that they have not voluntarily chosen and thinking about what benefit they might get from it. Counselors will likely need patience and persistence to stick with clients as they move back and forth between wanting a visitor relationship and wanting a customer relationship. The more counselors can give clients ownership and a meaningful stake in the outcome of counseling, the more likely it is that the clients will become customers.

But Is It Really Treatment?

Our approach to working with clients who want to establish a visitor relationship in treatment sometimes leaves substance abuse professionals in a quandary. Not confronting visitors about their addiction and its very real dangers can leave counselors feeling as if they are not doing good treatment, or even not practicing ethically. It may also seem as if we are suggesting that counselors side with the clients' denial by allowing them to set a goal other than substance abuse as the focus for the initial stages of treatment. Neither of these situations is the case. We are not banning discussion of substance abuse during the joining and goal-setting stage of treatment. Rather, we are suggesting that aggressively trying to force clients to go where they are not yet prepared to go is not effective. As systems thinkers, we are also convinced that all parts of clients' lives are intertwined, and that one will lead to another. Take the case of Shannon, for example. It will not be long before she begins to see that part of the reason her mother is on her case all the time has to do with Shannon's use of drugs and alcohol. At this point, Shannon can consider making a change in her drug use from a new perspective—not as something that is being forced on her by the courts or by her mother, but as a route to getting something else she wants and needs. Such a realization may not lead immediately to complete cessation of drinking and drug use, but Shannon is now seeing that choice as a potential benefit to her, and not as evidence that she has given in to the demands of an authority she wants to resist. When clients see issues more flexibly, they have more possibility for change.

A second struggle that counselors sometimes have with our approach to visitors is that often the goal that opponents suggest they want to work on is "getting out of coming here." By suggesting this goal, opponents typically hope the counselors will mount an effort to convince them that they need treatment, thereby setting up a struggle. In our view, the goal of ending treatment is a perfectly legitimate one. Every client should have it as their goal. Thus, we suggest that counselors not argue with opponents about this goal but invite them to begin planning how to achieve it. When clients propose provocative goals, it is usually helpful to move toward those goals with curiosity, rather than to initiate a struggle over them. One might ask an opponent whose goal is to get out of treatment, "What would it take to convince the judge (PO, your parents, your spouse, etc.) that you don't need to come here anymore? How could you go about convincing that person that alcohol is not a problem for you?" Similarly, an adolescent male, for example, might provocatively suggest that his goal is to become a dealer so that he can move out of his parents' home and thereby not have them trying to set limits on him all the time. Although it is tempting to try to educate the adolescent about all the dangers of dealing, interesting things happen when the counselor asks questions that move toward that goal, rather than opposing it. When we have asked questions such as "Who do you know who would set you up as a dealer? Where would you plan to live? How would you handle getting arrested and having to go to court?" we have often found that clients soon begin to tell us how impractical the goal of being a dealer really is. We are not trying to be tricky here or to use reverse psychology. Instead, we are respecting the appropriate part of the adolescent's goal—becoming independent of his parents—while trying not to get into a struggle about the inappropriate part of the goal—becoming a drug dealer as the means to independence. As always with visitors, our goal is to keep the conversation going.

As noted earlier, visitors are often difficult clients for counselors to deal with because their whole stance is to reject exactly what the counselor has to offer, namely, help. Although none of the strategies discussed here will miraculously convert a visitor to a customer, each holds the possibility of keeping the counseling conversation going and providing a way for the client to find some meaning and ownership in the process, if the client chooses to take it.

COMPLAINANTS

Some people come to see a counselor hoping to establish a relationship based on concern about a third person—a complainant relationship, in other words. These clients hope that through presenting the problems and failings of the other person, the counselor will be persuaded to enter into an effort to change that other person. Of course, changing someone who has not appeared for counseling—or is a visitor, if they have appeared—is a nearly impossible task for a counselor. Since we do not have reliable methods to change people who are not involved in the treatment process, we often suggest to clients who want to establish a complainant relationship that *they* are the ones who need to do something different. Sometimes we tell such clients that they have a problem that needs treatment. We say that their worry about someone else indicates that they are codependent. We diagnose "overfunctioning" when they describe all the unsuccessful efforts they have made to change the person about whom they are concerned. If they have tried to make the other person's life easier in some way, we wonder if they are not "enablers." Sometimes, when we are more candid, we tell complainants that, although it is unfair, the only people we know how to help change, are the people who come to our offices. Since they are there, and the person they are worried about is not, we propose to help them change with the hope that by doing something different they will provoke a change in the other person. Of course, none of these strategies make sense to people who come wanting to establish a complainant relationship. Complainants have a clear vision of what the person they are worried about needs to change, and little or no vision of any part they may play in the continuation of the problem. A counselor's suggestion to a complainant that he or she act differently as a means of solving the problem seems either naive or insulting under these circumstances. The complainant's most likely response is an increased effort to convince the counselor that someone else needs to change.

The initial focus with someone seeking a complainant relationship is the same as with a visitor, namely, to empathize with the client's view of the situation. Complainants expend a great deal of emotional and physical energy trying to solve the problem about which they are concerned. Although they are often angry and frustrated by the time they get to treatment and may have moved into a reactive blaming stance, it is important for counselors to remember that complainants care about the people they are focused on and want to solve the problem. Unfortunately, their focus on the other person typically does not result in change. So, rather than suggesting that the clients must do something different, counselors should begin by understanding the clients' view and empathizing with all the effort, worry, and concern they have put into the situation. Again, we are not suggesting that the counselors do this as some tricky intervention, but rather because it is true. Until clients are convinced that counselors can at least see their perspective, they are likely to continue their attempts to convince the counselors that they have no power to solve the problem.

The second step in working with complainants is to gently shift the focus of the conversation from the third person to the complainants themselves. This shift should not initially aim at getting them to take action but should ask them simply to reflect on their involvement in the situation. Counselors begin by accepting their clients' view of the seriousness and strain of the situation, and by asking how the clients have managed to survive in such difficult straits without giving up or going crazy. While not a call to action, this approach does ask clients to begin to look at themselves in the situation, but from the perspective of strengths, not problems. As this focus on self expands, counselors can gradually introduce ideas about what clients might do to ease the strain of the situation. Notice that the focus stays on what the clients can do to survive in the situation, not what they can do to solve the problem. Any hint that counselors expect clients to solve the problem is likely to be met with increased protest.

As an example, consider how Stephanie worked with Maria, who came to therapy very concerned about her husband, Ramon.

> Ramon was admitted to treatment after a second drunk and disorderly arrest for assaulting one of his employees. When Maria came to meet with Stephanie, the family counselor at the treatment center, she immediately began to describe the many difficulties she had endured over the course of her ten-year marriage to Ramon. Ramon had been verbally abusive, had had at least one affair that Maria knew of, worked long hours at the successful plumbing business he owned, and refused to have anything to do with Maria's family, who he felt were all against him. Along with her complaints, Maria also described in detail the many unsuccessful efforts she had made to get Ramon to change. She had tried to get him to go to marriage counseling, to AA, to

talk to their parish priest, and had even left him for three weeks when she found out about his affair.

Finally, Stephanie said, "When you tell me all the troubles that you and Ramon have had, it sounds like you would have left him years ago. But you didn't. That tells me that there is more to the story, that there is a good part of Ramon that is worth putting up with all this crap for. What is that good part?"

Notice that Stephanie's question accepts Maria's view of Ramon as a man with many troubles and problems but also asks her to enlarge that view to include the positive things she sees in her husband as well. It also depathologizes Maria's decision to stay with her husband by suggesting she had good reasons to do so.

Stephanie's question seemed to take Maria by surprise. She was so tuned in to seeing the difficult side of Ramon that she had to think for a moment about the positive side.

"It isn't very often," Maria said in answer to Stephanie's question, "but sometimes Ramon can be very nice. Last New Year's Eve, he got a baby-sitter for the kids without telling me and took me out to a dance. We hadn't been dancing for years. He told me how much he loved me, and how we were going to make things better, and he only had one glass of champagne to drink at midnight. I had a lot of hope after that night. But two days later, he started yelling at me again about why did I let the cleaners put too much starch in his shirts or something like that. He's never going to change."

"You've really gone through a lot with him, haven't you?" Stephanie said. Then, wanting to change the focus to Maria, Stephanie asked, "How do you put up with all the disappointments to stay around for the good times? What keeps you from giving up?"

Maria smiled. "Maybe I'm just stupid," she said.

"I doubt that," Stephanie replied. "Where does the strength come from to get through the hard times?"

"I guess it comes from the Church," Maria said. "The Bible says there is always hope."

"It sounds to me like you're a woman with strong faith," Stephanie said, "and your faith helps you endure the hard times with Ramon. What are the survival skills you use when things get really bad? How do you take care of yourself?"

"I pray," Maria said. "I have a friend who I can talk to. She has trouble at home, too, so she understands. I do some volunteer work at my daughter's school, and that takes my mind off of things. I guess I just get by as best I can."

As you can see, the questions that Stephanie asks help shift the conversation from all the things that are wrong with Ramon to the strengths that Maria has.

As always, written vignettes cannot accurately convey the back-and-forth nature of this work. It is likely that an entire session might involve working with Maria to draw out the strengths she uses to survive in her difficult relationship with her husband. Many clients do not make the shift readily, of course, and it is important to balance empathy for their plight with attempts to look at strengths and survival skills.

The stages of change literature (Miller et al., 1994) adds another dimension to understanding complainants. Complainants are often in the *contemplation* stage of change, a stage that is characterized by *ambivalence*. Complainants focus on others when they face difficult choices that appear to have no satisfactory outcome. Sometimes, they know the course of action they must take but are not yet ready to commit to doing it. At other times, they see only a limited range of options. Maria, for example, saw herself as able to do only one of two things—stay with Ramon and continue to be burdened by his actions or leave the marriage. Neither option was satisfactory, so she turned her attention to trying to make Ramon into the person she wanted him to be. This was a tempting thought because at times he *was* that person—considerate, temperate in his drinking, loving. Most of the time, however, Maria's efforts to change Ramon, and his reactions to those efforts, only polarized their relationship more and left Maria feeling hopeless and frustrated.

As the counselor succeeds at empathizing with the complainant and shifting the focus from complaints about others to considerations of the complainant's strengths and abilities, the client's ambivalence can also gently be addressed. We often talk with clients about their ambivalence as "voices in your head" or "parts of yourself." Stephanie used this language as she continued her work with Maria.

> "It sounds to me like there's a part of yourself, Maria, that says you should leave Ramon and get away from all the disappointments he causes. And there's another part that says you should stay because it's the right thing to do and because there are some good times. It must take an awful lot of energy to hold such opposite views."
>
> "It's like a wrestling match going on in my mind all the time," Maria said. Then she smiled. "Like on TV—Hulk Hogan against Steve Savage."
>
> "I get tired just thinking about it," Stephanie said. "What do those two parts of yourself say to you when they're really pulling you both ways at once?"
>
> "Well, one part says I'm pretty stupid to stay with Ramon when he treats me so bad. It's been going on a long time now, and what makes me think anything will ever change? But then the other part says that maybe things will get better, and it's important to have hope, and Ramon isn't always a jerk. Besides, how would I live on my own and support the kids? It just goes on and on like that."
>
> "Sounds like those voices only give you two choices," Stephanie said. "Either you shut up and take the abuse, or you leave. Maybe those aren't the only two choices."
>
> "What else is there?" Maria wanted to know.
>
> "I don't know for sure," Stephanie said, "but maybe we could spend some time trying to come up with something."

Stephanie's willingness to listen to Maria and to try to understand how trapped she felt in her marriage allowed her to shift the focus of the conversation to what changes Maria might be able to make. Thus, Stephanie moved closer to beginning to develop a customer relationship with Maria. Of course, not all clients are as willing as Maria was to consider alternatives. Sometimes clients wishing to have a complainant relationship remain adamant that nothing will change and that they can do nothing about it. In these cases, we again suggest that the counselor not try to counter the hopeless view but instead try to use it as the springboard for consideration of what the client will need to do in the face of such hopelessness. We call this the "survival skills" question, and we ask the following: "Since, in your view, the problems in your family are not likely to change, it seems clear that you will be living with those problems for some time to come. Given that, what are the skills you are going to need to use in order to sur-vive in this very tough situation?" This question acknowledges the hopelessness that the complainant feels but still turns the focus of treatment on what the client can do to make a difference, if only for his or her own psychological well-being. Often, it prompts the client to begin to think about self-care skills and to begin to disconnect a bit from the emotional intensity that has arisen around the problem.

When asking the survival skills question, it is important that the counselor not agree with the client that the situation is hopeless (unless, in fact, it is, as might be the case in terminal illness, for example). The counselor should always leave the door open for the possibility of change, but he or she can acknowledge that in the client's view, the situation is hopeless. This way the counselor remains respectful of the client's opinion but does not necessarily lend credence to it.

Summary

The basic strategy for joining with clients who want to develop a complainant relationship in counseling begins with the counselor not immediately trying to convince them that they have the power to make a change in their situation. It is important first to hear and acknowledge the pain and frustration clients feel about the problems they are facing and to recognize the efforts they have already put into trying to improve things. They can also be invited to discuss their ambivalence about making a change and their displeasure with the options they feel are open to them. Finally, the counselor can move the focus to the clients by asking about the strengths that have kept them going and the skills they will need to survive during such hard times.

CUSTOMERS

Clients who come to treatment seeking a customer relationship with their counselors both see a problem and are ready to take some personal responsibility for making a change in the problem. Such clients are the easiest to work with because the treatment relationship they seek is the one that most counseling theories and techniques prepare counselors to provide. We are best, in other words, at helping people make changes in their own actions as a means to solving problems. At times, discussions of how to work with customers have implied that counseling them is not complicated and does not require a great deal of effort on the part of the counselors, since change will occur naturally from clients' own motivation. This has not been our experience, however. Customers come to treatment at differing points along the road to change, and understanding each client's specific needs allows counselors to most effectively join with them. Again, we turn to the stages of change literature (Miller et al., 1994) to understand the steps customers take as they formulate a plan for change, put it into action, and learn to maintain the changes they have made.

Preparation

Clients in the preparation stage of change have made a commitment to doing things differently but have not yet taken steps to put that commitment into action. They may say such things as, "I know I need to make a change in my drinking, but I'm not sure where to start." Sometimes a dramatic event brings about the commitment to make a change. Recall the story of writer Caroline Knapp (1996), described earlier. Knapp's realization that she had come close to seriously injuring her friend's child led to her commitment to stop drinking. Being left by a spouse or partner, losing a job, or having a car accident are examples of other dramatic events that have led our clients to make a commitment to change. Sometimes the event is dramatic only in the eyes of the client. Eric quit smoking cigarettes within a few weeks of beginning a meditation program over twenty years ago. As he learned to concentrate on his breathing, he became dramatically aware of the effect that each cigarette had on him physiologically. As he felt his throat constrict and his lungs burn slightly with each puff, quitting became the only reasonable thing to do.

Making a commitment to change is not tied to a specific event. Sometimes clients are at a loss to say why they are now committed to change, stating simply that they woke up one morning and realized that they needed to do something different. Often this metamorphosis happens after an extended period of contemplating the pros and cons of change. Whatever the reason, a client's commitment to change is the starting point for the counselor to join with the customer in the preparation stage.

Once a commitment to change has been made, there is still much work for client and counselor to do. The primary task is to negotiate the specific goals for treatment, something we discuss in detail in the next chapter. When the goal has been set, the counselor then helps the client begin to formulate a plan for achieving it. Keeping with our collaborative stance, we do not prescribe a plan for clients to follow, as is traditional in most medical model-based treatment. Instead, we invite clients to think with us about how they can best meet their goals. This does not mean that we withhold information about possible treatment options or suggestions about how clients might proceed. Nor do we refrain from raising questions about plans that seem unrealistic. It does mean that we do not automatically assume that *we* can pick the best way for clients to make the changes they seek. In Chapter 6, we describe ways to help clients understand the change process and formulate a plan through looking at problem and solution sequences. At this point, we want to discuss, in general, some approaches that counselors can use to help customers in the preparation stage.

Klion and Pfenninger (1997) suggest several general steps that counselors can take to help their clients make realistic plans. Foremost is helping them choose a realistic rate and scope of change. At times, customers become so eager to make the changes they are now committed to that they set themselves up for failure by planning to do too much too quickly.

> Ralph came to treatment seeking to stop drinking, improve his marriage, go on a low-fat diet, begin a training program to receive a technical certificate, and renew a connection with his adult children, whom he abandoned when they were young. He assured his counselor that he would make a start on all of these projects before their next session a week later. Luckily, Ralph's counselor coached him to slow down and prioritize these goals, giving each one the time and energy it deserved. Ralph started by deciding to attend five AA meetings in the next week and to go to the community college to get a brochure on the training program he wanted to enter. Although important, starting a new diet, improving his marriage, and reconnecting with his estranged children were left for later in the process. Without the counselor's help in limiting the scope of change, Ralph would

likely have not been able to do as much as he had hoped and would have had to return to the next session feeling like a failure for not accomplishing all he had said he would do.

Klion and Pfenninger (1997) also suggest that counselors should help clients who are working on recovery build social support into their change efforts. People who abuse substances often center much of their social interaction around using. Efforts to stop using will disrupt these customary activities and sources of social support (dysfunctional though they may be) and may threaten the clients' change efforts. One way to address this issue is to help clients and their family members develop activities that are not centered on drug use to provide social support and recreation. Sometimes clients already have these drug-free activities in their repertoires. Counselors can ask about things clients and their family members used to do before substance abuse was a problem. At other times, substance abuse has become so pervasive that no area of the clients' lives remains untouched. Under these circumstances, new activities need to be developed. For many people, twelve-step or other recovery-oriented self-help programs provide the needed new activity and social support. However, counselors should not make formulaic suggestions about AA attendance and social support (e.g., "90 in 90"). Instead, involve clients in finding which drug-free activities and social support suit them best. The more ownership clients feel in developing the plan, the more likely they are to put energy into accomplishing it.

Action

Customers enter the action phase when they begin to put their plan into action. Sometimes this is a straightforward process that flows directly from the definition of goals to accomplishing them. More likely, however, the clients' efforts to change will be only partially successful, and they will need their counselors' help in evaluating and adjusting their strategy as time goes on.

Janie and Bob were working hard to reduce the frequency and intensity of verbal fights they had been having. Both were committed to change and had developed a time-out plan that they agreed to put into action whenever a difficult conversation turned into a fight. After developing this plan, they came to the next session saying that they had had only mixed success. They had used time-out successfully on one occasion, but two other conversations had turned into fights, and they had not used time-out. As Sharon, their counselor, asked questions about the two times they had not used time-out, Janie and Bob discovered that waiting until the conversation got heated didn't work for them. Both of them had the urge to "get in the last word" once they became angry, and this kept either of them from taking a time-out. With Sharon's help, they amended their plan by defining some of the earliest signals that their conversation was in danger of becoming an argument, and then taking a brief time-out at that point.

In the action stage of treatment, counselors serve as sounding boards, coaches, and coplanners. Again, the focus is kept on the clients' wishes and plans, but the counselors add their suggestions and opinions when appropriate. Counselors also often serve as cheerleaders during this phase, helping clients to notice the progress they are making and not to become discouraged in the face of setbacks. Relapse is part of any effort to change. In Chapter 7, we describe ways to work with relapse.

Maintenance

Maintenance begins when clients have a plan in place that allows them to regularly meet their goals. Counselors have a twofold job at this point. First, they help clients anticipate future events and stresses that might destabilize the plan. Second, they help clients "own" the changes they have made and see them as reflections of their strength and ability to solve their own problems. This is especially important, since research has demonstrated that believing one's own efforts are responsible for the positive changes made in treatment helps maintain those gains after treatment (Goldbeck, Myatt, and Aitchison, 1997; Lambert and Bergin, 1994; McKay, Maisto, and O'Farrell, 1993).

Janie and Bob, for example, entered the maintenance phase when they regularly used their time-out plan to interrupt potential fights and were then able to come back together later and discuss the hot topic successfully. Sharon now helped the couple look at any upcoming events that might be difficult to handle and that could precipitate a relapse into fighting. They identified an upcoming beach vacation with Bob's family as a potential source of stress. Bob's parents, his sister, her husband and children, and Janie and Bob would all be staying in a rented beach house for a week. In the past, Janie had found this situation difficult to cope with, and she and Bob both noticed an increase in fighting before, during, and after the trip. Sharon asked if they could use the time-out procedure at the beach, but Bob said it would be difficult since the house they were all staying in was small. She asked them to brainstorm other ways of reducing stress, and Janie suggested they set aside an hour in the morning and an hour in the evening to walk alone together on the beach. Bob would explain to his family that this was their time to "renew their relationship." Before starting each walk, they would agree whether to use that time to talk about issues or just to unwind. Both Janie and Bob thought this would help keep tension low between them. They also pledged to use time-out if necessary.

When they returned from the beach trip, Bob and Janie said it had gone better than either of them had expected. Their tension had been kept low, they enjoyed much of the time they spent with Bob's family, and they used their time-out procedure only once for a few minutes. Sharon used these experiences to increase their sense of efficacy, compliment them on all they had done to change their lives, and remind them that *they* had come up with the plan to walk on the beach.

"I think you two have what it takes to keep these changes going," she told them. "If you can do it while you're on vacation with Bob's family, you can do it anytime."

WORKING WITH VISITORS AND COMPLAINANTS IN THE SAME FAMILY

With individuals, counselors find it relatively easy to assess the motivational stance of the client and tailor their interventions accordingly. The process becomes more difficult when families come to treatment because each member may be at a different level of motivation and want to develop a different kind of relationship with the counselor. The counselor must be thoughtful about how to join with all family members under these circumstances. In substance abuse treatment, complainants and visitors often go together.

> Jason, for example, was over two years into his own recovery when he was seen with his wife, Lisa. Lisa herself had a long history of alcohol abuse and finally came to treatment by court order following a traffic accident and a DWI charge. Jason had spent the past two years telling Lisa that she needed to stop drinking and going into great detail about how he had done so himself. He dragged her to AA meetings, urged her to call the twenty-one-day inpatient facility that had helped him detox, and peppered her daily with sayings from his twelve-step group. Although Jason was initially delighted that Lisa had been ordered to treatment, by the time of their first couples session, he had become discouraged and irritated with her.
>
> "She isn't going to meetings every day like she's supposed to," he told Daneeka, their counselor. "And she's still stressing out about things. I keep telling her that she has to 'Let go and let God,' but it doesn't do any good."
>
> For her part, Lisa thought she was doing fine. She hadn't had a drink in three weeks—the longest she'd gone since she started drinking as a teenager. "I go to three meetings a week and that's enough for me right now," Lisa said. "I just wish Jason would get off my case. Living with him is like having The Big Book for a husband."
>
> Daneeka faced a real challenge with Lisa and Jason. If she tried to get Jason to reduce the intensity of his efforts to change Lisa, he was likely to feel Daneeka didn't understand how serious he felt Lisa's problem was, or that she was dismissing his concern. On the other hand, if Daneeka tried to push Lisa toward doing things she wasn't ready to do, counseling would become just another hassle to be avoided in Lisa's life. In either case, one or the other would see her as taking sides.

What counselors do when complainants and visitors come together to counseling depends on several things. First, it is important to understand how polarized family members have become in their positions. We usually begin by seeing if we can empathize with each person's position individually in the presence of the other. Remember that the polarized views may not reside only in individuals. Adolescent substance abusers and their parents sometimes represent two different levels of motivation, with the adolescent as a visitor and the parents as complainants.

> Daneeka began by letting both Lisa and Jason know that she was doing her best to understand their positions. She started with Jason.
>
> "Jason, I get the picture that you are doing your level best to help Lisa because you really care about her and want her to stop using."
>
> Lisa's reaction to this statement was a critical gauge of how polarized the pair had become.
>
> "I don't know what you're talking about when you say he cares about me," Lisa said. "This is all about him being the hot shit recovering person and rubbing my face in my problems." Not only did Lisa not see Jason's actions as helpful, she also doubted that his *motivation* was to be helpful.
>
> Daneeka was tempted to point out to Lisa how she saw Jason being concerned about her, but she wisely refrained from doing so. Instead, she tried to empathize with Lisa's point of view.
>
> "It sounds like you see Jason doing this more for his own reasons than anything having to do with helping you," Daneeka said.
>
> Although Lisa nodded her head in agreement, Jason got mad. "What am I getting out of this anyway? Most guys would have dumped Lisa years ago. In fact, that's exactly what her first husband did. Now I think I know why."

Obviously, Lisa and Jason have very different views of the problem and the kind of help they want. They are also unable to listen to each other's views without becoming reactive and argumentative. With couples such as this, we find it useful to meet with them individually for a while to begin to develop a relationship with each of them before coming back together. The counselor will find it almost impossible to join with both of them together when they are so reactive to each other. During the individual meetings, the counselor can use the skills described earlier in this chapter to join with both the visitor and the complainant. As her relationship with each of them develops, she can help each move to more self-focus that will set the stage for coming back together and working to find jointly shared goals.

Not all couples are as polarized as Jason and Lisa. Let us look at a different scenario. Suppose that instead of getting angry when Daneeka pointed out Jason's wish to help, Lisa had said something such as, "I know he wants to help me, but giving me advice all the time only pisses me off. The more he tells me what to do, the more I want to tell him to go to hell. I'm not a little kid."

Jason might have responded, "I just get so worried about you. I don't know what to do."

In this scenario, although Lisa rejects Jason's actions, she does not doubt his motivation. She believes he wants to help, in other words. For his part, Jason reiterates his worry and does not blame Lisa for not taking his advice. These responses to Daneeka's initial attempt to empathize with Jason's position indicate a less polarized stance and the possibility that Daneeka can join with this couple while seeing them together—empathizing first with one and then with the other until she has a strong relationship with each.

SUMMARY

Counselors, in part at least, can help develop relationships with their clients that are either marked by cooperation and movement toward change or characterized by conflict, resistance, and lack of motivation. The more accurately a counselor can assess client's level of motivation for change and accommodate to it, the more likely their relationship can grow into a productive one (see Table 5.2). Of course, counselors do not have unilateral power in treatment. The outcome of counseling also depends on clients' efforts and willingness to use what counselors offer. But the failures of the old model of the client having to accommodate completely to the counselor's view of what should happen in therapy or risk being dismissed as "unmotivated" are being recognized. Counselors must have thoughtful flexibility in their interactions with clients in order to build relationships that will support change.

TABLE 5.2. Summary: Assessing Motivation

Motivation is interactional.
It is a product of the quality of the therapy relationship.
Counselors must assess the clients' stage of change:
Precontemplation
Contemplation
Determination
Action
and therapy relationship type:
Customer
Visitor
Complainant
Level of intervention must match the clients' stage of change and the type of therapy they seek

Chapter 6

Negotiating a Contract for Therapy

A group of our students once joked that they had a 50 percent chance of knowing the first thing we would say in response to any supervision question they asked us. Whenever they brought a stuck case to supervision, they said, we invariably asked one of two questions: "How good is your relationship with the family?" or "What is your contract?" We had to admit that their observation was accurate. Having a sound therapeutic relationship and a clear therapy contract are the bedrock of successful treatment, in our experience. When therapy gets stuck, attending to these two elements is the first place to start fixing things. In Chapters 3 and 4, we examined the importance of developing a strong therapeutic relationship, or joining with a family. In this chapter, we discuss how to develop a workable therapeutic contract.

In our view, a therapeutic contract has two primary elements. First is the family members' vision of their preferred future. What do they want to get from coming to counseling? Where do they want treatment to take them? The second element is the translation of the family's vision of the future to more specific goals that will guide the day-to-day work of counseling. Throughout the chapter, we use the word *contract* to describe this set of shared visions and responsibilities. Although some counselors may, in fact, write out all the elements of the therapeutic contract, we do not think that a therapy contract must be a written document. We use the concept of a contract because it connotes a process of coming to a clear understanding about where treatment is headed. Negotiating a clear agreement—regardless of whether it is written down—is the basis for successful treatment.

A VISION OF THE FUTURE

When Lien [Lee-in] first met with Josh and his parents, she asked the family what they hoped to get from coming to family counseling.

"I just want them to leave me alone," Josh said, pointing to his parents.

"I could leave Josh alone if I was sure he wasn't going out drinking with his friends," Josh's mother said. "I can't just pretend things are great when I know they haven't been."

"I'm tired of his attitude," Josh's father said. "I wish he'd stop yelling and swearing at us every time we have to say no to something he wants to do. And I'm really tired of him sneaking out of the house all the time. We can't trust him an inch."

Similar to Josh and his parents, people invariably come to treatment able to describe in detail what they want to see *end* as a result of counseling. Drug abuse, alcoholism, family conflict, disappointment, and depression are all examples of things clients hope to stop with the help of the counselor. Few clients, however, have a clear vision of what they want to create or move toward as a result of treatment. Although nothing is wrong with wanting to end suffering, change efforts also need a positive direction in which to proceed. The counselor's first job, then, is to help families shift their view from what they want to stop doing to what they want to start doing. The shift is from working for the *absence* of something that has been happening to working toward the *presence* of something that the families would like to have as part of their future. Of course, family members' positive goals will typically be incompatible with the problems they want to go away.

There are three related reasons to make the switch from an absence goal to a presence goal. First, it is easier to work toward a positive goal than away from a negative one. A positive goal gives direction and points the way to action, whereas a negative goal points only to inhibition, to not doing something. Second, a positive goal gives both counselor and family a concrete gauge to assess progress and ultimately decide when therapy should end. A couple's success, for example, in their effort to reduce the number of fights they have is hard to judge in an absolute way. How long will a reduction in fighting have to be in place before they decide they have really reduced their conflict? Does a week when they fight more mean that they have failed in their efforts? Better questions to ask, and better goals to pursue, would consider what the couple would like to see take the place of their fights and what they want to do with the energy and interaction that have been concentrated in conflict. Living in separate homes and seeing each other only on Tuesday and Saturday evenings might reduce the frequency of the couple's fights, but it is probably not the outcome they are seeking. Finally, concentrating on not doing something keeps that action in the forefront of family members' thinking, like the paradoxical instruction not to think about a pink elephant. Setting a goal not to fight means that a couple must think about fighting, thereby keeping their conflicts in mind. In contrast, setting a goal to communicate calmly and regularly (actions that reduce conflict and fighting) guides a family's thinking toward positive actions they can take and reduces the amount of attention given to conflict.

To help family members create a vision of the future that they want, the counselor asks them to describe what they hope their lives will be like as a result of treatment. The counselor uses this line of questioning to elicit the family's broad vision of its preferred future. He or she then asks more questions to make the broad components of that vision specific. Wanting to be happy is a wonderful goal, one that all of us would endorse, but it is hard to know how to start being happy. What actions would someone undertake to start being happy? And how would they know when they are happy? Obviously, the larger vision the family has can only be achieved in a step-by-step process, and the counselor must help the family think through what those steps will be. When working with families, we usually find ourselves weaving back and forth between asking family members about their vision of the future and translating that vision into a series of specific, measurable, behavioral steps. We often start this process with the following question: "What will you see happening in your family in six months that will tell you that this treatment was useful?" This question is often a difficult one for family members to answer. While they are well able to describe to you what they want to stop happening, they have typically not spent much time thinking about what positive changes they want to make. The counselor must be persistent in his or her efforts to keep the family focused on what positive changes they want to create. Lien began this work with Josh and his parents in the following way:

"Suppose that Josh's work in treatment, and your work as a family, is successful. What will each of you see happening in your family in six months that will tell you that therapy has worked?"

"Well, Josh won't be drinking and going out with his friends all the time," Josh's mother began.

"Not drinking is certainly an important goal," Lien said, "and I know Josh has been working on that in group. As Josh continues his progress, what will you see him doing that is different from what he's done in the past?"

"He won't be so negative all the time," Josh's mother said. "His attitude is really bad when he's drinking."

"So, he'll be more positive," Lien said.

Josh's mother nodded her head in agreement.

"What does Josh do when he's being positive? If I had a video-tape of the three of you together at home, what would I see that would tell me that Josh is in a positive space?"

"He'd talk, for one thing," Josh's mother said. "When he's negative, he doesn't talk to me at all."

"What does he talk about? Anything in particular?"

"No, nothing in particular. He'll just say hello to me when I get home from work and tell me things that happened at school."

"So one of the things that you would see in six months that would tell you that this treatment had been helpful would be Josh spending some time talking to you. Would it happen every day? Once a week? How often?"

"At least every other day," Josh's mother said. "I'd like it if we had a little time to talk every day, but I also know that he's getting to the age where he's going to be spending a lot more time away from home, so I guess every other day would be reasonable."

Notice that Lien does a number of things in this brief interchange with Josh's mother. First, she acknowledges the importance of the goal of Josh not drinking. Although this is an absence goal, it is one that cannot be ignored when adolescents are in drug treatment. Then, Lien gently guides Josh's mother to describe other changes that will accompany the absence of drinking. Josh's mother first mentions a decrease in Josh's negative attitude, and Lien reframes this as Josh being more positive. Thus, Lien has moved from a goal of less negativity to a goal of a more positive attitude. She then asks a series of questions to define a positive attitude more specifically. Josh's mother replies that one primary indicator for her of Josh's positive attitude is when he talks to her. This is a clear, positive, and specific indicator.

MAKING GOALS MEASURABLE

With Lien's help, Josh's mother has defined a specific, positive goal that she wants the family to work on in treatment. Her goal is to increase the amount of communication between Josh and herself. But how much communication is enough? To gauge the amount of change that the family wishes to see, we use a scaling technique. Scaling questions were developed as part of the solution-focused therapy work done at the Brief Family Therapy Center (Lipchik and de Shazer, 1988). They ask family members to assign numbers to their views about the current situation. This not only gives the therapist and the family a representation of the current state of the family's movement toward a solution but also helps demarcate differences between family members' views and gives the family a concrete way to define what the next steps toward change are.

In the following section, Lien works with Josh and his parents to quantify the amount of change they want on a numerical scale:

> "Help me get a better picture of how you would like to see your communication change. Think of a scale between one and ten. Suppose that the worst communication you can imagine is at one, and the best communication you can imagine is at ten. Where would you say you two are today?"

> Josh's mother thought for a minute. "I guess I'd say we're at a four."

> "What makes you say a four?" Lien asked. "I'd have guessed that you would be lower than that."

"Well, Josh does talk to me sometimes. Not as much as I'd like, however."

Lien smiled. "That leads to my next question. On the one-to-ten scale, where would you like your communication to be?"

Josh's mother smiled too. "A ten, of course."

"I don't want to have to be talking to my mother all the time," Josh said. "I'm not some baby, you know."

Lien held up her hand to quiet Josh. "I'll give you a chance to talk about goals in a minute," she said. "Right now, I want to hear from your mom."

"Ten's a great goal," Lien said to Josh's mom. "But let's start with the steps in between. What would it take for you to go from a four to a five?"

"Like I said earlier, if he would talk to me every other day, I'd be pretty satisfied."

"So if you and Josh had a conversation every other day, that would move you from a four to a five on our ten-point scale?"

"Yes, I think it would," Josh's mother said.

Lien turned to Josh. "Do you think you and your mother could have a conversation every other day, Josh?"

"What's she want to talk about?"

"That seems like a fair question," Lien said. "Why don't you ask her?"

Josh grimaced. "So what would you want to talk about?"

"I just like to know what's going on with you," his mother said. "Maybe you could tell me about school, or about your friends."

"But whenever I talk about my friends, we always get into a fight because you don't want me to see them," Josh said.

Lien interrupted. "On the one-to-ten scale we keep talking about, Josh, where would you say your communication with your Mom is now?"

"Probably the same. About a four."

"For you, what would it take to move to a five?"

"I'd talk to her more if she didn't get on my case all the time when I did."

"So one thing that would help you move to a five is if your conversations with your mom didn't turn into criticism."

Josh nodded.

"Let me see if I've got this right. If the two of you had a positive conversation every other day, that would move you from four to five on our ten-point scale."

"I guess so," Josh said.

"It would sure be a good start," Josh's mom said.

Using a scale to evaluate goals not only provides a way to measure progress but also helps refine the goal. As Lien talked with Josh and his mother, the specifics of what good communication meant to each of them emerged more clearly. Not only did good communication involve talking more frequently, it also meant having positive interactions when they talked.

Scaling is helpful not only in the goal-setting process but throughout treatment. Using small steps on the scale helps clients manage change at the right pace. It also helps keep them from feeling overwhelmed when they have only a vision of the end they wish to achieve and not the steps they need to take to get there. Efforts to change can become discouraging without intermediate markers of success. At the beginning of subsequent sessions with Josh and his family, Lien asked them to rate their progress on the scale. When they came back the next week, for example, saying that they had talked every other day and had had positive interactions, Lien wondered what it would take for them to move from a five to a six. With that question, Josh and his mother began to define what their next small step would be. Seeing small successes along the way helped assure all family members that they were making progress toward their overall goal.

RESOLVING CONFLICTING GOALS

Not every family will agree on goals as readily as Josh and his mother did, of course. One of the challenges of working with families in treatment is learning to help them resolve conflicting goals. This involves the counselor helping the family members learn to negotiate.

Fisher and Ury (1992), in their book titled *Getting to Yes,* describe the skills needed to negotiate mutual goals in general life situations. We have found these skills particularly useful in working with families. Fisher and Ury observed that most negotiations are positional; that is, each party in the negotiation stakes out a position and then tries to convince the others to give ground. This sets up a win-lose situation. For one party to gain something, the other party must give up something. This is typically the negotiation style we see when we work with families in treatment. Consider the following vignette from Lien's work with Josh and his family. Although Josh was willing to accede to his mother's wish to have more frequent conversations with him, when it came to negotiating a weekend curfew, he and his father were adamant about their positions.

> "Is it my turn to bring up something I want to change?" Josh asked after he and his mother had worked on defining what a successful conversation would be like.
>
> "Sure. What did you have in mind?" Lien asked.
>
> "I really want be able to stay out later on weekends," Josh said. "All my other friends can stay out really late, but my parents won't let me. It really sucks."
>
> Josh's father spoke up. "This isn't a conversation we're going to have again," he said. "When you prove that you can be trusted, we'll talk about extending your curfew. Until then, ten o'clock on weekends is late enough."
>
> Josh gave Lien a disgusted look. "See, there's no point in even talking about it."
>
> "But it seems like having a later curfew is important to you," Lien said. "Maybe that's something we can work on."
>
> "There's nothing to work on," Josh's dad said. "He thinks he should stay out until one in the morning on weekends and there's no way he staying out past ten."

As you can see from this conversation, both Josh and his dad had staked out positions from which they are trying to negotiate. For one to gain ground, the other must give up something. In other words, if

Josh were to convince his dad to let them stay out until 11 p.m., his father would have to move away from his stance that 10 p.m. was when Josh needed to be home. Since most of us do not like to feel that we have lost in negotiation, positions quickly become hard and fast, and movement difficult.

In contrast to positional negotiations, negotiations based on common interests invite both parties to look at what they have to gain from a successful outcome. When done correctly, this takes the negotiation out of the win-lose paradigm and moves it to a win-win footing. Negotiations based on common interests are particularly useful in situations in which the parties have ongoing relationships. Positional negotiations not only lead to an adversarial stance, they also become "contagious." Working toward a win-win solution is less likely to alienate the parties and more likely to make future negotiations go smoothly. After all, if one party feels that he or she must "give in" in a particular negotiation, that person is likely to be even less willing to compromise in the future, since he or she will feel that the other person owes him or her something. Counselors need to be active in their interactions with family members to help them make the shift from positional to common-interest negotiations, however, because it is not the way we are accustomed to trying to resolve disagreements.

Fisher and Ury (1992) suggest several steps to successful common-interest negotiations. We have modified the steps somewhat for use with families. Our steps to goal negotiation are focus on interests, not positions; explore options that benefit both sides; and negotiate a mutually satisfactory goal. Although we present these steps in outline fashion, in practice, they usually blend together.

Focus on Interests, Not Positions

The counselor starts the process of reconciling conflicting goals by helping each person articulate his or her interests in the situation. Interests are the needs or perceptions that lead the person to see his or her position as a solution. We assume that people do not generally take positions simply to irritate other members of their family (although it can seem that way sometimes). Positions represent a way either to meet emotional needs or to solve the various problems the family is facing. However, positions also lead to increasing rigidity and a variety of negative perceptions about the others involved in the issue. As this happens, the interests behind the positions quickly get lost. In the case of Josh and his father, for example, Josh sees his father as tyrannical, while Josh's father sees his son as irresponsible. Josh may say to himself, "Dad's just against me. He never lets me do anything because he doesn't want me to be happy." In the same vein, Josh's father may think, "That boy is totally irresponsible and will never amount to anything. He just wants to stay out late in order to get in trouble." As negative attributions about the other person accumulate, mistrust grows and negotiations become even more difficult. Families typically come to counseling when they are in this state of mistrust, a state heightened by the many deceptions and lies that are typically part of the phenomenon of substance abuse.

The counselor plays a key role in helping reveal the interests underneath the rigid positions each side has taken. The counselor's first task is to help each family member describe his or her emotional position. Having each person talk to the counselor while the others listen is a useful technique to help the process proceed. This strategy serves two purposes. First, it helps maintain solid relationships between the counselor and each family member. In addition, it allows family members to hear one another discuss their emotional positions without becoming involved in heated arguments about them. Once an argument starts, the ability to listen to a different viewpoint vanishes quickly. Lien used this technique in her work with Josh and his father.

> "I want to make sure I understand each of you clearly," Lien said. "Let me start with you, Josh. You want a later curfew, right?"
>
> "Right."
>
> "Why?"
>
> "Isn't it obvious? So I can stay out later and not get in trouble."
>
> "You seem to know how to get in trouble no matter what time it is," Josh's father interjected.
>
> Lien stopped him. "I want to see the situation from Josh's perspective right now," she said. "Then I'll want to see your side of it too." She turned back to Josh.
>
> "So part of it is that you don't want to get in trouble with your parents. Is that right?" Lien asked.

"Uh-huh."

"But what about the other part, the part about staying out later? What's that all about?"

"It's a real drag to be the only one who has to go home at ten," Josh said. "I've been doing everything they told me to do when I got discharged from treatment. I've been going to group. I go to three AA meetings a week over at the church. I haven't used or been drinking at all. I think I deserve a later curfew."

"Sounds like part of it has to do with your friends," Lien said.

"They're starting to give me shit about it. Last week no one would give me a ride to the dance at the teen center because no one wanted to have to leave early to bring me home. The dance was over at eleven but my dad said I still had to come home at ten. I feel like a baby."

"So another reason you want a later curfew is so you can do more things with your friends, so you can feel like you fit in better."

"Yeah."

Lien asks questions that lead Josh away from his focus on his father's unfairness and the hour he has to be home. Instead, she tries to find out what his underlying *interests* are—what benefit he is looking for by extending his curfew. *Positions* ("I want a two a.m. curfew") are narrow and can usually only be met in one way, whereas *interests* ("I want to feel like I can fit in with my friends without getting in trouble at home") are broader and can be achieved in any number of ways. After Lien has helped Josh define his interests, her next step in the process is to make sure that Josh's father has understood his son. To begin the process of finding shared interests, the counselor must make sure that everyone involved in the negotiation understands the interests of the others.

"Before we go any further," Lien said, "I want to make sure that we're all understanding each other." She turned to Josh's father. "Tell me what you understand Josh wants to get from having a later curfew."

"He just wants to stay out later, probably to get in trouble."

Lien turned to Josh. "Did he get it?"

"Nope," Josh said.

"Try it again," Lien said. "What do you want to get from having a later curfew?"

"First, I don't want to have to choose between my friends and being in trouble with my parents. And second, I don't want to feel like some kind of baby because I have to be home earlier than everyone else."

Lien turned back to Josh's dad. "I'm not asking you to agree with what Josh said. I just want to make sure that you understand it."

"He doesn't want to get in trouble with us, and he still wants to stay out late with his friends."

"What about it, Josh? Better?"

"I guess."

Although both do so grudgingly, Josh and his father indicate that they have communicated clearly about what Josh's interests in the situation are.

Although the process can become laborious, we have found that it is a mistake to move ahead before everyone understands one another. Some families are so polarized that it may take the counselor a long time to ensure that all members understand one another. When the interests of the first one to speak are understood, the counselor turns to the others and helps them articulate their interests.

"Okay," Lien said to Josh's father, "now tell me about what you want."

"I want him home at ten o'clock every night."

"Why?"

"I'm his father. I can decide when he's supposed to be home."

"Of course, you're his father, and you can set his curfew. But I'll bet there's more to it than you just feeling you have the right to tell him when he has to be home. What happens for you when Josh isn't home by ten?"

Josh's dad got quiet for a moment. "I start to worry."

"What do you worry about?"

"I worry that he's getting in trouble. That I'm not there to protect him. I keep thinking of that night when the cops brought him home and he looked so sad, and I wondered where I'd gone wrong. I felt like I hadn't been a very good father to him or he wouldn't be in so much trouble."

"So, when you tell Josh he has to be home at ten, you're doing it to be a good father to him?"

"Yes."

"Well, stop trying to be a good father," Josh said. "You're screwing up my life."

"Your father gave you a chance to talk, Josh," Lien said. "I want you to do the same."

Josh sat back in his chair, and Lien returned to her conversation with his father. "It sounds like you really care about your son."

"Of course I do. I love him."

"And you're doing the best you can to help him get through this tough time?"

"Yeah. I feel like I have a lot of catching up to do."

Lien now has a clearer understanding of Josh's father's interest underlying his position on Josh's curfew. He is trying to be a good father to his son. Although it is tempting to suggest to him other ways that he might be able to parent Josh more effectively, the goal is for family members to come to an agreement together, not for the counselor to step in and solve the problem. Instead, Lien uses the same techniques she used earlier to make sure that Josh has heard his father's interests. When she is sure that he has, she is ready to move to the next step in the process.

Explore Options That Benefit Both Sides

Understanding the interests behind family members' positions allows the counselor to begin the process of exploring options that might lead to a mutually acceptable solution. As noted earlier, whereas positions lead to either-or solutions—either you accept the other person's position, or you do not—interests allow for a much broader range of actions that might satisfy both parties' interests. Lien begins the process of exploring options by reminding Josh and his father what they have each stated their underlying interests to be concerning Josh's curfew.

> "Josh, you've told me that you want a later curfew because there are times when having to come home at ten keeps you from feeling like you fit in with your friends. On the other hand, your dad wants to know that he's doing what he needs to be doing in order to be a responsible father to you. Let's see if there are some ways you can both meet those needs."
>
> "They could just stay out of my business," Josh said.
>
> "I don't think that's going to happen," Lien replied. "Let's just brainstorm some options—no matter how ridiculous."
>
> Both Josh and his father were silent.
>
> "Okay, I'll start it off," Lien said. "One option would be for Josh to be able to stay out as long as he wants, as long as he takes his father with him. So, Josh, next time you want to go to a concert, you'll have to get a ticket for your dad too."

Humor and exaggeration can be useful tools to break a stalemate between family members. Polarized positions lead to constricted thinking, as all parties become invested in defending their positions and are unwilling to see any other alternatives. Sometimes the counselor can model expanded thinking by coming up with a suggestion that is so unexpected, or ridiculous, that it shakes the family out of the stalemate. Lien did that with her suggestion that Josh and his father go everywhere together. The counselor must be careful to make sure that the family is amenable to the use of humor, however. The counselor must be able to communicate that she is trying to help in a funny way, and that she is not making fun of the family or its dilemma. When the intensity in the family is high, or when family members have not given any evidence of being able to step back from their difficulties enough to laugh at themselves, the counselor should not use humor or exaggeration so as to avoid offending family members.

Somewhat to Lien's surprise, it was Josh's father who spoke first. "I don't think Josh has to be treated like a baby," he said. "I just want to make sure that Josh is safe." Then he smiled a little bit. "Besides, I don't know if I could stand going to one of his rock concerts anyway. I'm more of a Beach Boys guy myself."

Lien turned to Josh. "See if you can work something out with your father so that you can find a way to reassure him you'll be safe."

"He should just trust me," Josh said.

"I don't think he's talking about not trusting you," Lien said. "I think he's talking about making sure you're safe and not using." She looked at Josh's father. "Is that right?"

Josh's dad nodded.

"I'm not going to use again, Dad," Josh said. "Why won't you believe me?"

"Most of the time, I do," Josh's father replied. "But when you're out late at night with people I don't know, I start to worry."

"What would make you feel more secure if Josh wanted to be out later and had a good reason?" Lien asked.

"It would help a lot if I knew the kids he was hanging out with. The kids he used to drink and use drugs with were kids I'd never met."

"Josh, could you work that out?"

"You mean bring my friends over to meet my dad so I could get permission to stay out late? I'd really feel like a baby then."

"I'm not trying to embarrass you, Son," Josh's dad said. "I just want to make sure you're okay. How about if you would just bring your friends by the house a few times so I could get to meet them?"

"Would that be a fair trade for permission to stay out later sometimes?" Lien asked.

"I guess," Josh said.

"Why don't the two of you start there and see how it works," Lien said.

In this example, the last step in the negotiation process—negotiating a mutually satisfactory goal—flowed directly from the process of generating alternatives. Of course, our example is designed to illustrate the process clearly. In practice, the negotiation of a mutually satisfying goal may take much longer and may be spread over several sessions. Family members may develop a plan that they find does not work. They may need help refining it or they may abandon it altogether to try to find a different solution. As in all work with families, the counselor needs patience and persistence to keep the goal negotiation process moving in a positive direction.

CONTRACT PROBLEMS

Counselors encounter a variety of contract problems in their work with families. We present a few of the most common here along with suggestions about how to deal with them.

Does a Focus on Substance Abuse Have to Be Part of the Family Treatment Contract?

Sometimes families define goals they want to work on as families that do not seem to be directly connected to helping the addicted family member stop using. For instance, family members may say they want to work on the parents' marital conflict when their adolescent daughter is in treatment. In general, we feel that family members should set their own goals, even if they do not directly address the issue of substance abuse. Although it may seem to the counselor as though this is siding with the family's denial, we recommend it for two reasons. First, as systems thinkers, we are convinced that substance abuse does not exist apart from the rest of the family system. Making whatever change the family wants to make in the system will affect all other parts of the system, including substance abuse. Sometimes this effect is felt when the family solves one set of problems and then decides to address the issue of substance abuse directly. At other times, the systemic effect is felt when the family works on issues that are seemingly unrelated to substance abuse, yet a change occurs in the family members' drinking or drug use. The second reason we suggest beginning with the family's goals is that this model is designed to be part of a comprehensive treatment model, with substance abuse issues dealt with elsewhere in treatment. Thus, the counselor has the luxury of joining with the family members wherever they want to start, thereby building a relationship with them that respects their ability to identify changes they want to make as a group and to work toward them.

Two situations may require that the counselor raise the issue of substance abuse directly with family members who have not defined it as a problem they want to deal with in their family counseling. If family members are behaving in such a way that they are actively undermining the substance abuser's efforts to abstain, the counselor may need to raise this issue directly. Consider the following example:

> Andy insisted on keeping beer in the refrigerator even though Jeff, his gay partner, was only a couple of weeks into recovery. The presence of alcohol in the home was a serious and continuous challenge for Jeff. Their family counselor finally helped Jeff raise this issue with Andy. Andy claimed that since he wasn't an alcoholic, he should be able to have a beer when he wanted one. The counselor was able to help Jeff communicate to Andy the degree to which having beer so easily accessible threatened his recovery. They were able to come to an agreement that Andy would not bring beer, or any other alcohol or drug, into the house until he and Jeff had discussed and agreed on the issue.

A second situation that may lead the counselor to raise the issue of substance abuse as a family issue is when the substance-abusing family member is repeatedly relapsing or otherwise demonstrating that he or she is struggling to remain engaged in treatment. At a time such as this, family support (sometimes even carefully planned family pressure as in an intervention) can help the substance abuser through a difficult time.

Although the counselor may have to raise the issue of substance abuse with families from time to time, we urge restraint in this area. We trust families' abilities to plan their own course, as well as the reality of systemic effects, to lead the family and counselor to a solution that includes the end of substance abuse.

What If the Family Does Not Want to Work on the "Real" Problem?

At times, it seems as though families pick a trivial issue to work on in family counseling when it is clear to the counselor that there are other, much more serious problems they should be attending to. Our approach to this situation is related to the stance we take about including substance abuse as an explicit family treatment goal. We begin with the goal the family sets, unless there is a compelling reason to do otherwise. While an outsider may be convinced that family members are missing the most important issues they must tackle, we trust their sense about where they should start to make changes. As noted previously, we also trust the interconnectedness of a system and are convinced that a change in one part of the family's relationship patterns will affect all other parts of the system. Finally, we send a mixed message about our belief in the family's strengths and abilities if we ask family members to set their own goals and then tell them that they have chosen the wrong ones.

Despite our preference to trust the family's goals first and foremost, there are times when the counselor must raise issues that the family might prefer not to address. In the previous section, we described the importance of focusing on substance abuse when the substance abuser is relapsing seriously or is not participating in other aspects of the treatment program. Violence between adults in the family and child abuse are two other situations that require the counselor to impose his or her focus on the family. In a later chapter, we describe ways in which counselors can both identify situations that indicate a risk for violence and take actions to safeguard family members.

What If the Family's Goal Shifts Every Week?

We are well familiar with families in treatment who seem to have a different goal each week. One week they want to work on communication between the adults and the children. The next week they are concerned about a fight between the parents. The week following, they come in the midst of a crisis because they are being evicted from their home. If the counselor focuses on the *content* of their difficulties, each session is like starting over—defining the solution the family wants for the week's problem, coming up with specific steps that need to be taken to reach the solution, having the family contract with one another to take those steps, and so forth. The problem is, however, that the following week's crisis overshadows the previous week's crisis, leaving little time in subsequent sessions for the counselor to review with family members how much progress they have made on the previous week's problem, or to refine the solution.

To work with a family that seems to have an ever-changing multitude of problems, the counselor should pull his or her focus back to look at the overarching pattern that surrounds each of the problems. In other words, we would suggest that the counselor begin to focus on the family's *process,* instead of the content of their problems. For example, the counselor may determine that one common aspect to all the problems the family presents is unclear communication. The counselor can then help the family to see the importance of clear communication and determine if family members are willing to set this as a goal. If they are, working on clear communication can take place regardless of the specific problem the family brings to the session. One can work to develop clear communication about an adolescent's household chores, a couple's decision about how to deal with a financial problem, or the ways in which family members can support the substance abuser in recovery. No matter what the content, by focusing on the process, the counselor can help the family make progress toward improved functioning.

What If the Family Does Not Have a Goal?

In contrast to the family that comes with a new goal or problem every week, some families find it almost impossible to set a goal. Often these families are in treatment seeking a visitor relationship, as described in the previous chapter. They see no need for help and are coming either because the agency requires their child or spouse to get treatment or they have been coerced into participating in treatment by the court, a probation officer, child protective services, or some other entity that has power over them. In Chapter 5, we described some strategies for working with clients or families who wish to establish a visitor relationship in therapy. In general, the counselor should remain open and curious about the situation in which family members find themselves but not push them to take action until they see a need to do so.

Although many families without a goal assume a visitor stance toward treatment, some seem genuinely interested in getting help but are still seemingly unable to set a goal. The counselor dealing with such a family should remain both persistent and patient—allowing family members to tell their stories while keeping the issue of what they want to achieve in treatment as part of the conversation. The counselor should also try to understand the extent to which unclarity about goals is a snapshot of the family's process. Are family members typically unclear about everything? In these cases, helping the family assess its situation, agree on a goal, and move toward achieving it is not the prelude to the treatment process, it *is* the bulk of treatment. As in the case in a family with too many goals, the family without a goal needs help working on its interactional process. (Therapy contracts are summarized in Table 6.1.)

TABLE 6.1. Summary: Therapy Contracts

Develop a Vision of the Future	• "How will you know treatment has helped?" • "What will be the first small signs of change?" • "What positive things will take the place of negative things?"
Make Goals Measurable	• "On a scale of one to ten, where are you now and where would you like to be?" • "What would you be *doing* differently when you get closer to your goal?" • "If we had a videotape of your family after you have met your goals, what would we see?"
Resolve Conflicting Goals	• "What is important to you about the position you have taken in this conflict? What are your interests?" • "Where do your interests overlap?" • "How can each of you get some of what you want in this situation?"

Whenever our supervisees find themselves stuck with a case, we still find it useful to ask them to explain their understanding of the treatment contract they have negotiated with the families. As we discuss in the next chapter, having a clear idea of what the families want from treatment structures the rest of the counselors' work with them. To miss that crucial first step leaves both counselors and families unsure of where they are going and how they will know when they have gotten there.

Chapter 7

Problem and Solution Sequences

"I don't see why I should have to come to counseling," Tina told her counselor, Rasheed, after he had recommended that couples counseling be part of her husband Patrick's treatment. "Patrick's the one with the drinking problem. I don't drink at all."

"But you're married to him, and you're part of what goes on in the family," Rasheed told her. "I think it's important that you be here. You've got changes to make, too."

"But I don't make Patrick drink," Tina went on. "He does that all on his own. And if he would just stop his drinking, I'm sure our fights would stop, too. That's the only thing I get mad at him about. Every time he drinks, we get in a fight. It isn't my fault."

In many ways, Tina is right. She does not make Patrick drink. Drinking is a choice that he makes on his own. From the interactional perspective, however, we know that Patrick makes that choice in a complex context of factors, including Tina's actions and responses to his actions, his own past experiences, his relationships with his children and his extended family, even his genetic makeup. Research tells us, however, that if we leave out the family context, clients are less likely to complete treatment successfully (Anglin et al., 1987; Berger, 1981; Collins, 1990; McAuliffe, 1975; McCrady et al., 1986; O'Farrell, 1991; Zweben and Pearlman, 1983). For Rasheed, of course, the issue is not what *he* knows about the importance of family involvement, but how he can make a credible case to Tina for why she needs to become part of the change effort. Simply telling her that she needs to contribute to the changes being made obviously is not enough. Similar to most family members, Tina has a firm conviction that the problem "belongs" to Patrick, and that she can do nothing to improve how things go for them as a couple. So Rasheed must gather the right data to present an *interactional view* of the problem to both Patrick and Tina. Creating an interactional view connects the problem to the family's interaction in a way that does not relieve the substance abuser of responsibility for his or her actions but does give all family members a way to contribute to making changes in the family.

Family therapists have developed a number of techniques to create interactional views of problem behavior. In our work training substance abuse professionals to work with families, we have found Haley's (1976) concept of a behavioral sequence to be the most helpful. Haley's observation is that problems occur as part of regular, predictable patterns of interaction in families. He further observed that changing any step in the pattern often changes the outcome.

Consider a biological example—the hiccups. Everyone who has had the hiccups knows that they take on a life of their own that is outside our control. No one hiccups on purpose, after all. And trying to stop yourself from hiccuping seems only to ensure that they continue. You try to keep the spasm in your throat from developing. You tighten your muscles when you feel it start. You keep your mouth closed, trying to control the annoying sound that is making everyone look at you. None of these strategies works very well, however, because hiccups are the result of a biological sequence that causes your throat to spasm. Most of the "cures" for hiccups are based on trying to interrupt that sequence. Remember the old recommendation that scaring someone who has the hiccups will cure them? Fright will sometimes interrupt the biological sequence because it affects the neurological system. Holding your breath is an attempt to do the same thing. Interpersonal sequences that surround family problems are a bit like the hiccups—although far more serious. No one engages in problem sequences on purpose, and often such sequences take on lives of their own, seeming to control the family members who are caught in them. Efforts to change the sequence by force of will—such as trying to stop a hiccup after it has already begun to develop—are rarely successful. Just like a cure for the hiccups, the solution for problem sequences in the family is to change the steps.

Substance abuse counselors are already familiar with the idea of an individual behavioral sequence, as they help clients in recovery anticipate the "triggers" that might lead them to using drugs again. In this case, however, the sequence is an individual one because the assumption is that triggers are stable parts of the environment and that only the client's response to his or her triggers can change. In contrast, an interactional view suggests that, at least in the context of the family, not only can the client's responses to triggering events change, *the events themselves can also be shifted* by changing the interactional patterns of the family.

DEFINING PROBLEM SEQUENCES

Although our family treatment model focuses primarily on strengths and competencies, we begin the search for behavioral sequences by looking at the pattern of interactions surrounding whatever problem the family has decided to work on. We do this in order to begin creating the interactional view that will illustrate the part each family member can play in helping to achieve the goals all have agreed to pursue.

Let us begin by looking at an example of a therapist working with a client to construct an interactional sequence. Although this vignette is based on a therapist working with only one client, we include it here because it makes the interactional sequence very clear. It is the slightly edited transcript of part of a session with Rose.

Counselor: So is that one thing that the fights are usually about?

Rose: Umm hmm.

Counselor: You remember the last time you talked about that?

Rose: About a week ago . . .

Counselor: Can you take me back to that time and tell me—

Rose: Oh yeah, we went to a party. It was a little girl's birthday party, and the next thing I know is I go outside to get my phone book to write down an address from a friend—

Counselor: A male friend or a female friend?

Rose: It was a female friend. And I just rushed into the bathroom to primp myself up, and I stood there for about ten minutes in the bathroom, and when I came out, Joe was gone from where we were sitting. I asked the people around us, quite a few people. "Oh, look, he's around here somewhere." So I went back outside to look. I didn't see him in the car. And then they told me, "Oh, he walked into the bathroom." So I knock on the bathroom; he didn't respond. Anyway, so I stood there, and the next thing I know he started accusing me of being out there with some guy. I was like "What?"—you know, shocked—and I mean that really pissed me off by accusing me of being out there with someone else.

Counselor: Do you remember exactly what he said?

Rose: Huh?

Counselor: Do you remember exactly what he said?

Rose: Yeah, he goes, "What are doing out here? Were you here with someone else?" I go, "No." He said, "Oh, yes, you were." I was like, "What? How dare you say that I was with someone else out here. What type of person do you think I am?"

Counselor: And then what did he say?

Rose: Then he goes, "Oh well, dah, dah, dah, what took you so long and where were you at?" I said I was in the bathroom. I didn't have to explain to him every little minute I did from the time he's away from me. I just got mad. I got mad. I felt I didn't need to explain to him. If he didn't believe me then, "Go take me home; let's go home. I'm not going to sit here and argue with you. This is ridiculous."

Counselor: So you get in the car . . .

Rose: So we went to the car and I just told him I didn't want to talk to him about it anymore, I thought it was ridiculous, and I thought he was wrong, and I wasn't about to explain myself if he didn't want to believe me. We drove for about ten minutes and went without saying anything, and the next thing you know, he apologizes to me, and I was just too angry to take his apology at that point.

Counselor: Is that pretty typical—his apologizing?

Rose: Yeah, he apologizes a lot of the time because he doesn't know what he does wrong.

Counselor: And you were feeling too angry to accept the apology?

Rose: Yes, to accept it at that time.

Counselor: Did you say anything at that time?

Rose: I said that, "I don't think you believe anything I say or do. So I just don't want to talk about it." So when I came home, I went straight upstairs and got ready for bed, took a shower and got into the bedroom. The next thing I know he's trying to apologize to me. So I thought that I had to accept his apology just because of the fact that I wanted to fall asleep. Otherwise he would have bugged me all night. He wouldn't go to bed unless . . .

Counselor: And how does he try to apologize to you?

Rose: Well, he hugs me and kisses me, and he says he's sorry and, you know, he's wrong. I just didn't want to deal with him hugging and kissing me anymore. It's happened way too many times.

Counselor: After that did you have sex?

Rose: No, we didn't. I told him I was tired and I wanted to go to sleep. But it's happened too many times where I try to avoid the possibility of getting into a fight with him. I just ignore him. He's got a jealous rage in him where he accuses me all the time of talking to other guys or men or whatever. I've got a personality where I like people very well. I like to talk; I like to carry on a conversation. But he doesn't like that . . . he thinks I should just talk to him only.

Counselor: Would you ever argue about it, or would it ever make you want to go out and get high?

Rose: Yeah, a few times. A few times I did.

Counselor: So when was the last time you got high?

Rose: I guess about a month ago.

Counselor: Do you remember what happened? Can we go back—

Rose: Well, we got into a big old fight. The same situation.

In Rose's case, the sequence that she and Deborah defined was directly related to her use of drugs. This may not always be the case, since some families will define other problems they want to work on together. Regardless of the problem being addressed, the process of defining a sequence remains the same. First, we look at the skills that Deborah used to elicit the sequence as she talked with Rose and then discuss the sequence itself.

Interviewing for Sequence

In Chapter 3, we noted that one of the skills that counselors working with families must develop is the ability to attend to the process of a family's interactions, rather than solely to the content of those interactions. Nowhere is that skill more essential than when it comes to discovering problem and solution sequences. If Deborah had asked Rose what about her relationship with her husband was related to her decisions to get high, Rose would have probably replied with a content description. She might have said, for example, "He's such a jerk, I just get fed up," or "He's always on my case. If he'd just leave me alone, I could relax and deal with my stress better." While each of these statements reflects Rose's view of the situation, neither gives us much information about the interactional process that accompanies her decision to use. Notice, too, that Rose leaves herself out of these content descriptions. She describes actions or qualities of her husband that irritate her, but she does not include her part in the cycle. To get a clear picture of the problem sequence, and thereby begin to discover the interactional pattern or process that helps to maintain problems in the family, the counselor must ask the right questions.

The Right Questions

We suggest a specific process that counselors can use to assess sequence. In our experience, this series of steps helps counselors new to the idea of looking for interactional sequences get started. With experience, looking for sequence will become second nature, and counselors will not need to stick so closely to the steps we describe here. Asking about, and identifying, interactional sequences becomes something that counselors do without thinking about it. For beginners, however, some guidelines are helpful.

Begin by asking the family to recall the most recent time that the problem arose. Most families will not have trouble remembering such an incident. Notice, in the previous example, how Deborah begins by asking Rose if the fight she is describing happened recently, and Rose confirms that it did.

When constructing a problem sequence with more than one family member in the room, therapists' session management skills are essential to keep the family from plunging back into the content of the problem. Remember that the goal is not to find out *what* the family was arguing about, or who was right or wrong (if conflict is the problem they want to work on). Rather, counselors are trying to help family members get a picture of *the pattern* of their conflicts so that they can see how to change that pattern.

How can counselors steer the family away from the content of the problem? We have found a couple of strategies useful. First, we suggest that counselors create a sort of visual diagram as they construct the problem sequence with the family. A blackboard or flip chart works well, giving all family members a chance to see the diagram of the sequence as it evolves. However, therapists can also use a simple piece of paper on a clipboard, or a newsprint pad, if something larger is not available. Not only does creating a visual representation of the sequence give counselors and family members a record of what they have done, but it also decreases the intensity in the session by changing the dynamics of the interaction. Asking family members to focus on what the counselors are drawing as they talk draws their attention away from one another and makes it less likely that they will become mired in the content of the issue. With particularly volatile or contentious families, counselors may even want to stand up and work at the board or flip chart while family members respond to their questions. This creates a classroomlike atmosphere that also decreases the likelihood of family members beginning to argue about the details of the last time the problem occurred.

The second strategy counselors can use to help family members focus on the steps of their interactional sequence is to ask specific, factual, behavioral questions to track the events leading up to the problem event. Ask each family member to answer for himself or herself, and block any attempts to attribute motives or emotional states to other family members. Similar to the old advice for newspaper reporters, counselors who are trying to interview for interactional sequence information should stick to "Who?" "What?" "Where?" and "When?" questions (see Table 7.1).

TABLE 7.1. Interviewing for Sequence

- "Describe a typical time when the problem happened."
- "Who was there?"
- "What happened first?"
- "What did each of you do at first?"
- "What was the next step?"
- "What did each of you do then?"
- "How did it end?"

Nguyen used these strategies to begin constructing the problem sequence as he worked with the Ramierez family, a family whose seventeen-year-old son Eddie was in intensive outpatient treatment for using marijuana regularly. Present in the session were Eddie and his parents.

Nguyen: Okay, I'm going to ask you all some questions about what happens when Eddie goes out and gets high. I want us to get a picture of what all three of you are doing at those times. Eddie, when was the last time you smoked?

Eddie: It was last weekend . . . on Saturday night.

Mrs. Ramierez: Eddie! You lied to me! You told me you were over at Maria's house. That's the only reason I let you go out of the house . . . because I trust Maria not to use drugs. Where did you really go?

Eddie: [To Nguyen] See. This is the kind of shit that happens all the time. She's always bitching me out, trying to pick my friends, getting on my case.

Mr. Ramierz: Shut up, Eddie. I don't want to hear you talking about your mother that way—

Nguyen: Let me interrupt. It's very important that I get a clear picture of what happens when Eddie gets high. Where was everyone on Saturday evening just before Eddie said he was going over to Maria's house? [Nguyen stands up and moves to the flip chart.]

Mr. Ramierez: I didn't have anything to do with it. I just got home.

Mrs. Ramierez: Like always. You never have anything to do with it. I'm trying to help our son stay off drugs, and you're never around.

Nguyen: So, Mr. Ramierez, you had just gotten home. [Writes on the flip chart—"Dad gets home."] Where were you, Mrs. Ramierez?

Eddie: She was watching TV. That's all she does, watch the stupid *Oprah* show and stuff like that.

Nguyen: Hang on, Eddie. I want to hear from your mom.

Mrs. Ramierez: I was watching TV like Eddie said.

Nguyen: Where were you actually? In what room?

Mrs. Ramierez: I was in the living room where the TV is. [Nguyen writes "Mom watching TV in living room" on the flip chart.]

Nguyen: And Eddie, what about you? What were you doing?

Eddie: I was in my room listening to music.

Nguyen: So what happened next? Dad comes home, and what happens?

Eddie: They start fighting right away.

Nguyen: Who?

Eddie: Them [points to his parents].

Nguyen: [To Mr. and Mrs. Ramierez] Is that what happened?

Mr. Ramierez: Well, she started in on me with an attitude right when I walked in the door. I'd worked a full day plus four hours of overtime, and I was beat.

Nguyen: So you were pretty tired, and when you got home, you and your wife had an argument. [When Mr. Ramierez nods in agreement, Nguyen writes "Mom and Dad argue" on the flip chart.]

Notice some of the things that Nguyen does as he works with the Ramierezes. He stays with defining the interactional sequence even when content issues arise. For example, when Eddie admits that he lied about where he was on Saturday night, Nguyen does not pursue this issue. Trust may be an important thing for the family to discuss in the future, but having that conversation now will not help Nguyen construct the interactional sequence. In the same way, Nguyen does not respond to Eddie's complaint that his mother is always trying to choose his friends. Pursuing this would only lead the session into content.

In addition to *not doing* some things, Nguyen also *actively works* to structure the session. He begins by telling the family why he is asking the questions he asks. He works to have each family member speak for himself or herself. He stands up and uses the flip chart to give the family a focus other than on one another. And, although it is not evident in a written transcript, he also uses a calm tone of voice and a relaxed rate of speech to counter the family members' efforts to escalate the conflict.

The interactional sequence that Nguyen and the Ramierez family finally construct reveals a great deal of useful information. We have condensed it into a representation of what Nguyen drew on the flip chart (see Figure 7.1). As you look at the diagram Nguyen made, notice that he did not stop at the point where the problem occurred—when Eddie got high, in other words. He continued to track the sequence of events until emotions had returned to relative calm in the family. Why is this important? Since sequences are *repetitive* cycles, sometimes the possibility for change lies in the events that follow the problem in one sequence but set the stage for it to happen again when the cycle repeats. We discuss this more later.

Notice, too, that Nguyen includes all three of the Ramierezes in the sequence. The sequence diagram includes the actions of Mr. and Mrs. Ramierez as well as Eddie. Since defining an interactional sequence helps to see the part each family member can play in arriving at a solution, counselors must be sure to include all family members. Sometimes family members claim that they played no role in what happened. For instance, Mr. Ramierez tells Nguyen, "I didn't have anything to do with it. I just got home," when Nguyen begins to ask about the last time Eddie got high. Nguyen puts this step in the sequence diagram anyway, and we quickly see the part that Mr. Ramierez plays in the process. Even "nonactions" should be included in the sequence diagram, including such behaviors as "Dad kept quiet," "Mom left," and so on.

Finally, counselors should check with the family members to make sure that they are diagramming a typical sequence. Ask family members if this diagram rings true for them and whether the particular inci-

FIGURE 7.1. Ramierez Family Sequence

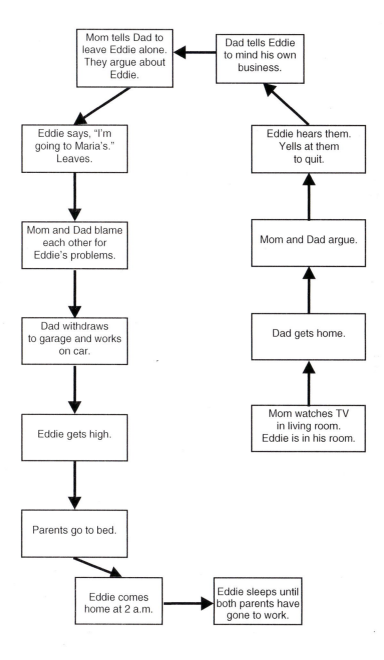

dent they have described is a typical one. Sometimes, by asking for the most recent example of a problem sequence, counselors may unwittingly guide the family to describe an unusual situation. The goal of defining a problem sequence is to find the pattern that flows through most occurrences of the problem, not an isolated event.

SOLUTION SEQUENCES

Up to this point, we have described problem sequences as if they encapsulate all of a family's experience with a given problem. In other words, we have been acting as if the only possible outcome for a problem sequence is the problem occurring. Although this is the kind of language families often use to describe their experiences ("He's *always* a jerk" or "She *never* agrees with me"), recall that one of our underlying assumptions is that life is a fluid process, not a fixed entity. Based on this view, we assume that there are times when family members begin the sequence that usually leads to the problem, yet they find a way to short-circuit that process and prevent the problem from happening. In solution-focused terms, there are *exceptions* to the sequence. It is hard for any of us who are caught in the midst of a problematic interactional sequence to see exceptions. Since they do not fit our idea of an unvarying process ("It *always* happens this way"), we tend to regard them as anomalies that do not have much use. However, exceptions often contain the seeds of a solution. One way to help families make a change in their typical interactional patterns is to help them find those exceptions and amplify them. We call this process *constructing a solution sequence*.

The counselor begins the search for a solution sequence by asking a seemingly simple question: "Tell me about a time when this cycle started but it didn't end up with the problem happening." As you might guess, the most common answer families give to this question is an absolute one: "There's *never* been a time when the problem doesn't happen." This can be frustrating for the counselor who wants to move on to constructing a solution to the problem, but it is important to be patient with the family members' view. After all, they have lived with the problem for a long time, and if it were easy to solve, they would already have done so. It is important for counselors to both *empathize* with the absolute view of family members and be politely persistent in their pursuit of an exception (see Table 7.2).

TABLE 7.2. Interviewing for Solutions

- "Describe a typical time when the problem sequence started but the problem didn't happen."
- "What made the difference?"
- "What did each of you do to help make a solution instead of a problem?"
- "What did each of you do at first?"
- "What can each of you do to make this solution cycle happen the next time?"

In his work with the Ramierez family, Nguyen moved to searching for exceptions this way:

Nguyen: [Looking at the sequence diagram with the family] What I'd like to do now is talk about a time when all this got started but it didn't end up with Eddie using.

Eddie: Good luck. They're always at each other, and it drives me crazy. You'd get high, too, if you had to live with them. .

Nguyen: [To everyone in the family] You must all be pretty discouraged with the way things have been in the last few months. But I'll bet they weren't always that way. Tell me about a time when the sequence we've been working on started, but, Eddie, you didn't get high.

Mr. Ramierez: He never talks to me. I wouldn't have any way of knowing.

Mrs. Ramierez: Why do you think he doesn't talk to you? You're always yelling at him.

Nguyen: Let me stop you there. It's really important that we find a time where you all were able to do this sequence differently. I've worked with a lot of families, and even though they think it always goes the same way, we've always been able to find at least once when it didn't, if we looked hard enough.

Eddie: You know, a couple of weeks ago, Dad came home and started fighting with Mom, and I was starting to get all tense and everything, and then they just stopped. I turned up my headphones really loud, thinking they were really going to get into a bad one . . . but nothing happened.

Nguyen: And did you get high after that?

Eddie: No. I just kept listening to my music and being cool.

Nguyen has managed to help the Ramierez family find an exception to their habitual pattern that is part of the context for Eddie using drugs. He has empathized with the family's struggles while gently pushing them to think of a time when the problem did not occur. Now that they have found an exception, Nguyen will help the family construct the solution sequence that contributed to that exception. Just as he did with the problem sequence, Nguyen will work to make the solution sequence *interactional*. Since Eddie identified the exception, it would be tempting to focus on him and what he did differently. However, we want to include his parents as well.

Nguyen: Okay, so just a couple of weeks ago, you guys all did something different. [To parents] Do you remember the time Eddie is talking about?

Mrs. Ramierez: I think so. It was on Wednesday night, I think.

Nguyen: How did you all make that evening go differently?

Mr. Ramierez: I don't think it was that different. You know, we don't fight all the time.

Mrs. Ramierez: But you came home pretty mad that night. You told me the house was a mess and you were tired of coming home to a mess all the time—

Mr. Ramierez: It *was* a mess—

Nguyen: But, according to Eddie, that night it didn't turn into a big fight. What did you do differently?

Mrs. Ramierez: I just told myself to let it go. Usually, I get really mad when he does stuff like that, but that night I just said, "To hell with it." I wasn't going to let it get to me.

Nguyen: [To Mr. Ramierez] What did you do then? Do you remember?

Mr. Ramierez: I just let it drop, I guess. I was tired. I didn't have the energy for a big fight. I went in the living room and turned on the TV and tried to cool down.

Nguyen: And Eddie, what about you? What did you do to keep yourself from using?

Eddie: Nothing. I just stayed in my room, listened to my music, and worked on homework.

Nguyen: Sounds like you did a lot of stuff. You didn't get involved in the conflict between your parents, you didn't go out where you might be tempted to use if you were upset, and you turned your energy to something positive—school.

Eddie: Well, if you say so.

Nguyen: [Smiling] I say so!

Nguyen's work with the Ramierez family gives a hint of the process of defining a solution sequence. In actual practice, of course, it may take a whole session—or even several sessions—to complete this task. When it is done, the next step is to help the family plan to increase the frequency at which the solution sequence occurs.

Increasing the Occurrence of the Solution Sequence

Solution sequences give both families and counselors clues to what a problem solution might look like. However, counselors need to be active in helping families identify the contributions each member has made to the solution and in making plans to do what they did again. In moving to this phase of the process, counselors must do their best to keep each person focused on what *he or she* could do differently. Talking about future action provides a tempting point for contentious families to return to blaming and focusing on the alleged shortcomings of other family members. To the degree that counselors can preserve self-focus on the part of each family member, the more likely families are to devise a workable plan that they will make an honest effort to accomplish.

In addition to self-focus, counselors should also promote a sense of *balance* in the plan. That is, each person should have a part to play. In Nguyen's work with Eddie and his parents, for example, it would be easy for Eddie's parents to tell him just to ignore their fights. In addition to this not having worked in the past, it also puts the entire burden of change on Eddie's shoulders. Nguyen worked with this situation in the following way:

> **Nguyen:** So, Mrs. Ramierez, on that Wednesday night we're talking about, you just let it go when your husband came home in a bad mood. Mr. Ramierez, you didn't keep after your wife, instead you went and watched TV and tried to cool down. And Eddie, you didn't get involved in trying to get them to calm down, like you might have other times. Seems to me we've got a lot of clues to things each of you could do differently to solve things.

> **Mr. Ramierez:** If Eddie would just mind his own business and stop using drugs, that would about take care of it. What happens between me and his mom isn't any of his business.

> **Eddie:** Well, you could keep it down a little bit. It's pretty hard to ignore two people screaming at each other—

> **Nguyen:** Let me stop both of you. I think there are things that both of you can do to make things better at home. And it's only fair that everyone pitches in to change things, since everyone benefits from a better atmosphere, right? Eddie, what's one thing that you could do?

> **Eddie:** Well, I'll just keep out of it from now on. If they want to get a divorce or kill each other, that's their problem.

> **Nguyen:** [Smiling] So, you're going to try not to be your parents' marriage counselor, huh?

> **Eddie:** My parents' marriage counselor? . . . That's a gross thought.

> **Nguyen:** How about you, Mr. and Mrs. Ramierez? What can each of you do?

> **Mrs. Ramierez:** I guess I can work on letting things go a little more, if he'll work on his attitude. I wouldn't mind him coming home from work in a good mood sometimes.

> **Nguyen:** [To Mr. Ramierez] What about it? Want to make a deal with her? She'll get off your case and you'll work on your attitude?

Mr. Ramierez: I guess.

Nguyen: Well, that's your homework for the week. I want each of you to try making the changes you've just talked about and we'll see how it goes. If you can do it, I think you'll all be surprised at the results.

Nguyen gets each person's commitment to make a change and then asks the family to work on that during the week. Notice that the changes he asks them to make are not necessarily large. Our model of working with families relies on helping them make the adjustments that will ease the difficulty of life and let them live without using substances. We often find that small changes have far-reaching repercussions.

What If the Family Cannot Find an Exception?

Sometimes, despite their best efforts and a fair amount of persistence, counselors cannot help families find exceptions to their problem sequences. When this happens, counselors should consider a number of options.

First, examine the state of the therapeutic relationship. In earlier chapters, we discussed the importance of *joining, empathizing, assessing motivation,* and *goal setting* as foundations for successful work with families. Anytime counselors find themselves stuck (e.g., a family cannot find an exception to the problem sequence), it is important to revisit each of these areas to make sure that the therapy relationship is "on track" before moving on to the following two techniques. For example, are family members unable to find an exception because the counselor has not adequately empathized with their experience of how difficult and draining the problem is? Until the counselor has communicated his or her understanding of the seriousness of the struggle the family is having, family members may be unwilling to discuss exceptions, since doing so appears to negate their own experience. Or are family members unable to find an exception because they are in the precontemplation or contemplation stage of motivation and the counselor is pushing them to take action before they are ready?

When counselors have assured themselves that the difficulty in finding an exception is not a reflection of a problem in the therapeutic relationship, they can turn to two techniques we have found useful in helping families work on solution sequences. First, counselors can have families reflect on the problem sequence and brainstorm ways that they might change it. As in constructing the solution sequence, counselors should ask each member to focus on what *he or she* can change in the sequence, and not on what other family members should do differently. The first part of this process is a brainstorming period during which families generate a list of possible changes they can make. The next step is for counselors to help the families select from the list the changes they feel they can actually make and develop a plan to make them. As discussed earlier, the issue of balance is important here as well. The burden of change should be shared, not given to only one or two family members.

Sometimes, family members are unable even to brainstorm changes to their problem sequence. In this case, and as a last resort, counselors can suggest a plan of action for them to take. We feel this strategy should be used as a last resort because it jeopardizes the family's sense of ownership in the solution. Our clinical experience tells us that the more ownership people feel in the changes they make, the more likely those changes will be effective and lasting. The research on self-efficacy (discussed in Chapter 2) supports our experience. Therefore, when offering a suggestion for a way to change the sequence, counselors should do so tentatively, leaving the door open for family members to either reject or modify the suggestion. This will tend to give them a chance to develop at least some sense of ownership in the task they are sent home to do.

SUMMARY

Working with problem and solution sequences offers counselors an *interactional* approach to involve all family members in creating change in the family, even when one member has been identified as the one with the problem. Constructing interactional solution sequences allows all family members to participate in positive changes and gives everyone a feeling of some control over what happens as a result of therapy. Although working to find a solution sequence is a relatively straightforward approach, it is not without its ups and downs. In the next chapter, we address techniques for keeping change going once it has started and for dealing with relapses. (Table 7.3 summarizes problem and solution sequences.)

TABLE 7.3. Summary: Problem and Solution Sequences

Construct the Problem Sequence	• "Tell me about a time when the problem happened." • "Who was involved?" • "What happened?" • "How did it end?"
Look for Exceptions to the Problem Sequence	• "When did the problem cycle start but you kept the problem from occurring?" • "What happened?"
Make It Interactional	• "How did each of you contribute to the solution?"
Increase the Frequency of the Solution Sequence	• "What can each of you do to help that solution happen again?"

Chapter 8

The Ups and Downs of Change

Beth was looking forward to her fifth session with Milt and LaTanya. They had worked hard in previous sessions to understand their problem sequence and had begun to experiment with a solution sequence. Both seemed dedicated to making a change in their relationship, and Milt had been working hard in the intensive outpatient program to deal with his drinking. In addition, they both were bright and articulate and easy to work with. For once, Beth thought, maybe what happened in therapy would actually match the "miracle cure" case vignettes in all the textbooks. But when she met them in the waiting room, Milt looked a little distracted and LaTanya's smile was tense.

"How's it going?" Beth asked after they had settled into the chairs in her office.

LaTanya erupted like a volcano at the question.

"Terrible," she said. "Things were going okay for a while, but now we're back where we started. Maybe we're even worse than when we started."

"What happened?" Beth asked.

"Same old, same old," Milt told her. "We had a fight. I went out for a while—took a time-out like we planned. When I came back LaTanya accused me of drinking, said she could smell it. I got so mad I couldn't see straight. I figured if no one was going to believe me when I said I didn't drink, what was the point? I went down to the bar where I used to hang out all the time. I must have sat there for an hour, talking to a couple of my friends, trying to decide if I was going to have a beer or not. I told one of my buddies what was going on, and he told me to just go home, that it wasn't worth throwing away all I'd gained because of a little fight."

LaTanya interrupted. "But did you have a beer?"

Now Milt's anger rose to the surface. "No, I didn't. Damn it, LaTanya, I've been telling you that ever since this thing all blew up. Why won't you believe me?"

"I've been disappointed too many times before, Milt," LaTanya said.

Beth felt her stomach sink as she listened to Milt and LaTanya talk. What had gone wrong for her "miracle" couple? Why had things blown up? A hint of discouragement crept into her thoughts, too. Maybe the problem was something that she'd done.

If Beth made any mistake in her work with Milt and LaTanya, it was in assuming that their progress in therapy would not be interrupted by periods when things did not go very well. Few clients come to therapy, make the changes they need to make, and never suffer a setback. That is not to say that it does not happen from time to time. We do not want to leave counselors thinking that *everyone* has to suffer a setback or two in the course of treatment, and that if they do not, something suspicious is going on. Instead, we want to be clear that most clients go through ups and downs in the course of therapy. Many clients will become discouraged when they hit a down period in therapy—a time when solutions are overpowered by old habits and problems. It is up to counselors to have patience and confidence, and to keep family members on track under such circumstances. Doing so requires that counselors themselves have a clear vision of the ups and downs of therapy and the skills to guide the family through the downs.

Two major categories of "ups and downs" demand a counselor's attention during the middle stage of therapy. First, the counselor must be able to help family members recognize and capitalize on improvements in their interactions. Sometimes the counselor has to point out such changes and help the family see them. The second thing the counselor must be able to do is to help the family deal with setbacks—the return of old problems or old interaction patterns. The following sections discuss the skills needed for both of these activities.

MAKING CHANGE BIGGER

Sixteen-year-old Kristen and her mother Anne had been seeing Tom for family counseling while Kristen took part in an outpatient drug treatment program. They were working on calming down their arguments and learning to communicate better. Tom knew that midterm grade reports had just come out and that Kristen had been worried about how she was going to do. One of the things that she and Anne argued most about was school.

"How have things been going?" Tom asked.

"Not so great," Kristen said.

"What's the problem?"

"We had an argument in the car on the way over."

"Did it have anything to do with grades?" Tom asked.

Anne looked puzzled. "Why would it have anything to do with grades? Kristen's midterms were fine. I'm just worried because she wants to go to a concert Friday night with some boy she barely knows."

"Brian's my *boyfriend,* Mom. You can't say I hardly know him."

"Well, then I don't know him, and that's important, too. Why don't you invite him over to the house for dinner so I could get to know him?"

"I would if you didn't act weird all the time."

Tom stopped them.

"I want to back up for a second," he said. He turned to Anne. "Maybe I got confused," he said, "but I thought I heard you say that Kristen's midterms were fine."

"Yes," Anne said. "What about it?"

"If I remember right, last semester she had all Ds and Fs and she was worried that she might have to go to summer school." Tom turned to Kristen. "What were your midterms?"

"Mostly Bs," she said. "And a C."

"And an A," Anne said. "Don't forget the A."

"That was no big deal," Kristen said. "It was only Art. I always do good in Art."

"You didn't last semester," Tom said. "It sounds to me like you've made a big improvement."

"So what?" Kristen said. "What's the point if she never lets me go anywhere?"

"You can go lots of places," Kristen's mother said. "You just can't go to a concert with a boy I don't know."

Tom interrupted again. "Wait a second. You two are missing something important here. Kristen's made a major improvement in her grades. How did you two make that happen?"

It may seem incomprehensible that a family would not notice when long-standing and painful problems begin to change, but, in reality, this is not that unusual. Kristen and Anne seemed to forget that Kristen's raising her grades to mostly Bs was a big change as they rushed on to the next area of conflict—Kristen's boyfriend. Although such a seemingly irrational act may appear to be evidence of "resistance," or a wish to keep having problems, counselors should try to remind themselves that when in the midst of a family crisis, sometimes you cannot see the forest for the trees. Families dealing with drug and alcohol abuse (as well as many other kinds of problems) often have a problem-saturated view of their lives (White and Epston, 1990). Because they have faced so many problems, they come to feel as if their destiny is to always have trouble, and that they must stay on the lookout for the next problem on the horizon. Such a view makes improvements and successes hard to see. When you are anxiously looking for a gas station because your gas gauge is on empty, you do not pay much attention to all the fast-food restaurants you pass. In the same way, families do not pay much attention to improvements because they are so focused on anticipating problems. With Kristen and Anne, Tom's job was to keep them from glossing over the improvement in Kristen's grades so that they could learn from that experience what works for them. A number of skills are involved in helping families slow down and examine their successes.

Seek Successes

Since clients may have trouble seeing successes, one of the counselor's jobs is to seek them out (see Figure 8.1). Simply listening is one important way to do this. Because Tom knew that grades and fighting about grades were major concerns for Kristen and her mother, Kristen's offhanded remark about her grades improving intrigued him. He tried to keep himself tuned in to finding ways in which Kristen and Anne were succeeding in solving their problems, so when he heard about Kristen's improved grades, he made a point to ask about it.

Whereas Tom chose to let his clients bring up changes in their own way, another strategy is to ask directly about successes. This can be done in a number of ways. Tom might have begun his session with Anne and Kristen by saying, "Tell me what evidence you've seen this week that you are moving yourselves closer to your goals." He could also have asked, "What's been going well for the two of you since I saw you last?" or "What have you seen happening that tells you we're on track in counseling?" Notice that in all of these questions; Tom assumes that something has gone well and asks questions based on that assumption. Doing so cues the client to focus on evidence of success. If he asked, "Has anything gotten better since I saw you last?" he is more likely to hear Anne and Kristen's problem-saturated view of their situation and not help them notice and understand their successes.

When Tom first heard about Kristen's good grades, he immediately asked about them and thereby implied that this was an important topic for therapy. And he did not ask only once. When Kristen returned to discussion of her complaints about her mother not letting her go to the concert, Tom once again called attention to Kristen's grades. It does not do much good, after all, for only the therapist to notice that a success has occurred. If family members are to profit from their own experience, they need to notice the change as well. Sometimes it takes persistence to counter their view that they only have problem experiences, not success experiences. Whether done actively or passively, seeking and calling attention to success is an important job for counselors (see Table 8.1).

"Enlarge" Successes

After successes have been found and highlighted, it is often helpful to enlarge them. By enlarging a success, we mean asking detailed

FIGURE 8.1. Keeping Change Going

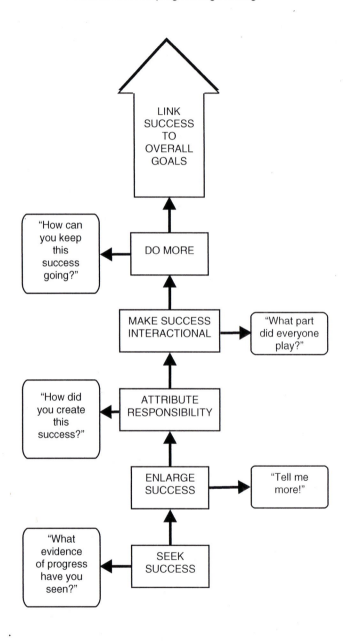

TABLE 8.1. Success-Seeking Questions

- "What evidence have you seen since we last met that you are getting closer to meeting your goals?"
- "What was the best thing that happened in the family this week?"
- "What have you seen happening since we last met that tells you you are 'on track' as a family?"
- "Tell me how you handled a tough situation in a new and better way since we last met."

questions about it, exploring all the nuances of it, and generally making it a "big deal." The more time and energy the counselor devotes to a particular topic in session, the more important it becomes. Let us return to Tom's session with Anne and Kristen for a moment:

"Tell me about your grades," Tom said to Kristen. "You said you got an A in Art. That sounds pretty good."

"Like I said, it wasn't a big deal." Kristen told him.

"What do you have to do to get an A?" Tom asked. "You must have to do something. If I remember right, you got a D in Art last semester."

"Well, we had this big project we had to do," Kristen said. "You had to, like, choose something that was really important to you and then show it three different ways."

"What did you choose?"

"I picked my cat, Amber. I know that sounds stupid—"

Tom interrupted her. "It doesn't sound stupid to me. What was the project?"

"I did a drawing of her, and then I took a bunch of pictures of her and put them together in a collage, and then I made a sculpture of her out of clay."

"Wow, that's a lot of work."

"I guess," Kristen said.

Tom turned to Anne. "Was it a lot of work? You must have seen all the trouble Kristen was going to, to finish her project."

Anne smiled for the first time in the session. "It was a lot of work. Kris spent one whole afternoon chasing that cat around with her camera."

Kristen smiled too. "Yeah, I think she's camera shy . . . like me."

Tom's questions elicit more and more details from Kristen about her improved grades. For something as important as Ds and Fs becoming mostly Bs, Tom might spend most of the session in this kind of conversation. He might go from subject to subject, asking Kristen what she did in each class to improve. While such an exercise might appear to be overly detailed, it is not. By devoting so much time to Kristen's improvement, Tom is telling her in a very concrete way how important her efforts have been. In addition, encouraging Kristen to talk about her accomplishments in school helps to counter her and her mother's view that their family only has troubles. Tom's questions make Kristen's school success "bigger" emotionally in the life of this family (see Table 8.2).

Attribute Responsibility for the Change to the Family

Although important, it is not enough for counselors simply to notice and magnify changes. They also have to help family members take responsibility for the good things that have been happening in their lives. As discussed in Chapter 3, a sense of *self-efficacy* is a powerful predictor of success in clients' self-change efforts (see, for example, Holden, 1991; Kores et al., 1990; Yates and Thain, 1985). The primary way that counselors can help family members develop a

TABLE 8.2. Enlarging Success

- "I want to hear all the details on the progress you've made."
- "I know this is starting to sound repetitious, but I really want to know what happened. Go over it again so I'm sure I have the complete picture."
- "Wait a second. You're acting like this is no big deal. I think it's really important. Tell me what happened."
- "I'm really impressed with what you've been able to accomplish."

sense of self-efficacy at this stage in treatment is to link their own actions to the positive outcomes they are experiencing. Tom began this work with Kristen and her mother after he had thoroughly explored the improvement in her grades.

"You must have put a lot of work into raising your grades so much," Tom said to Kristen.

"It wasn't a big deal," she said.

"What did you do to raise your English grade from an F to a B?"

"I don't know."

Tom turned to Anne. "Do you know how Kristen managed to raise her English grade?"

"I talked to her teacher a couple of weeks ago, and he said Kristen was turning in her homework on time. That seemed to help a lot. Last semester she was always losing points because she either turned her homework in late or didn't turn it in at all."

"That sounds like a big change," Tom said. Then he asked Kristen, "How did you manage to make such a big change?"

"You keep saying it's a big deal, but it isn't. I just started making sure I put my English homework in my backpack when I did it at home. When I got to school, it was there and I turned it in. Why are you trying to make such a big deal of it? You make me sound like I'm some kind of baby and that turning in my homework is some kind of wonderful thing."

"I didn't mean at all to make you sound like a baby, Kristen," Tom said, "because I know you're not. In fact, the point I was trying to make is that your efforts paid off in raising your grades. That seems important to me, and I want to make sure we pay attention to it."

Tom's gentle persistence in helping Kristen and her mother examine the way in which Kristen had raised her grades is important. Too often, clients downplay their part in positive change or attribute it to something outside their control. Adolescents sometimes say that they are no longer using because the friend they used to get high with has moved away. Adult couples sometimes tell counselors that their conflicts have decreased "because we've been too busy to fight." We are not suggesting that clients in either case are lying, only that they need help in attributing their success to their own efforts. The counselor's job is to provide that help (see Table 8.3).

Make the Change Interactional

In addition to helping an individual see how his or her efforts have contributed to a positive change, the counselor should also search for the actions taken by other family members that aided the success. There are two reasons to do so. First, it reflects how life really works. None of us can attribute the successes in our lives solely to our own actions. All of us have relied on others to get where we are. As individuals, it is important that we recognize the ways in which others have helped us, so that we get a clear picture of the resources we have available to us in times of stress. In addition, if the counselor does not recognize other family members' roles in an individual reaching his or her goals, counseling will seem increasingly irrelevant to everyone else in the family.

The counselor helps the family see the interactional nature of success by continuing to track the solution sequence surrounding the most recent success. Tom did this with Kristen and Anne after he had gotten a clear picture from Kristen of what she had done to raise her grades.

"What do you think your mom did that helped you get better grades this semester?" Tom asked Kristen.

"I don't think she did anything."

"Really? Seems to me you two have been working pretty hard together. Anne, what do you think? What part did you play in Kristen raising her grades?"

"I guess I have to agree with Kristen. I don't think I did anything. In fact, I tried really hard not to do anything. Remember, we agreed that her grades were going to be her responsibility unless she asked me to do something to help her. She didn't ask, so I didn't do anything."

Often, people mistake stopping an action (for example, not always checking up on children's homework, or not asking partners if they

TABLE 8.3. Helping Clients "Own" Change

> - "What part did you play in making this success happen?"
> - "I'm sure there was more to all that's happened than just luck. What did *you* do to make it happen?"
> - "You know, maybe you did a get a lucky break when you heard about the new job. But not everyone would have gone down right away to apply for it. What gave you the motivation to go down and put in your application right away?"
> - "What did you say to yourself to keep yourself from getting all bent out of shape about this situation like you would have in the past?" (for situations where the success was the absence of an old pattern)
> - "It sounds to me like you had a lot to do with how things worked out for the better this time."

have been to their AA meetings) for inaction. They are not the same thing, and it is important that the counselor not fall into the trap of believing they are. For people who are used to overfunctioning for other family members, stopping themselves from taking the actions that get in the way of success can require even more energy than continuing to overfunction. Tom made this point with Anne as he continued to ask about her part in Kristen's school success.

"It sounds to me, Anne, like you did a lot. You created some space for Kristen to be in charge of her own success or failure."

"I guess so."

"I'll bet it was hard, too. How did you do that?"

"I didn't really do anything. I just didn't nag her about her homework, and I didn't call the school to check on how she was doing."

"There must have been times when you got really curious."

Anne laughed. "Oh yeah! After about two weeks of hearing Kristen say she didn't have any homework because she did it all in study hall, I was sure she was still failing everything. I really wanted to call Mrs. Diego, her counselor, and see what was going on."

"What did you say to yourself to stay on track?"

"I just reminded myself that I had to let Kristen take responsibility for herself." Then she smiled. "I also told myself that if Kristen had to go to summer school, I wouldn't have to stay around home so much to watch her. I could go out with my friends more!"

It took Kristen a moment to figure out that her mother was teasing her. "That's cold, Mom," she said.

"Well, it doesn't look like you're going to have to go to summer school, so I guess I'm stuck with you."

Tom summarized what he'd heard so far about Anne's part in the change. "It sounds to me like you really helped Kristen by giving her the responsibility for her grades and letting her live up to that responsibility. While on the outside it may look like you didn't do anything, I think it probably took a lot of effort not to get in there and try to make sure she was doing her work. I think you did a lot, Anne."

Making change interactional is outlined in Table 8.4.

Link This Success to the Family's Overall Goals

In Chapter 4, we discussed the importance of using goals to help both counselors and clients stay on track in treatment. Having clear goals helps keep treatment focused and gives each session coherence

TABLE 8.4. Making Change Interactional

- Make sure that everyone in the session participates in describing the success.
- Ask each member of the family to describe his or her part in the successful change.
- Ask each member of the family to describe what other members did to help create the change.
- Define taking no action as helpful. For example, "It sounds to me like your deciding not to nag Tom about going to AA was a very helpful contribution to the good week the two of you have had."
- Draw the new solution sequence on the board or on a sketch pad, making sure to include everyone in the family.

by linking it to the overall plan. Therefore, the counselor's final task as he or she helps a family or couple recognize and enlarge a successful experience is to link this particular experience to the overall goals for treatment. In this way, a single success is also seen as part of a larger picture of progress. Consider how Tom helps Anne and Kristen link Kristen's success in school to their two larger goals of decreasing their arguments and helping Kristen not use. He uses the family's problem sequence, constructed in earlier sessions, as a way of doing this.

> "If I remember right, when you two first came to see me, you were having a lot of arguments about Kristen's grades, her homework, and her attendance at school, right?"
>
> "All the time," Kristen said. "She was always on my case about something. Even when I got a D in PE, she grounded me. That's so stupid. My friends cut PE all the time and their parents don't mind."
>
> "I guess you and Kristen haven't been fighting so much about school lately," Tom said to Anne.
>
> "No. It's been a real relief, too. I'm sick of fighting."
>
> Tom continued. "And if I remember right, Kristen, one of the times you were most likely to go out and get high was when you and your mom had a fight."
>
> "I guess so. I haven't done that in a long time, though."
>
> "I know," Tom said. "And I think one of the reasons you haven't is that you and your mom are working pretty hard together to get along. When you mom backs off a little and you take on the responsibility and pull up your grades, the two of you don't have so much to fight about, and then you aren't so tempted to use. Good work!"
>
> "Well, maybe school isn't a problem anymore, but she better let me go to the concert with Brian or I'm gonna really be mad."

As Kristen's last statement shows, even though her grades are better, she and Anne have not solved all their conflicts. However, progress in treatment is like building a brick wall—each success provides a foundation for the next one. Using what has been learned from the success with grades, Tom can help guide Anne and Kristen toward the resolution of other problems. As they become better and better at solving problems, they will need less and less of Tom's help.

WHEN CHANGE GETS DERAILED

Kristen and Anne represent clients who had made a change but were having trouble seeing it because they were so used to seeing only problems. Milt and LaTanya, in the vignette at the beginning of this chapter, represent a different challenge for the counselor—a family in which old problems or interaction patterns recur. In the alcohol and drug treatment field, such occurrences are usually labeled *relapses*.

Milt and LaTanya, for example, had been doing well for several weeks before their session with Beth when they reported that they had returned to the old pattern of LaTanya pursuing and Milt distancing. In this instance, the return of the old pattern did not end in Milt drinking, as it so often had in the past. However, it is easy to imagine that if the cycle continued, Milt would be even more at risk for drinking. At the same time, Milt's return to drinking would likely cause LaTanya such anxiety that she would pursue him even more intensely in an effort to keep him sober, thus triggering an escalation of the old interactional pattern. The connection between these two things is at the heart of our understanding of relapse.

People generally take one of two positions when trying to understand the return of drinking or drug use after a period of abstinence. Those who see substance abuse as the result of a biological or psychological illness (the disease model) view relapse as a nearly inevitable part of the course of a chronic disease. The disturbances in family relationships that accompany relapse are understood as a reaction to the individual's drinking or drug use. The disease is substance abuse, and the interpersonal turmoil in the family is simply a symptom of that disease. The other position that one might take (the interactional model) is that substance abuse flows primarily from a disturbed network of relationships. From this perspective, relapse is understood as the result of a return of old interactional patterns—what we have called the problem sequence—that "support" drug use. In the case of a pursuing-distancing cycle, such as the one we described in Chapter 7 concerning Rose and her boyfriend Joe, drinking or using again is just another step in an elaborate interpersonal dance. The solution is not to change the single step of drinking but to change the entire dance.

We are neither disease model purists nor interactional model purists. Our position is that it does not make sense to try to figure out whether relapse causes a return to old relationship patterns or vice versa. The two views are so inextricably linked; they represent different aspects of a larger phenomenon. Thus, we take the same approach to relapse regardless of the form it takes—chemical or interactional.

A counselor can take several useful steps when family members report that they have experienced a relapse. The most important thing to do, however, is not to panic. Relapse is an expectable, though not inevitable, part of the process of change. After all, few of us would expect to recover from a period of depression without some up days and some down days along the way. Whereas traditional approaches hold that relapse means that the client has made no progress at all, we take a different view. Neither a return to drinking or drug use nor the recurrence of interpersonal conflicts means that previous progress is invalidated. Rather, the return of problems is simply an indication that the solution sequences the family has been working on are not yet firmly in place and need to be refined. This process begins with the counselor not becoming discouraged or panicked. As Milt and LaTanya's session with Beth illustrates, families are often understandably discouraged by relapse and fear that all their previous progress was merely an illusion. In these situations, the counselor must hold the hope for the family and coach them through the relapse experience (see Figure 8.2).

Realistically Assess Relapse

The first step in the process of working with relapse is to realistically assess the situation. The recurrence of old problems is often presented to the therapist in extreme form. Recall that when Beth asked LaTanya how the week had been, LaTanya said that things had been going okay, but that now they were terrible, maybe even worse than when she and Milt started counseling. Beth's job at this point is to ask questions that will allow her and her clients to realistically assess the extent of the relapse. Although it is theoretically possible for events to occur that would make a family's situation worse than when counseling began, our experience tells us that this rarely happens. At the same time, when clients tell us that a relapse represents disaster, we

FIGURE 8.2. Dealing with Setbacks

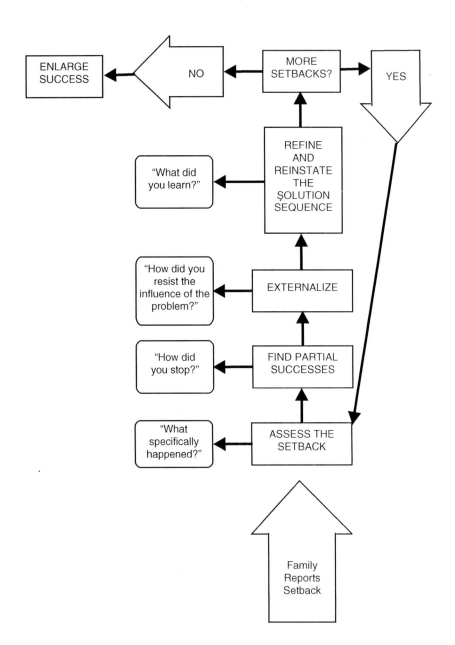

do not believe that they are lying to us or purposefully exaggerating their feelings. Instead, they are describing their *affective* experience of their situation, the emotional reality they perceive. The counselor's job is to help them evaluate the situation from a more rational perspective. However, this process must begin with an empathic response. Clients must know that their counselor understands their emotional reality before they are willing to reevaluate it. Otherwise, it seems as though the counselor is simply minimizing their concerns. When clients feel their concerns are being minimized, they typically react in one of two ways. They either intensify their efforts to convince the counselor that, indeed, the situation is terrible, or they feel so misunderstood that they give up trying to get anything from counseling. Beth began the process of helping Milt and LaTanya evaluate their rough week by letting them know that she understood their emotional experience.

> "You both seem pretty discouraged," Beth said, after Milt and LaTanya finished talking. "It must feel like all the good work you've done is down the drain."
>
> "Well, isn't it?" LaTanya asked. "I'd say we're right back where we started."
>
> "Yeah," Milt added. "LaTanya was acting like she trusted me again, but obviously she didn't. I don't think we've gotten past square one."
>
> "Let's begin by you two helping me get a clearer picture of exactly what happened," Beth said. "I want to make sure I understand the situation. Now what day did you have the argument?"

Beth makes clear that she understands Milt and LaTanya's disappointment and discouragement, without agreeing that their feelings are an accurate interpretation of the facts of the situation. Notice that she does not argue with them about their feelings by trying to convince them that the situation is not as dire as it seems to them. Rather, she asks them to begin to describe what happened so that together they can more realistically assess it.

> As Milt and LaTanya described their argument and the events surrounding it, it became clear to Beth that they have done a

number of things differently than they would have in the past. Most notable was that Milt didn't drink, even though he was tempted to do so. However, LaTanya also made some changes. She didn't go out searching for Milt when he left to take his time-out, as she would have before, and she called a friend to help her calm down during his absence. Obviously, some of the old problem sequence was present, but some of it wasn't. Beth decided to begin trying to shift the couple's view of this incident by commenting on the changes she saw.

"It sounds to me like even though this was a pretty tough time, both of you did some things differently than you would have in the past," Beth told them.

"Seems like the same old shit to me," Milt said.

"Well, let's begin with you, then," Beth said. "You didn't drink, even though you went down to the bar when you got mad. That seems like a huge difference to me. That must have taken a lot of effort, Milt."

"If my buddy hadn't been there telling me not to throw away everything I've gained, I don't know what I'd have done. I think it was just luck that he was there."

"You didn't have to listen to him, did you?" Beth asked. "How many times did people tell you not to drink before and you went ahead anyway?"

"I guess so," Milt said.

Beth went on. "And, LaTanya, you told me that before you used to panic so much when Milt left after a disagreement that you would race after him and try to follow him. You didn't do that this time."

"I was just sick of fighting. I didn't care what happened at that point."

"I'm sure you were," Beth said. "But at the same time, you didn't make things worse by chasing Milt and keeping the argument going."

In this interchange, Beth begins the process of realistically assessing the relapse by pointing out ways in which they have changed their old problem sequence, even though they did not achieve a perfect solution this time. By listening closely and asking factual, sequence-defining questions, Beth is able to find a number of differences she can point out to Milt and LaTanya. This begins to break down their view that the current events are an exact replay of all their past conflicts. It also helps them to see ways in which they have been successful in the midst of what feels like a failure. She continues this process by asking them how they were able to limit their conflict.

"In one of our first sessions, you two told me that when you got mad at each other, the arguments usually went on for days. If I remember right, there was a lot of yelling and screaming and even some threats of hurting each other. Did that happen this time?"

"No," LaTanya said.

"How'd you decide not to let things get that far?" Beth asked. "It must have been tempting to get back into the old pattern completely."

"I don't think we decided to do anything. It just stopped."

"What do you think, Milt?" Beth went on. "How do you think the two of you decided to stop this conflict before it got completely out of hand, like it used to?"

"Well, I made up my mind when I left the bar that I was going to go home and I wasn't going to fight with her. It never gets us anywhere, and I realized how easy it still is for me to go back to drinking. When I got home, I told LaTanya we should just put all of this stuff on hold until we came here today so we could talk it out with a third party. She kind of surprised me. I didn't think she'd go for it, but she said okay."

"I was just sick and tired of the fighting," LaTanya said. "We weren't going to settle anything that night."

"So even though you got into an argument, and that was disappointing, you were able to limit the extent of it," Beth said.

"I guess so," Milt said. LaTanya nodded.

The final step in helping families realistically assess a relapse is to look at the extent of the experience. Beth does this with Milt and LaTanya by asking them how they limited their argument. Sometimes families will come to a session with a bad experience fresh in their minds, and this prevents them from talking about how most of the intervening week went well. Counselors need to help them see that what would have been an unending series of arguments in the past was kept to a fairly short duration now.

Fine-Tune the Solution Sequence

After counselors and clients have a realistic view of the relapse experience, the next step is for clients to consider what they have learned from this event that will help them the next time such a conflict occurs.

> "You two aren't going to make it through the rest of your life without some arguments," Beth told Milt and LaTanya as their session neared its end. "What did you get from your experience this week that will help you the next time you hit a situation like this?"
>
> "I think I need to tell LaTanya I'm taking a time-out and not just stomp out of the house, like I did this week," Milt said. "Maybe we could agree on where I'll go when I need a time-out. I know she worries when I leave without her knowing where I am."
>
> "That would help a lot," La Tanya said. "And I'm going to work on not jumping to conclusions when he does leave. It's hard for me to trust that he won't go back to drinking, but I'm going to try to trust him. If he decides to drink, there's nothing I can do about it anyway."

TROUBLESHOOTING RELAPSE WORK

Sometimes a setback may so upset family members that they are unable to step back from it enough to look at it realistically. This usually takes the form of family members' personalizing the situation and accusing one another of doing what they did in an effort to cause one another pain. In these circumstances, externalizing the problem—especially if it has been used previously in treatment—can help family members shift their view of the problem from a personal attack to the resurgence of an "outside" problem that is trying to disrupt the family. Externalizing was described in Chapter 3. When using this concept to explore and deintensify the personalization of a setback, counselors should ask family members how they see the externalized problem—be it Alcohol, or Marijuana, or Conflict, or Messages from the Past—

trying to disrupt their progress and convince them that the situation is hopeless. Then counselors can do their best to help family members unite to fight the influence of the externalized problem.

At times, counselors may find themselves working with families in which the relapse was not limited. Perhaps an individual started drinking or using again and then was unable to stop, or an interpersonal conflict sequence began again in the family and family members were unable to stop it. What should counselors do under these circumstances? As we emphasized earlier, the first task is not to panic. Although the situation may indeed be serious, adding the counselors' anxiety to that of the family members is not helpful. Instead, we encourage counselors to return to the process of defining the problem sequence and helping the family members brainstorm ways to interrupt it. When the continuing relapse involves substance use, intensive outpatient treatment or even residential treatment may be part of interrupting the sequence. Likewise, if the interpersonal conflict is severe, it may be useful for counselors to help family members negotiate a brief separation, or a period of no discussion of difficult issues. For example, an adolescent may need to go to an emergency shelter to give both the youth and the family a cooling-off period. Although these measures are extreme, and should only be undertaken after careful consideration, they can be useful ways to interrupt an ongoing relapse and help the family again consider ways to build a solution sequence.

A final difficulty that counselors sometimes encounter when dealing with relapse in the way we suggest is that they begin to feel that they are simply siding with the clients' denial of the seriousness of the situation. We do not mean to minimize the danger clients put themselves in when they return to either substance use or ineffective relationship patterns. At times, counselors may need to address these negative aspects of relapse directly. However, we have found it more helpful to begin with a focus on the solutions embedded in relapse experiences, and not on the clients' already strong sense of failure. The motivation for further effort in the face of relapse comes from the recognition that all is not lost.

SUMMARY

Change is an up-and-down process, and clients will report both successes and failures in the course of treatment (see Table 8.5). The counselor's job is to continue to guide the process toward the search for solutions even in the face of setbacks.

TABLE 8.5. Summary: Ups and Downs of Change

| **Focus on Successes** |
| **Make Success Bigger** |
| **Look for the Potential Solutions Within Relapses** |

Chapter 9

Ending Treatment

We have described a way to work with families in which drug abuse is a problem that is different from many approaches to treating chemical dependency. With its focus on resiliency and solutions, rather than weaknesses and problems, this approach offers a more engaging, collegial, positive counseling experience for both the family and the counselor. So far, we have focused on finding a family's previous exceptions and solutions to both alcohol and drug abuse, and to the concomitant family problems that serve as a context for substance abuse. This process takes place in two stages. During the first stage of counseling, relationships are formed with the family and the specific interactional patterns that contribute to the substance abuse are identified. Finally, the counselor helps the family set goals that will lead to a future without drugs and alcohol. In stage two, the interactional patterns that were previously identified are disrupted, using solution-focused techniques of searching for exceptions and previous solutions, and then enlarging the influence of these exceptions.

Counseling does not last forever, of course. There comes a point when it is clear that family members have made significant changes in their drug use and interactional patterns and now have stronger, more positive feelings for one another. This point marks the transition to stage three, which we call *consolidation*. We call it this because it is the stage at which family members solidify or *consolidate* the changes they have made during the previous months of counseling. Basically, they need to learn to *feel* the differences that the counselor and others *see*. This stage also provides the structure for a positive termination, one that does not have the clients just "fizzle out" by missing appointments or dropping out of treatment. One of the mistakes newer family counselors make is not to structure the ending of counseling so as to provide this sense of positive closure.

STRUCTURE OF THE SESSIONS

In consolidation, the goal is to help the couple or family solidify and punctuate the changes they made during stage two. This is a very important stage, and we have found that *not* attending to it can lead to a renewal of previous problems and conflict, even though the family has learned strategies to cope. The number of sessions that families need in the consolidation stage varies. If counseling has moved quickly—lasting, for example, only four to eight sessions—then there may be only a need for one or two consolidation sessions. If counseling has taken longer, more consolidation sessions may be needed. No matter the number of sessions, the counselor should tailor the consolidation stage to the family's needs. Frequently, at this point time between sessions is increased. Doing so gives the family a chance to "try it on our own" without totally severing ties to the counselor. Whatever the structure, the main theme for consolidation sessions is, "You are a different family, with different skills than the family who first came to treatment. Let's focus on that difference."

There are four main types of consolidation interventions:

- Difference punctuating interventions
- Strategies to maintain change
- Plans for postcounseling challenges
- Termination interventions

To the extent possible, all of these areas should be addressed during the last few sessions of counseling.

DIFFERENCE PUNCTUATING INTERVENTIONS

Many times the changes a family has made are quite apparent to the counselor but not to the family. The main purpose of difference punctuating interventions is to help family members learn to *feel* the changes they have made. When we say *feel*, we mean to make both the cognitive and the internal, emotional experience of change available to them. The more family members feel they are different, the more likely they are to respond to problems in a different way. Conversely, the more solidly they feel the changes they have made, the less likely they are to respond using old patterns. A number of specific interventions are used to punctuate the differences for a family.

How Is the "New Family" Different from the "Old Family"

With this intervention, the counselor continually reminds family members of their "newness," speaks "as if" they have changed and are not like they were before, and uses language that confirms that the counselor believes the family is different. The counselor asks, whenever the opportunity arises, "How would the *old* Smiths have handled that situation?" "What would you two have done if your son came home after curfew *before* you came into counseling?" "What would you have felt *before counseling* when he told you that he wanted to have a drink?" If the family is truly in stage three, they will very clearly be able to state the differences between pre- and postcounseling. Consider how Aaron uses this approach with Bobby Tyler and his parents.

Aaron: So, how are you all doing today?

Father: Well, we had á bit of a problem this week.

Aaron: Oh?

Father: Yeah, Bobby got into a bit of a car wreck last Saturday night.

Aaron: He did?

Bobby: Yep. I backed into another car at the parking lot at the movies.

Aaron: Were you hurt?

Bobby: No, but I bashed in the front of this other car pretty bad.

Father: And broke off the taillight of my car, too.

Mother: I was just happy no one was hurt.

Aaron: So what happened?

Father: Well, Bobby came home, kind of upset, and told me about it. He didn't end up seeing the movie, I guess.

Bobby: No, I just came home.

Aaron: What happened then?

Father: What do you mean?

Aaron: What did he say, what did you say, what did Mother say?

Father: Nothing really. Bobby came in, told me about it, I asked what had happened . . .

Aaron: Bobby, what did your dad say?

Bobby: Well, we just talked about it, how it happened. I told him I'd pay for it, and he said "Well, let's see what the insurance will pay, and how much is left."

Father: Yeah, we have a high deductible. The insurance guy didn't get back to us yet.

Aaron: So, Dad, did you scream or yell or throw a lamp at Bobby? [Laughter] Or punish him in any way?

Father: No, not really. We just talked about it. Why, should I have thrown a lamp at him? [Laughter]

Aaron: [Laughing] No, of course not. But this is *really* different from how the old Tyler family would have handled this, don't you think?

Father: I guess so.

Aaron: You guess so? The old Tylers would have had a huge fight about it, as I remember. Mom, how do you think your old family would have handled this, if Bobby would have come home after having a car accident?

Mother: Well, first thing, we would have thought he had been drinking. I guess it crossed my mind, but when I saw Bobby I knew that wasn't it. I guess we would have really blown up at him. Dad would have grounded him. Bobby would have called him names.

Aaron: Bobby, how do you think the old Tylers would have handled this situation differently from the new Tylers?

Bobby: Oh God, Dad would have screamed and hollered about the car and how much it cost and how I wasn't responsible and I was just a kid drunk. . . . It would have been awful.

Father: [Laughing] Wait a second. I don't think I was that bad.

In this interchange with Bobby and his parents, Aaron emphasizes how this family is a new family by asking sequencing questions that punctuate how they deal with problems differently than they would have in the past. The major task in this intervention is merely for the counselor to ask comparative questions once a sequence that demonstrates the family's changes is identified—"How are the *new* Tylers different from the *old* Tylers?" The family then should be able to articulate those differences and do so with vigor and enthusiasm. An inability to do so may be a sign that the family has not truly reached consolidation.

Role-Play

It is sometimes useful, and fun, to have a couple or family role-play their old patterns and styles. Here, the counselor brings up an old situation or problem, then asks family members to act out how they would have handled it at the beginning of counseling. This usually results in an exaggerated form of their previous patterns, which not only punctuates the differences and how they have changed, but which is often quite funny and playful. Aaron might have used role-play with Bobby and his parents this way:

Aaron: You know, I'd like to do something a little different, a little wacky, okay?

Bobby: I guess so . . .

Mother: Sure.

Aaron: What I'd like you all to do is, think back to the way you were when you first came in here, back in September.

Father: Okay. . .

Aaron: And what I'd like you to do is to pretend that you are now like you were then. Then I want you all to act out what you would have done and said then if Bobby had backed into someone in a parking lot.

Bobby: You mean you want us to do it exactly like we would have done it?

Aaron: That's right, just like you would have done it then. Okay?

Mother: I don't know if we remember how we were exactly.

Aaron: It doesn't have to be exact. Just get into how you remember it then, and then act it out. Okay? Bobby, why don't you get up, and come in the door? (Bobby gets up and goes out of the office, then slowly opens the door and tries to sneak in so his parents don't see him.)

Mother: Is that you, dear?

Father: [In a harsh voice] What the hell you coming in so late for? Don't you know what time it is? Where have you been?

Bobby: [Not looking at either of his parents] Out.

Father: [Angry] Out where?

Bobby: Just out. Went out with some friends. [Bobby tries to move quickly past them. Father reaches out and grabs Bobby's arm, but Bobby yanks it away.]

Father: [Very loudly] Don't pull away from me? You been drinking?

Bobby: No!

Father: Why won't you talk to us? What the hell is going on?

Bobby: Okay, I guess you're going to find out about it, anyway. I had a little accident with the car.

Father: [Jumps up out of his seat and knocks it over. Everyone laughs.]

Aaron: No, stay in character. What would you have done now?

Father: What the fuck do you mean you had an accident? What happened? Did you wreck the car??!! [Everyone slowly starts to laugh as they realize what he emphasized.]

Father: [Breaking character again] I guess I worried more about the car there, huh?

Aaron: Well, you were mad, and you saw that Bobby was okay. Anyway, go back to it.

Father: How did you have an accident? What happened? Were you drinking?

Mother: Was anyone with you? Was anyone hurt?

Bobby: I just backed the car up into someone else's car in the parking lot at the movies. It was just an accident.

Father: I'll bet you just drove off, too. I'll bet you were drinking.

Bobby: [Screaming] I was not drinking, goddamn it, but I wish I was to have to come home to this. [Father jumps up and pretends he is going to punch Bobby. Bobby grabs his arm and pretends he is going to hit him, too. Then they look at each other and start laughing.]

Aaron: What's wrong?

Bobby: This is really really weird. It seems so stupid now.

Aaron: But isn't this how you all would have been?

Mother: Oh yeah, even worse.

Aaron: How does it feel for you, Dad?

Father: Strange. Silly.

Bobby: Feels like we are exaggerating.

Aaron: Well, you are, now. But again, isn't this pretty much how it was?

Bobby: Yes.

Aaron: Why do you think it feels so weird?

Bobby: [Thinking] It just isn't how we are anymore.

An intervention such as this has some obvious risks. First, if the family is not really in stage three, but somewhere in the middle of stage two, having them role-play may be more of an enactment of current problems than punctuating differences between now and the past. The counselor needs to be well assured that the family does indeed sequence differently, and that doing this exercise will be fun rather than traumatic. Second, it is probably best not to role-play old, but still very painful scenes. For example, if a previous fight had escalated to the point of abuse, it would be better not to role-play *that* fight even at this later, safer time. It is not worth the risk of bringing back very painful feelings when doing an exercise designed for playfulness. It is better, we believe, to pick a current problem that the counselor has seen handled well and role-play *that* as the "old family." Third, even while being aware of these issues, the counselor needs to be ready for a role-play to go awry. It is possible, although we have rarely seen this happen, for the role-play to escalate into a real dispute and not be resolved as the counselor would like the "new family" to resolve it. Here, it is best for the counselor to use this as a vehicle to discuss changes, how far family members have come, and what feelings and issues have perhaps not been dealt with. The counselor can always "take the blame" and apologize for moving the family a bit too fast, before each of their individual concerns had been addressed. More often than not, if a problem occurs at this point at the end of counseling, either it is a transient problem, which the counselor can point out will occur the rest of their lives, or the family is not fully in stage three, and counseling may need to move back a few paces.

Pre-Posttest Results

If the counselor used any standardized test instruments at the beginning of counseling (either as part of a research study or for clinical purposes), it can be very helpful to go over the posttest changes with the family. Hopefully, if stage two has been successful, and the family's vulnerabilities are reduced and their coping mechanisms increased, this should be reflected in the posttest scores. Going over these with the family can add a certain external validity to the counselor's enthusiasm about the changes the family has made. Consider how Shauneeka uses the Dyadic Adjustment Scale (Spanier, 1976)—

a measure of a couple's satisfaction with several aspects of their relationship—in a consolidation session with Pete and Marie.

Shauneeka: Before we finish, I just want to go over some of the results from those questionnaires you filled out the other day.

Pete: Yeah, I was wondering about those.

Marie: Me too.

Shauneeka: I was particularly interested to see your marital satisfaction scores. Both of you moved quite a ways in the direction of being more satisfied with your marriage compared to when you filled these things out right when we started counseling.

Pete: [Smiling] Well, we are doing better. I think we are having more fun, and doing more things.

Marie: What did the questionnaire say?

Shauneeka: Well, both of you scored higher in communication ...

Marie: Oh yes, we are talking a lot more. The TV stays off more when we come home from work now, and we just talk.

Shauneeka: So you agree with the test?

Pete: Yep. It's much better.

Shauneeka: Well, these tests are usually pretty accurate, so I was certainly pleased, but the most important thing is that the two of you feel it.

As can be seen, Shauneeka uses the test results as a vehicle for discussing Pete and Marie's changes from the beginning of counseling to the end of counseling. Although Shauneeka could just tell Pete and Marie that she thought they were doing better, a certain power is associated with a more neutral-feeling test. Of course, if the results are negative or more tentative, those should be discussed with the couple as well. The first question to ask is if the couple agree with the test results. If the couple believe that they are doing better, the counselor must be sure that the test results do not override the couple's own perceptions. Tests are certainly fallible, and it is the couple's experience of their own relationship that is most important. Of course, if the test results show that the couple have made little change, and they concur, the counselor would probably not be as likely to move to stage three interventions. Instead, the counselor would likely negotiate a new set of goals with the couple, goals that focus on ameliorating the difficulties they still feel they are having.

STRATEGIES TO MAINTAIN CHANGE

Besides interventions designed to punctuate the changes the couple or family has made since the beginning of counseling, stage three lends itself to interventions that encourage strategies to maintain those changes. The problems associated with *relapse* among chemically dependent individuals are well documented. However, family *systems* can also relapse, although family counselors usually do not use that concept when referring to family problems. Families and couples may have learned new patterns of interacting and may demonstrate them in most aspects of their lives. However, for a number of reasons (including the fact that even larger systems can impact a couple or family, just as a family system may impact an individual), families may have difficulty maintaining those interactional changes which they have made under some circumstances. Therefore, these stage three interventions are offered to help families keep changes going.

How to Keep Change Alive

A straightforward intervention is to ask what strategies the couple or family plans to use to *maintain* all the changes members have made. These should include, of course, a list of the major strategies the couple or family has used to *make* the changes to begin with, and also include new ideas for maintaining them. Sometimes it is useful to use a blackboard or a drawing pad to list the strategies so that they become concrete in the family members' minds. Aaron used this technique to help Bobby and his parents plan how they could maintain the gains they had made.

> **Aaron:** You know what I'd like to do today? I'd like to talk about ways you all can make sure that all of the wonderful changes the *new Tylers* have made keep going.

Bobby: What do you mean?

Aaron: Well, last week when we talked about your fender bender, you saw how different you all are from when you first came in.

Bobby: Yeah, I almost got a bruise from my *old father* grabbing at me! [Laughs]

Mother: We sure do want to keep these changes going. It is really a lot better.

Aaron: My question is, How are you going to do it? Here, let me write it down on the board. [Walks over to blackboard to write.]

Father: What do you mean?

Aaron: Tell me, for example, one thing you can do, Dad, to keep these changes going.

Father: Well, I need to control my temper. That used to get me in a lot of trouble.

Bobby: [Grinning] That's for sure!

Aaron: [Writing it on the board] "Dad will work to control his temper." How will you do that, Dad?

Father: Need to think before I act. Like when Bobby told me last week about the car. My very first thought was to get mad, and I felt it boil up in me. Then I took some deep breaths like we talked about here, and thought about it, like what it meant and what would happen if I got mad, and I calmed down. Then we just talked, and it was better. [Counselor writes that down.]

Aaron: Okay. Mom, how about you? What is one thing you can do to keep the changes going?

Mother: I can definitely speak my mind. I used to hold things in so, until I couldn't take it anymore. Then I'd explode. It has helped to tell Art or Bobby what I feel when feel it. That's hard for me, but I do it. [Counselor adds this to the list.]

Aaron: Bobby?

Bobby: Well, it's helped that I stopped drinking, that's for sure. I need to keep that up. It does affect me and my parents.

Aaron: That's great. Hard, but great. How will you manage to do that?

Bobby: I'm going to keep going to the meetings and stay in counseling with Jan. [Counselor adds Bobby's goal to the list.]

Aaron: Anything your folks can do to help with this hard one?

Bobby: Just keep letting me do it without worrying or getting into it and all. I know what I need to do, and them asking about it, or sniffing for booze, or anything like that—it doesn't help. It just makes it worse really.

Aaron: Does that make sense to you two?

Mother: We don't do that anymore. He is right. He has to be in charge of that part of his life. We have been pretty good about that, I must say.

Aaron: Is there anything you all can do as a family to keep the changes you have all made going?

Bobby: I know this is going to sound weird, 'cause I hated coming so much at first, but I think if we came back to see you once in a while, you know, not every week, but once every couple of months maybe, it would help us stay honest. You know, just knowing we have to see you and answer to you, I think that would help.

Aaron: What about that? I sure am willing to, in fact was going to suggest it later.

Mother: I think that is a good idea. It's not that we can't do it alone, just that to have an outsider seeing things we can't see. [Counselor adds "booster sessions" to the list.]

Father: So, Bobby, [laughing], you gonna pay for these sessions?

Bobby: Well, I can always sell some drugs to pay for the sessions. [Groans from mother and father.] *Just kidding!*

Here, the counselor merely leads the discussion on keeping changes going. The family members were able to identify some important vulnerabilities that they will have to watch, and each of them had reasonable suggestions for personal interventions. As when looking for solution sequences, it is important that each family member focus on what he or she can do to maintain change. In fact, if family members cannot focus on their own responsibilities and actions, this may signal that they have not truly reached the consolidation stage.

Although Bobby's joking reference to selling drugs to pay for counseling may have felt a bit "close to home," we consider it a good stage three indicator when couples or families can joke about their problems. Humor often helps "detoxify" the negative emotions associated with painful experiences in the past and also helps family members further punctuate the differences between how they are now and how they used to be.

Journal of Changes

Some couples and families find it helpful after they have generated a list of strategies for maintaining change to keep a notebook with a page for each strategy. For example, one page might contain a heading "Go Out on a Date" for the couple. Each time they go out on a date with each other, they record the date, where they went, and how it helped their relationship. If the counselor plans to meet with the couple in the future, he or she can tell them to bring in their journal of changes with them to review, thus providing external motivation to keep this intervention going. Shauneeka used this intervention with Pete and Marie.

> **Shauneeka:** Now that we have some ideas on how you two are going to keep your changes going, you know what I would like you to do with them?
>
> **Pete:** [Laughing] Stick them …
>
> **Marie:** [Feigning horror] Pete!
>
> **Shauneeka:** Not quite. I'd like you to keep track of them, of which ones you are doing, and how it is going. [Gives them each a small notebook.] Here, a gift for each of you. Now, write the three things each of you said you would do to keep the changes going on the top of a page. So you have three pages, one with

each heading. [They do it.] Good. Now, every time you do one of these things, I want you to write it down. Put the date, the time, what you did, how it went, and how you felt.

Pete: Why are we doing this?

Shauneeka: Two reasons. First, these changes are so important to keep going, and your ideas on how to keep them going are so good that I want to make sure that they are on your minds all the time. The second reason is that when I see you next month, I'd like to see who is working the hardest, what you are doing, if it is going well, et cetera. We can then make any additions or adjustments. How does that sound?

Marie: Fine with me.

Pete: Let's do it.

Exploring Coping Mechanisms

Many couples and families, even in stage three, are not aware of how many coping mechanisms they possess, and how these can be mobilized to maintain change. To help families recognize their abilities to cope, counselors can list the common coping mechanisms, ask them which ones *they* possess, and then generate ideas on how each mechanism can be used to maintain change.

Aaron: You know, I want to tell you all that you possess some qualities as a family that will make it easier to keep these changes going.

Bobby: [Laughing] Like we scream loud?

Aaron: Well, maybe the energy you have as a family—which can get reflected sometimes in screaming loud—the energy is a strength, one of those qualities. Do you know how having a lot of energy may help keep changes going?

Mother: Well, I think it makes us make things happen.

Aaron: Great! That is just what I was thinking. What other qualities do you have as a family that will help you keep these changes going? Mind if I write these on the board?

Father: Well, I think we love each other a lot. Even when we used to fight, we really did care.

Bobby: My dad, an old softy!

Mother: But it's true.

Aaron: I sure see it. Hell, sometimes families who love the most fight the most, too. It is that energy I was talking about. But I agree that genuine love and caring, which I see you all having, will really help sustain the changes. Do you have any idea how they might?

Mother: Well, it makes me not want to give up, even when things are toughest. It should also help when things are going better.

Aaron: How about another quality that might help. I have seen one continuously with you all, especially in Bobby. Know what it is?

Bobby: [Rather sarcastically] My brilliant sense of humor?

Aaron: Actually, that is exactly what I was thinking of. You all have a great sense of humor and have used it during your saddest times. I'll bet you will also use it during better times. How can you use a sense of humor to keep these changes going?

Father: Maybe by making sure we always have fun with each other, have some laughs. You know, I was just thinking, Bobby is getting to the age when he and I can start having some fun together, not like a kid and his dad, but like two grown-ups.

Bobby: [Smiling] Great, Dad, let's go to Vegas!

PLAN FOR POSTTREATMENT CHALLENGES

Dealing with Expected Challenges

In addition to helping families and couples plan ways to keep change going, it is also useful to review briefly some of the common developmental events in the life of a family that can cause stress (for an excellent review of the family life cycle, see Carter and McGoldrick,

1999). Then the counselor can have the couple or family members outline how they will realistically cope with these events. Anticipating such challenges not only prepares the family for them but also makes the point that stress and challenge are a part of life and will not cease, even after successful counseling. In the wake of a period of sustained change, some families may find it difficult to think that they will ever experience problems again. Preparing them for the reality of ongoing stress and challenge is important. Shauneeka uses this technique with Pete and Marie in the following vignette:

> **Shauneeka:** Okay, we have talked about how you two are very different than you were many months ago, how your relationship is different, how you feel closer. We also saw how in the past, you, Marie, when things got too much, you would withdraw, and you would go get high. I want to talk today a little about the normal things that can happen to couples as they progress through life which might add stress and then might throw you two back into your old patterns.
>
> **Marie:** Like what?
>
> **Shauneeka:** Well, I can think of one offhand: having a baby. You two are planning to have kids, right?
>
> **Pete:** We're kind of trying now.
>
> **Shauneeka:** Children can be the greatest source of joy, but they sure change things, fast. How do you think having a child might affect what we have worked on here?
>
> **Marie:** I also worry about that. We are kind of selfish. I wonder if I could handle all that responsibility.
>
> **Shauneeka:** Well, it feels to me like you will do just fine.
>
> **Marie:** But you are right, I didn't deal well with stress before.
>
> **Shauneeka:** And give me an example of one thing you two are doing different when you get under stress?
>
> **Marie:** Well, I don't run away from Pete. Just the opposite. I have been going to him more, looking toward him for support. And he's there for me now.

Pete: So isn't that something we could do then? I mean, having a baby is a family thing. You wouldn't have to do that alone.

Shauneeka: So what you are saying is that what you have learned here, the big thing you do differently, is to come toward each other when in crisis or stress, instead of going away from each other. You could do that when you have a baby?

Marie: We'll have to. Otherwise it doesn't work for me.

Shauneeka helps Pete and Marie build on the solution sequence they have developed (moving toward each other rather than pursuing and distancing) and apply it to a not-so-distant future developmental change. Not only does she help them anticipate predictable stresses, she reminds them of the skills they already have to deal with such stresses.

Dealing with Unexpected Challenges

All lives take unexpected twists and turns. One of the keys to life-long mental health for couples and families seems to be possessing the coping mechanisms to deal with these challenges. In addition to having couples or families anticipate predictable challenges, it is also helpful to have them make provisionary plans for how they might deal with crises or challenges that may not be expected but could realistically emerge. They may look back to their families' history to come up with some of the problems and challenges that can face families. Then, as in the previous intervention, they can outline how they might cope with these challenges.

Shauneeka: Okay, we have talked a bit about challenges that can occur as part of normal life development. What about the unexpected? It's one thing to deal with something you have time to plan for. What about something you don't plan to happen? All of us face these someday.

Marie: Like what?

Shauneeka: Oh, there are so many things—death, divorce, accidents, losing jobs. I do know that in the past, Marie, every crisis, major or minor, set that pattern in motion that ended up with you two not talking and you getting high. My question is, What will you two do to maintain even in the face of the unexpected?

Pete: That is hard to say, you know, because you never know what will happen.

Shauneeka: Well, I seem to remember, Pete, that your family tended to stick together in crisis, even kind of thrived on it, brought everyone closer.

Pete: Right. I have thought about that. I think that is why I always tried to pull Marie back in.

Shauneeka: And Marie, your family, maybe because of all the drug abuse, tended to draw apart, to go into themselves. In your family, most of the bad stuff that happened around drugs happened during crises.

Marie: Mostly, yeah.

Shauneeka: So here is my question again: Can you two overcome that powerful pattern, both that you two have had and that preceded you in other generations?

Marie: We have to. I like us the way we are now. I like being able to lean on Pete. I like not being a damn drug addict. I think we can manage the crises, if we do it together.

Shauneeka: Well, I think you can, too. I would like to say that it is all right to get some help, though. I will always be here. If and when something unexpected comes up, some crisis or problem, even if it feels like you are handling it okay, please feel free to give me a call, come back in for a session, just to get a little pep talk from me, and maybe I can remind you of what you were doing that was so successful in changing your relationship while you were here.

Pete: Sounds good to me.

How Will You Know If You Need to Return to Counseling?

Using counseling as a lifelong coping strategy can be one of the most important things families with drug and alcohol problems can learn. This does not mean that families need to be in counseling for a lifetime, only that they know when it is time for them to come back. Counselors should ask what signs couples or families should watch for to suggest they may need a "booster session" or two in the future. Counselors should also add warning signs to the list. Framing "returning to counseling" as a "booster" is consistent with the stage three theme that they are new couples or families with new skills, and that returning to counseling is really a "coping mechanism," not a sign of failure.

> **Aaron:** I have a question that is really important. We have talked about crises that might come up that will make maintaining all these good changes you have made difficult. We've talked about the normal developmental stages that can be tough. My question is—whether it happens because of something planned or un-planned—How will you know when you need to come back to counseling?
>
> **Father:** [Laughing] Jeez, we are about to finish and Aaron already wants us back in!
>
> **Mother:** No, but that's a good point. I have been thinking about that. I mean, we didn't know at first how bad it had gotten until it was too late.
>
> **Aaron:** So how will you know? What will be the signs?
>
> **Bobby:** [Smiling] I know! I get strung out, OD, then get arrested on my way out of the hospital.
>
> **Mother:** Bobby, please not even as a joke!
>
> **Bobby:** [Laughing] Sorry, Mom. But I am kind of not kidding—if I started using again.
>
> **Aaron:** Sure, that would be an important time. Hopefully you guys might see some signs even before that.
>
> **Father:** Well, yes, I think if we stopped talking to each other. If Bobby felt he couldn't talk to us anymore, especially after all we have been through here, that would be a sign to me to get ourselves back.
>
> **Mother:** Right, the biggest change, to me, is that those two talk to each other. It was so different before. But if that stopped or changed or slowed down, I agree, I'd want us to come back in.

Aaron: [Writing it on the board] Okay, so we have two things. Bobby getting high again. And then Dad and Bobby starting to not talk. Anything else?

Mother: Well, I think if he and I start fighting like we used to, when Bobby was younger, and we stopped being as close, that would worry me. I never was totally convinced that maybe some of our stuff wasn't related to Bobby's.

Aaron: [Writing that on the board] Okay, so you and your husband having marital issues might be a good reason to check back in. Anything else?

After getting a list, counselors should negotiate a verbal agreement with the couples or families to come in for a booster session if any of the listed signs occur. We always tell families that it is better to call sooner, rather than later, because interrupting problem sequences is easier the more quickly they are addressed. It also would be useful for counselors to call the families periodically, list in hand, to check to see if any of the listed items are occurring. Family systems are very powerful, with a strong pull to return to the way they were. Helping families to become vigilant to such a return, and even making occasional calls to families, can help circumvent this systemic tendency.

TERMINATION INTERVENTIONS

Counseling can end in a number of ways. Many times, of course, clients just seem to "fizzle out," that is, they start missing appointments, and then never come back. We believe that the resiliency-based and solution-focused nature of this model helps to prevent dropouts because the counseling process tends to be more positive and cooperative. Even when termination is planned, however, there are still different ways to end. One way is to reduce the number of sessions from weekly, to biweekly, to monthly, and then to "come back as you need to" sessions. Another way to end is with a final celebratory session that includes a strong celebration ritual.

Celebration Rituals

Counselors can use many different celebration rituals with their clients. Some bring in coffee and cake for the last session; some bring a small, meaningful gift; some have a "Certificate of Merit" printed for the couple or family, and so forth. The more counselors are able to tailor the ending ritual to the specific work families have done, the better, of course. One couple we know of had used the metaphor of running a marathon throughout their counseling. In the final session, their counselor gave each of them race numbers, similar to those worn by marathoners, and also a certificate stating that they were able to "finish the race" as a couple. Whatever is done, it is important to send the message that ending counseling is a cause for celebration, similar to a graduation, and that the counselors are proud of their couples or families and the changes they have made. And, just as a graduation does not preclude more education, neither does "graduating" from counseling preclude more counseling, if and when it is needed.

BOOSTER SESSIONS

If couples or families do return for counseling in the future, this should be seen as a continuation of stage three rather than a beginning of stage one. A follow-up session, then, is a booster session, not an intake interview. Booster sessions are designed to give further support to the work the families or couples have done and to help keep them on track. The structure of such sessions is illustrated through the following questions and interventions.

"How Is It Going?"

As in all of the interviews during the course of counseling, it is important to refer back to the original goals of treatment. Counselors can use these goals as a structure for evaluating what progress families have made and maintained. As in the rest of this model, counselors should also keep an eye out for gains or positive changes that have happened so that these can be emphasized. The following vignette illustrates a planned booster session, where it is easy to focus on strengths and progress:

Aaron: So, how has it been going since I saw you last?

Father: Pretty good, pretty good.

Aaron: You know, I just have to tell you, in the *old days*, when you all first came in, I never got a *pretty good* answer from any of you.

Mother: No, it really is going nicely. In fact, we kind of wondered why we were coming in.

Aaron: So you talked about whether you even needed to come today?

Mother: Yes.

Aaron: Well, I'm happy you did. I really have been wondering about you all. Since it is going pretty good, want to tell me some of the good things that have happened since you were here last?

Bobby: Well, I made the basketball team.

Aaron: You did? I didn't even know you were interested in basketball. Shows how much I know.

Bobby: Yeah, just never thought I was good enough to go out for it.

Father: He really is good, real quick. The coach actually came to him to see if he wanted to be on the team.

Aaron: Now, just so I'm not missing anything, this is different from when you all first started coming in, right? I mean, you weren't playing basketball then?

Bobby: No, that would have seemed too jock to me then.

Aaron: What is different? Isn't it still "jock"?

Bobby: Nah, it's just fun. I always liked to shoot hoops.

This interaction shows a couple of things. First, when the family first mentioned things going well, Aaron went full force with it. Some counselors "perk up" primarily when given negative information, which leads to problem talk and moves away from a focus on resiliency. As in previous stages of counseling, the counselor using this model focuses as much as possible on the bits of resiliency information given and builds on that. Second, Aaron begins this booster session where he left off, that is, with a stage three punctuating-the-differences intervention. When Father says the family is doing "pretty well,"

Aaron points out how different that beginning is compared to their first sessions. Then when told Bobby is playing school sports, he again punctuates *that* difference. So in a few short minutes, with a few questions, the family again *feels* how different and successful they are.

"If You Slipped, How Did You Get Back on Track?"

Of course, not all couples or families will come in with a complete success story. More commonly, they will relate a few months of a life that is filled with ups and downs. The skill of the resiliency-based, solution-focused counselor is most apparent here. He or she should be able to, while listening and understanding the difficulties experienced, gently emphasize how the "new" family or couple was able to get itself back on track. Consider Shauneeka's work with Pete and Marie in a booster session.

Shauneeka: So how has it been going since I last saw you two?

Pete: Well, kind of up and down.

Shauneeka: That sure is to be expected.

Pete: Yeah, there were some screw-ups, that's for sure.

Marie: Well, it really wasn't that bad, except for that one time.

Shauneeka: So it was only one time that there was a problem?

Pete: Well, she relapsed.

Marie: I didn't relapse. I had one drink. And that was two months ago.

Shauneeka: Two months ago? Not too long after we finished regular couples counseling?

Marie: Yeah, about a month after our last session, I think.

Shauneeka: What happened?

Marie: I just screwed up.

Shauneeka: What was going on with you two? Anything going on right before?

Marie: Well, we had a fight. And then it felt like the same old thing. Pete started watching me like my father, then I got pissed, finally just wanted to get out, went out with my friend. We went to this bar; she and I just talked, but I did have one beer.

Shauneeka: So, you two had a fight, then you, Pete, started being more vigilant with Marie, then Marie felt overwhelmed, then went out and had a drink.

Marie: Yeah.

Shauneeka: What happened then?

Marie: I came home, he smelled it on my breath, we had a huge fight, he called me names, I cried, you know, the whole thing.

Pete: I was just so frustrated. You had come so far and then that.

Marie: But it was different. I only had one. I stopped myself. I felt bad about it. I went to a meeting the next day. Jeez, the group was better about it than you were.

Shauneeka: Hold on, so you went out after your argument. Did it feel like you went out because of the argument? You know, like that old pattern we talked about?

Marie: Yes, exactly.

Pete: I thought that might be an excuse.

Shauneeka: And you went out with your friend. Did you go out to drink? Did you have a craving?

Marie: I know what you are talking about. No, it definitely wasn't a craving, just a craving to get out, have some fun, get away from him for a while.

Shauneeka: Then how did you manage to only have one drink? In the past, you would have had a lot more trouble stopping yourself at one.

Marie: I don't know. I know I didn't want to start again. I wanted to see if I could do it. Maybe I was just trying to get back at him, but not enough to hurt myself, hurt us. I had the one, then talked about it with my friend. She only had one, too. I felt pretty guilty having the one; it really wasn't that much fun.

Shauneeka: So you were able to stop at one, to keep your wits about you and stop. And then you felt bad about it. What then?

Marie: Like I said, I went home, and we had a screaming fight about it. But then he stopped; he kind of backed off.

Shauneeka: So what happened, Pete?

Pete: I started to think about what we had talked about in here, about how my sniffing and smelling her, going after her, that it didn't work. I saw that all we were doing was fighting about it, and it made it worse. So I left the room, let things cool down for awhile. Then I went back in and just took her in my arms and hugged her.

Shauneeka: What happened then?

Pete: It got better.

Marie: I just cried. He told me he loved me and was sorry that he pushed so hard.

Shauneeka: What did his saying that do?

Marie: It helped. It really did. I told him I was sorry too, that we needed to not do our old thing.

Shauneeka: And then?

Marie: I went to a meeting the next day. Like I said, they weren't too worried about it. And then I told my counselor about it. We just watched it. I haven't had a drink since then. Haven't missed it.

Shauneeka: How are you two doing?

Pete: Much better now. I'm just giving her space, like we used to talk about here.

Marie: He is doing much better.

Shauneeka: You both are. I am really impressed with how strong you two have become, how far you have come, how different you are. Look how you settled this. What would have happened if this occurred during the first few weeks you were here, you know, last year.

Pete: God, it would have been terrible. First, she would have drunk a lot more, maybe did drugs. And I would have been a zombie, would have kept after her. We would have fought the whole time.

> **Shauneeka:** See, I cannot guarantee that you will never have problems, but look how differently the *new couple* deals with them.

Notice how Shauneeka both lets Pete and Marie tell their story and guides them to look for the strengths and competencies contained in it. She does not shy away from hearing about the difficulties, but she also does not let the picture become one-sided through a focus only on the negative parts of the story. She also quickly links this experience to the pursuing-distancing pattern that Pete and Marie had identified in their earlier counseling.

"Did You Slip and Not Get Back on Track?
If So, How Can You Get Back on Track Now?"

Sometimes, of course, couples or families will come back for their booster sessions having had a problem and *not* gotten back on track; that is, they still are struggling with the problem. In Pete and Marie's case, for example, Marie might have had a drink a week ago, but she and Pete are still fighting about it—a return to some of their old patterns. What can the counselor do in these circumstances? In essence, the counselor should use the same guidelines we presented earlier in the section on dealing with relapse during the regular course of therapy. Recall that a relapse can either be the return of alcohol or drug use, the return of old conflict patterns, or both.

First, counselors should help families or couples gauge the seriousness or depth of the slip—in other words, see it more realistically. When clients put their slips in perspective, they are less likely to see them as events that lead them to abandon their goals entirely. It can be helpful to rate the slip on a ten-point scale, compared to how they were when they first came in. For example, Marie having one drink one night with a friend and then stopping, going to an AA meeting, and going back to her counselor might be scaled as a "2" (a minor problem), compared with her earlier pattern of drinking extensively and with a good deal of denial.

Second, counselors can focus on how couples or families dealt with similar problems when they were in counseling. They can look specifically at previously helpful interventions, explore any barriers to doing those, and then reassign them. This is usually low risk, since these same interventions worked well before. Counselors can also normalize this process: "You know, it took your family many years to develop these patterns, and it will take a while for the changes you have been so good at to fully stick."

Third, counselors can encourage couples or families to generate alternatives to how they are currently handling the situation: "What do you think you can do to get back on track? Think about what worked well before." Clients' ability to remember previous successes will reinforce their stage three position as competent and put the responsibility back onto them. Counselors, then, should act as coaches rather than headmasters, helping families or couples build on previously demonstrated strengths. If clients cannot come up with any specific interventions, counselors might suggest some alternatives. These should be consistent with the themes of the previous counseling, should be something that previously worked, and should aim at interrupting dysfunctional sequences.

Depending upon the seriousness of the setback, counselors can determine if the couples or families should return soon or can wait for the next scheduled booster session. If the problems seem serious, counselors may have to reinstitute counseling and recontract for a certain number of sessions. Usually, the counseling can then be primarily stage three interventions, but in more serious cases, counselors may decide to move back to stage two. This should not be seen as a failure for the couples or families. Instead, counselors should try to normalize this:

> You know, it is not at all uncommon for families to need to come back for some more sessions after they have finished. Some see counseling as a lifelong experience. Some see it like going to the doctor: You are doing fine most of the time, but now and then, when things are a problem, you may need to return to get back on track. Now you all have the skills to make changes and keep them going. You have shown that many times over the last few months. Let's get back and see what was going on.

TERMINATION

Termination occurs when clients think that they are far enough along on the road to meeting their goals that they can go without counseling for awhile. Obviously, if they run into major difficulties, they can return for further sessions. However, the brief, resiliency-based, solution-focused model is predicated on the notion that the job of counseling is to help clients get a good start on change, not see them through until the very end. In that way, it is respectful of clients' strengths and resources.

The final session with the couple or family should have a tone of celebration. We often bring in food. Sometimes we have the couple or family bring in photos of the whole family. Sometimes we make up certificates using commonly available computer programs. The counselor should look back with family members to the original goals for treatment that they set at the end of the assessment period. He or she should acknowledge what goals have been accomplished. As much as possible, this last session should leave the family with a sense of accomplishment, and of pride. (A summary of ending treatment is presented in Table 9.1.)

TABLE 9.1. Summary: Ending Treatment

Emphasize Changes	• "How is the 'new' family different from the 'old' family?"
Plan for Problems	• "What stresses and problems do you antici-pate?" • "How will you handle them in a way that will tell you you are still 'on track' with the changes you have made?"
Booster Sessions	• "How is it going?" • "How have you kept on track?" • "What do you need to do to get back on track?"

References

American Medical Association (1992). Violence against women: Relevance for medical practitioners. *Journal of the American Medical Association, 267,* 3184-3189.

Anglin, M. D., Kao, C. F., Harlow, L. L., Peters, K., and Booth, M. W. (1987). Similarity of behavior within addict couples. Part I: Methodology and narcotics patterns. *International Journal of the Addictions, 22,* 497-524.

Atkinson, R. M., Tolson, R. L., and Turner, J. A. (1993). Factors affecting outpatient treatment compliance of older male problem drinkers. *Journal of Studies on Alcohol, 54,* 102-106.

Bachelor, A. (1991). Comparison and relationship to outcome of diverse dimensions of the helping alliance as seen by client and therapist. *Psychotherapy, 28,* 534-549.

Berg, I. K. and Miller, S. D. (1992). *Working with the problem drinker: A solution-oriented approach.* New York: Norton.

Berger, A. (1981). Family involvement and alcoholics' completion of a multiphase treatment program. *Journal of Studies on Alcohol, 42,* 517-520.

Bowen, M. (1978). *Family therapy in clinical practice.* New York: Jason Aronson.

Breunlin, D. C., Schwartz, R. C., and MacKune-Karrer, B. (1992). *Metaframeworks: Transcending the models of family therapy.* San Francisco: Jossey-Bass.

Brown, T. G., Werk, T., Caplan, T., Shields, N., and Seraganian, P. (1998). The incidence and characteristics of violent men in substance abuse treatment. *Addictive Behaviors, 23,* 573-586.

Burling, T. A., Reilly, P. M., Moltzen, J. O., and Ziff, D. C. (1989). Self-efficacy and relapse among inpatient drug and alcohol abusers: A predictor of outcome. *Journal of Studies on Alcohol, 50,* 354-360.

Carter, E. and McGoldrick, M. (Eds.) (1999). *The expanded family life cycle: Individual, family and social perspectives* (Third edition). Boston: Allyn & Bacon.

Cascardi, M., Langhinrichsen, J., and Vivian, D. (1992). Marital aggression: Impact, injury, and health correlates for husbands and wives. *Archives of Internal Medicine, 152,* 1178-1184.

Cervantes, O. F., Sorensen, J. L., Wermuth, L., Fernandez, L., Menicucci, L. (1988). Family ties of drug abusers. *Psychology of Addictive Behaviors, 2,* 34-39.

Collins, R. L. (1990). Family treatment of alcohol abuse: Behavioral and systems perspectives. In R. L. Collins, K. E. Leonard, and J. S. Searles (Eds.), *Alcohol and the family* (pp. 285-308). New York: Guilford.

Connell, G., Mitten, T., and Bumberry, W. M. (1999). *Reshaping family relationships: The symbolic therapy of Carl Whitaker*. Philadelphia: Brunner/Mazel.

Conners, G. J., Carroll, K. M., DiClemente, C. C., Longabaugh, R., and Donovan, D. M. (1997). The therapeutic alliance and its relationship to alcoholism treatment participation and outcome. *Journal of Consulting and Clinical Psychology, 65*, 588-598.

Diamond, G. S., Serrano, A. C., Dickey, M., and Sonis, W. A. (1996). Current status of family-based outcome and process research. *Journal of the American Academy of Child and Adolescent Psychiatry, 35*, 6-16.

Doherty, W. S. and Simmons, D. S. (1996). Clinical practice pattern of marriage and family therapists: A national survey of therapists and their clients. *Journal of Marital and Family Therapy, 22*, 9-25.

Duncan, D. F. (1978). Family stress and the initiation of adolescent drug abuse: A retrospective study. *Corrective and Social Psychiatry, 24*(3), 111-114.

Falloon, I. R. H. (1988). *Handbook of behavioral family therapy*. New York: Guilford Press.

Fals-Stewart, W., Birchler, G. R., and O'Farrell, T. J. (1996). Behavioral couples therapy for male substance-abusing patients: Effects on relationship adjustment and drug-using behavior. *Journal of Consulting and Clinical Psychology, 64*, 959-972.

Fals-Stewart, W., Birchler, G. R., and O'Farrell, T. J. (1999). Drug-abusing patients and their intimate partners: Dyadic adjustment, relationship stability, and substance use. *Journal of Abnormal Psychology, 108*, 11-23.

Fals-Stewart, W., O'Farrell, T. J., and Birchler, G. R. (1997). Behavioral couples therapy for male substance-abusing patients: A cost outcomes analysis. *Journal of Consulting and Clinical Psychology, 65*, 789-802.

Federal Bureau of Investigation (1993). *Uniform crime reports*. Washington, DC: Department of Justice.

Feld, S. L. and Straus, M. A. (1989). Escalation and desistance of wife assault in marriage. *Criminology, 27*, 141-161.

Fisch, R., Weakland, J. H., and Segal, L. (1982). *The tactics of change: Doing therapy briefly*. San Francisco: Jossey-Bass.

Fisher, R. and Ury, W. (1992). *Getting to yes: Negotiating agreement without giving in* (Second edition). Boston: Houghton Mifflin.

Fishman, D. B., Rotgers, F., and Franks, C. M. (1988). *Paradigms in behavior therapy: Present and promise*. New York: Springer Publishing.

Friedman, A. S. (1989). Family therapy vs. parent groups: Effects on adolescent substance abusers. *American Journal of Family Therapy, 17*, 335-347.

Garrett, J., Landau, J., Shea, R., Standon, M. D., Baciewicz, G., and Brinkman-Sull, D. (1998). The ARISE intervention: Using family and network links to engage addicted persons in treatment. *Journal of Substance Abuse Treatment, 15*, 333-343.

Garrett, J., Landau-Stanton, J., Stanton, M.D., Stellato-Kabat, J., and Stellato-Kabat, D. (1997). ARISE: A method for engaging reluctant alcohol- and drug-dependent individuals in treatment. *Journal of Substance Abuse Treatment, 14,* 235-248.

Garrett, J., Stanton, M. D., Landau, J., Baciewicz, G., Brinkman-Sull, D., and Shea, R. (1999). The "concerned other" call: Using family links and networks to overcome resistance to addiction treatment. *Substance Use and Misuse, 34,* 363-382.

Gelles, R. J. and Straus, M. A. (1990). The medical and psychological costs of violence. In M. A. Straus and R. J. Gelles (Eds.), *Physical violence in American families: Risk factors and adaptations to violence in 8145 families* (pp. 425-430). New Brunswick, NJ: Transaction Publishers.

Goldbeck, R., Myatt, P., and Aitchison, T. (1997). End-of-treatment self-efficacy: A predictor of abstinence. *Addiction, 92,* 313-324.

Gomberg, E. S. (1993). Women and alcohol: Use and abuse. *Journal of Nervous and Mental Disease, 181,* 211-219.

Greenwald, A. F. and Bartmeier, L. H. (1963). Psychiatric discharges against medical advice. *Archives of General Psychiatry, 8,* 117-119.

Haley, J. (1976). *Problem-solving therapy: New strategies for effective family therapy.* San Francisco: Jossey-Bass.

Haley, J. (1997). *Leaving home: The therapy of disturbed young people* (Second edition). New York: Brunner/Mazel.

Hare-Mustin, R. T. (1978). A feminist approach to family therapy. *Family Process, 17,* 181-194.

Hecker, L. L. and Deacon, S. (1998). *The therapist's notebook.* Binghamton, NY: The Haworth Press, Inc.

Hecker, L. L. and Trepper, T. S. (2000). REM approach to conflict resolution for couples therapy. *Journal of Family Psychotherapy, 11*(1), pp. 47-57.

Henggeler, S. W., Borduin, C. M., Melton, G. B., Mann, B. J., and Smith, L. A. (1991). Effects of multisystemic therapy on drug use and abuse in serious juvenile offenders: A progress report from two outcome studies. *Family Dynamics of Addiction Quarterly, 1,* 40-51.

Holden, G. (1991). The relationship of self-efficacy appraisals to subsequent health-related outcomes: A meta-analysis. *Social Work in Health Care, 16*(1), 53-93.

Iguchi, M. Y., Belding, M. A., Morral, A. R., Lamb, R. J., and Husband, S. D. (1997). Reinforcing operants other than abstinence in drug abuse treatment: An effective alternative for reducing drug use. *Journal of Consulting and Clinical Psychology, 65,* 421-428.

Imber-Black, E. (1988). *Families and larger systems: A family therapist's guide through the labyrinth.* New York: Guilford Press.

Joanning, H., Quinn, W., Thomas, F., and Mullen, R. (1992). Treating adolescent drug abuse: A comparison of family systems therapy, group therapy, and family drug education. *Journal of Marital and Family Therapy, 18,* 345-356.

Kavanagh, D. J., Sitharthan, T., and Sayer, G. P. (1996). Prediction of results from correspondence treatment for controlled drinking. *Addiction, 91,* 1539-1545.

Klion, R. E. and Pfenninger, D. T. (1997). Personal construct psychotherapy of addictions. *Journal of Substance Abuse Treatment, 14*, 37-43.

Knapp, C. (1996). *Drinking: A love story*. New York: Dial Press.

Kores, R. C., Murphy, W. D., Rosenthal, T. L., Elias, D. B., and North, W. C. (1990). Predicting outcome of chronic pain treatment via a modified self-efficacy scale. *Behaviour Research and Therapy, 28*, 165-169.

Krueger, D. W. (1981). Stressful life events and the return to heroin use. *Journal of Human Stress, 7*, 3-8.

Lambert, M. J. and Bergin, A. E. (1994). The effectiveness of psychotherapy. In A. E. Bergin and S. L. Garfield (Eds.), *Handbook of psychotherapy and behavior change* (Fourth edition, pp. 143-189). New York: Wiley.

Lee, W. V. and Weinstein, S. P. (1997). How far have we come? A critical review of the research on men who batter. In M. Galanter (Ed.), *Recent Developments in Alcoholism*, Volume 13: *Alcoholism and Violence* (pp. 337-356). New York: Plenum Press.

Lewis, R. A., Piercy, F. P., Sprenkle, D. H., and Trepper, T. S. (1990). Family-based interventions for helping drug-abusing adolescents. *Journal of Adolescent Research, 50*, 82-95.

Lipchik, E. and de Shazer, S. (1988). Purposeful sequences for beginning the solution-focused interview. In E. Lipchik (Ed.), *Interviewing* (pp. 105-117). Rockville, MD: Aspen.

Livingston, L. (1986). Measuring domestic violence in an alcoholic population. *Journal of Sociology and Social Welfare, 13*, 934-953.

Madanes, C. (1981). *Strategic family therapy*. San Francisco: Jossey-Bass.

Madanes, C. (1984). *Behind the one-way mirror: Advances in the practice of strategic therapy*. San Francisco: Jossey-Bass.

Matthews, D. J. (1995). *Foundations for violence-free living: A step-by-step guide to facilitating men's domestic abuse groups*. St. Paul, MN: Amherst W. Wilder Foundation.

McAuliffe, W. E. (1975). Beyond secondary deviance: Negative labeling and its effects on the heroin addict. In W. R. Gove (Ed.), *The labeling of deviance: Evaluating a perspective* (pp. 205-242). New York: Halsted Press.

McCollum, E. E. and Trepper, T. S. (1995). "Little by little, pulling me through": Women's perceptions of successful drug treatment, a qualitative inquiry. *Journal of Family Psychotherapy, 6*(1), 63-82.

McCrady, B. S., Noel, N. E., Abrams, D. B., Stout, R. L., Nelson, H. F., and Hay, W. M. (1986). Comparative effectiveness of three types of spouse involvement in outpatient behavioral alcoholism treatment. *Journal of Studies on Alcohol, 47*, 459-467.

McKay, J. R., Maisto, S. A., and O'Farrell, T. J. (1993). End-of-treatment self-efficacy, aftercare, and drinking outcomes of alcoholic men. *Alcoholism, Clinical and Experimental Research, 17*, 1078-1083.

Miller, S. D., Duncan, B. L., and Hubble, M. A. (1997). *Escape from Babel: Toward a unifying language for psychotherapy practice*. New York: Norton.

Miller, W. R., Benefield, R. G., and Tonigan, J. S. (1993). Enhancing motivation for change in problem drinking: A controlled comparison of two therapist styles. *Journal of Consulting and Clinical Psychology, 61*, 455-461.

Miller, W. R., Zweben, A., DiClemente, C. C., and Rychtarik, R. G. (1994). *Motivational enhancement therapy manual: A clinical research guide for therapists treating individuals with alcohol abuse and dependence* (NIH Publication No. 94-3723). Rockville, MD: National Institute on Alcohol Abuse and Alcoholism.

Minuchin, P. (1985). Families and individual development: Provocations from the field of family therapy. *Child Development, 56*, 289-302.

Minuchin, S. (1974). *Families and family therapy.* Cambridge, MA: Harvard University Press.

Minuchin, S. and Fishman, H. C. (1981). *Family therapy techniques.* Cambridge, MA: Harvard University Press.

Morgenstern, J., Labouvie, E., McCrady, B. S., Kahler, C. W., and Frey, R. M. (1997). Affiliation with Alcoholics Anonymous after treatment: A study of therapeutic effects and mechanisms of action. *Journal of Consulting and Clinical Psychology, 65*, 768-777.

Myers, M. G. and Brown, S. A. (1990). Coping responses and relapse among adolescent substance abusers. *Journal of Substance Abuse, 2*, 177-189.

Myers, M. G., Brown, S. A., and Mott, M. A. (1993). Coping as a predictor of adolescent substance abuse treatment outcome. *Journal of Substance Abuse, 5*, 15-29.

Napier, A. and Whitaker, C. A. (1978). *The family crucible.* New York: Harper & Row.

Nelson, T. S. and Trepper, T. S. (Eds.) (1994). *101 interventions in family therapy.* Binghamton, NY: The Haworth Press, Inc.

Nelson, T. S. and Trepper, T. S. (Eds.) (1998). *101 more interventions in family therapy.* Binghamton, NY: The Haworth Press, Inc.

Nichols, M. P. (1984). *Family therapy: Concepts and methods.* New York: Gardner Press.

Noone, R. J. (1980). Drug abuse behavior in relation to change in the family structure. In P. G. McCullough and J. C. Carolin (Eds.), *Pittsburgh family systems symposia: Collection of papers 1979-1980* (pp. 174-186). Pittsburgh: Western Psychiatric Institute and Clinic.

O'Farrell, T. J. (1989). Marital and family therapy in alcoholism treatment. *Journal of Substance Abuse Treatment, 6*, 23-29.

O'Farrell, T. J. (1991). *Using couples therapy in the treatment of alcoholism.* Paper presented at the Annual Convention of the American Psychological Association, San Francisco, CA.

O'Farrell, T. J., Choquette, K. A., Cutler, H. S., Floyd, F. J., Bayog, R., Brown, E. D., Lowe, J., Chan, A., and Deneault, P. (1996). Cost-benefit and cost-effectiveness analyses of behavioral marital therapy as an addition to outpatient alcoholism treatment. *Journal of Substance Abuse, 8*, 145-166.

O'Farrell, T. J. and Feehan, M. (1999). Alcoholism treatment and the family: Do family and individual treatments for alcoholic adults have preventive effects for children? *Journal of Studies on Alcohol* (Supplement), *13*, 125-129.

O'Farrell, T. J., Hooley, J., Fals-Stewart, W., and Cutter, H. S. (1998). Expressed emotion and relapse in alcoholic patients. *Journal of Consulting and Clinical Psychology, 66*, 744-752.

O'Farrell, T. J., Van Hutton, V., and Murphy, C. M. (1999). Domestic violence before and after alcoholism treatment: A two-year longitudinal study. *Journal of Studies on Alcohol, 60*, 317-321.

O'Leary, K. D., Barling, J., Arias, I., Rosenbaum, A., Malone, J., and Tyree, A. (1989). Prevalence and stability of physical aggression between spouses: A longitudinal analysis. *Journal of Consulting and Clinical Psychology, 57*, 263-268.

Osborn, C. J. (1997). Does disease matter? Incorporating solution-focused brief therapy in alcoholism treatment. *Journal of Alcohol and Drug Education, 43*(1), 18-30.

Prochaska, J. O. and DiClemente, C. C. (1982). Transtheoretical therapy: Toward a more integrative model of change. *Psychotherapy: Theory, Research and Practice, 19*, 276-288.

Prochaska, J. O. and DiClemente, C. C. (1984). *The transtheoretical approach: Crossing traditional boundaries of therapy.* Homewood, IL: Dow Jones/Irwin.

Prochaska, J. O. and DiClemente, C. C. (1985). Processes and stages of change in smoking, weight control, and psychological distress. In S. Schiffman and T. Will (Eds.), *Coping and substance abuse* (pp. 319-345). New York: Academic Press.

Prochaska, J. O. and DiClemente, C. C. (1986). Toward a comprehensive model of change. In W. R. Miller and N. Heather (Eds.), *Treating addictive behaviors: Processes of change* (pp. 3-27). New York: Plenum.

Prochaska, J. O., DiClemente, C. C., and Norcross, J. (1992). In search of how people change. *American Psychologist, 47*, 1102-1114.

Raynes, A. E. and Patch, V. D. (1971). Distinguishing features of patients who discharge themselves from psychiatric wards. *Comprehensive Psychiatry, 12*, 473-479.

Robinson, S. M. and Walsh, J. (1994). Cognitive factors affecting abstinence among adolescent polysubstance abusers. *Psychological Reports, 75*, 579-589.

Rogers, C. (1951). *Client-centered therapy: Its current practice, theory and implications.* Chicago: Houghton Mifflin.

Rosenberg, C. M., Gerrein, J. R., Manohar, V., and Liftik, J. (1976). Evaluation of training of alcoholism counselors. *Journal of Studies on Alcoholism, 37*, 1236-1246.

Rosenberg, C. M. and Raynes, A. E. (1973). Dropouts from treatment. *Canadian Psychiatric Association Journal, 18*, 229-233.

Rounds-Bryant, J. L., Flynn, P. M., and Craighead, L. W. (1997). Relationship between self-efficacy perceptions and in-treatment drug use among regular cocaine users. *American Journal of Drug and Alcohol Abuse, 23*, 383-395.

Sadowski, C. J., Long, C. K., and Jenkins, L. R. (1993). Does substance abuse treatment have self-schematic effects? *Journal of Psychology, 127*, 323-327.

Satir, V. (1972). *Peoplemaking.* Palo Alto, CA: Science and Behavior Books.

Satir, V. (1983). *Conjoint family therapy* (Third edition). Palo Alto, CA: Science and Behavior Books.

Schmidt, S. E., Liddle, H. A., and Dakof, G. A. (1996). Changes in parenting practices and adolescent drug abuse during multidimensional family therapy. *Journal of Family Psychology, 10,* 12-27.

Smith, D. B. (1997). Penicillin therapy. Unpublished paper.

Snyder, W. (1992). Seeing the troubled adolescent in context: Family systems theory and practice. In W. Snyder and T. Ooms (Eds.), *Empowering families, helping adolescents: Family-centered treatment of adolescents with alcohol, drug abuse, and mental health problems* (Technical Assistance Publication Series: Number 6) (pp. 13-37). Rockville, MD: SAMHSA.

Solomon, K. E. and Annis, H. M. (1990). Outcome and efficacy expectancy in the prediction of post-treatment drinking behaviour. *British Journal of Addiction, 85,* 659-665.

Spanier, G. B. (1976). Measuring dyadic adjustment: New scales for assessing the quality of marriage and similar dyads. *Journal of Marriage and the Family, 38,* 15-28.

Stanton, M. D. (1997). The role of family and significant others in the engagement and retention of drug-dependent individuals. In J. D. Blaine and J. J. Boren (Eds.), *Beyond the therapeutic alliance: Keeping the drug-dependent individual in treatment* (National Institute on Drug Abuse [NIDA] Research Monograph #165) (pp. 157-180). Rockville, MD: NIDA.

Stanton, M. D. and Shadish, W. R. (1997). Outcome, attrition, and family-couples treatment for drug abuse: A meta-analysis and review of the controlled, comparative studies. *Psychological Bulletin, 122,* 170-191.

Stanton, M. D., Todd, T. C., and Associates. (1982). *The family therapy of drug abuse and addiction.* New York: Guilford Press.

Steinmetz, S. K. (1977-1978). The battered husband syndrome. *Victimology: An International Journal, 2,* 499-509.

Stephens, R. S., Wertz, J. S., and Roffman, R. A. (1993). Predictors of marijuana treatment outcomes: The role of self-efficacy. *Journal of Substance Abuse, 5,* 341-353.

Stets, J. E. and Straus, M. A. (1989). The marriage license as a hitting license: A comparison of assaults in dating, cohabiting, and married couples. *Journal of Family Violence, 4,* 161-180.

Stith, S. M., Rosen, K. H., McCollum, E. E., Coleman, J. U., and Herman, S. A. (1996). The voices of children: Preadolescent children's experiences in family therapy. *Journal of Marital and Family Therapy, 22,* 69-86.

Straus, M. A. and Gelles, R. J. (1990). *Physical violence in American families: Risk factors and adaptations to violence in 8145 families.* New Brunswick, NJ: Transaction Publishers.

Strawderman, E. T., Rosen, K. R., and Coleman, J. (1997). Therapist heal thyself: Countertransference and the treatment of a battered woman. *Journal of Family Psychotherapy, 8,* 35-50.

Substance Abuse and Mental Health Services Administration (SAMHSA). (1998). *Addiction counseling competencies: The knowledge, skills and attitudes of professional practice* (Technical assistance publication series: Volume 21). Rockville, MD: Author.

Szapocznik, J., Perez-Vidal, A., Brickman, A. L., Foote, F. H., Santisteban, D., Hervis, O., and Kurtines, W. M. (1988). Engaging adolescent drug abusers and their families in treatment: A strategic structural systems approach. *Journal of Consulting and Clinical Psychology, 56,* 552-557.

von Bertalanffy, L. (1968). *General systems theory.* New York: Braziller.

Walters, M. and The Women's Project in Family Therapy (1988). *The invisible web: Gender patterns in family relationships.* New York: Guilford Press.

Watzlawick, P., Weakland, J. H., and Fisch, R. (1974). *Change: Principles of problem formation and problem resolution.* New York: Norton.

Weiner, N. (1948). *Cybernetics, or control and communication in the animal and the machine.* Cambridge, MA: Technology Press.

Weiner, N. (1954). *The human use of human beings: Cybernetics and society.* New York: Doubleday.

Whitaker, C. A. and Bumberry, W. M. (1988). *Dancing with the family: A symbolic-experiential approach.* New York: Brunner/Mazel.

White, M. and Epston, D. (1990). *Narrative means to therapeutic ends.* New York: Norton.

Williams, C. N. and Klerman, L. V. (1984). Female alcohol abuse: Its effects on the family. In S. C. Wilsnack and L. J. Beckman (Eds.), *Alcohol problems in women: Antecedents, consequences and interventions* (pp. 280-312). New York: Guilford.

Wilsnack, R. W., Wilsnack, S. C., and Klassen, A. D. (1984). Women's drinking and drinking problems: Patterns from a 1981 national survey. *American Journal of Public Health, 74,* 1231-1238.

Yates, A. J. and Thain, J. (1985). Self-efficacy as a predictor of relapse following voluntary cessation of smoking. *Addictive Behaviors, 10,* 291-298.

Zweben, A. and Pearlman, S. (1983). Evaluating the effectiveness of conjoint treatment of alochol-complicated marriages: Clinical and methodological issues. *Journal of Marital and Family Therapy, 9,* 61-72.

Index

Page numbers followed by the letter "f" indicate figures; those followed by the letter "t" indicate tables.

Abrams, D. B., 6, 139
Absence, 120
Absentee, 98-99
Abuse, spousal, 6
Action stage, 93
  case example, 111-112
Active interventions, 29
Activity, direct, 29
Addict. *See also* Case examples
  adolescent, 7, 96
  adult, 5-7
    and self-efficacy, 43-44
    and violence, 70
Addiction Counseling Competencies, 8
Addiction counselor. *See* Counselor
Adolescents. *See also* Case examples
  as drug addicts, 7, 96
  as opponents, 97
Adult addict, 5-7. *See also* Case
    examples
  and self-efficacy, 43-44
  and violence, 70. *See also* Domestic
    violence
"Adult talk," 60
Aftercare programs, 35
Aitchison, T., 43, 112
Al-Anon, 32, 35
Alateen, 32, 35
Alcoholic, woman, 1, 5-6. *See also*
    Case examples
Alcoholics Anonymous, 35, 44, 45

Ambivalence, 106
American Association for Marriage and
    Family Therapy (AAMFT), 27
American Medical Association, 73
Anglin, M. D., 5, 139
Angry session, 67
Annis, H. M., 43
Arias, I., 72
Assessment, relapse, 173, 175-178
Atkinson, M. D., 6

Bachelor, A., 49
Baciewicz, G., 7
"Bad kid," 47
Balance, 153-154
Barling, J., 72
Bartmeier, L. H., 89
Bayog, R., 6
Behavioral family therapy, 25, 52
Belding, M. A., 51
Benefield, R. G., 97
Berg, I. K., 9, 89, 90t
Berger, A., 139
Bergin, A. E., 39, 58, 112
Biofeedback therapy, 52
Biologically based disorders, 31
Birchler, G. R., 6
Blame, parent, 30-31
Blended families, 18

"Booster sessions," 199, 201-207, 208t
  case example, 201-202, 203-206
Booth, M. W., 5, 139
Borduin, C. M., 4
Boundaries, family, 20
Bowen, M., 22
Breunlin, D. C., 59
Brickman, A. L., 4
Brief Therapy Center, 123
Brinkman-Sull, D., 7
Brown, E. D., 6
Brown, S. A., 43
Brown, T. G., 70
Bumberry, W. M., 24
Burling, T. A., 43

Caplan, T., 70
Carroll, K. M., 48
Carter, E., 25, 195
Cascardi, M., 72
Case examples
  absentee, 98
  action stage, 111-112
  adolescent substance abuse, 1, 3-4
  adult substance abuse, 1-2, 5-6
  booster sessions, 201-202, 203-206
  challenge
    expected, 196-197
    unexpected, 197-198
  change, maintaining, 190-192
  complainant relationship, 104-106, 107
  coping mechanisms, 194-195
  customer relationship, 91, 110-111
  family therapy, 55
    emotional intensity, 57
    power, 56
  focus, 135, 159-160
  goals, finding meaningful, 100
  interactional change, 168, 169-170
  interpersonal process, 84-85
  journal of changes, 193-194
  maintenance stage, 112-113
  motivation, assessment of, 87-88
  mutual acceptance, 132

Case examples *(continued)*
  negotiation, 126, 128-131, 133
  "new" family, 183-185
  opponent, 96
  overlooking change, 161-162
  pre-posttest results, 189
  problem sequences, 141-143,
    146-147, 151-153, 171
  quantifying change, 123-125
  raising intensity, 80-81
  relapse, 175-177, 178
  role-play, 185-187
  self-efficacy, 167
  solution sequence, 154-155
  success, 159-160, 165-166
  therapy contract, 120, 122
  visitor to complainant, 114, 115
Categorical organization, 36
Cause, 13, 15
Celebration rituals, 200-201
Cervantes, O. F., 7
Challenges
  expected, 195-197
  unexpected, 197-198
Chan, A., 6
Changes. *See also* Relapse
  commitment to, 109-110
  increasing, 161-172
  journal of, 193-194
  maintaining, 190-195, 208t
  overlooking, 161-162
  process of, 27, 46-47
  quantifying, 123-125
Choquette, K. A., 6
Circular causality, 15
Client contributions, 40-47, 53t
Closeness, family, 19-20
Codependency, 32
Cognitive family therapy, 25
Coleman, J., 60, 79-80
Collins, R. L., 139
Communication, family, 19, 28
Communications family therapy, 24-25
Complainant relationship, 90, 90t,
    103-108
  case example, 104-106, 107

Compliment, 97, 98
Conflict, REM approach and, 66-69, 69t
Conflicting goals, 125-134
Connell, G., 24
Connors, G. J., 48
Consolidation
  difference punctuating interventions, 182-190
  plans for postcounseling challenges, 195-200
  strategies to maintain change, 190-195
  termination interventions, 200-201
Construction of problem sequence, 144-150, 157t
Contact, establishing, 60-61
Contemplation stage, 92, 106
Content, 136
Contract, therapy
  case example, 120, 122
  develop a vision of the future, 120-123, 138t
  make goals measurable, 123-125, 138t
  problems with, 134-138
  resolve conflicting goals, 125-134
Controlled-outcome studies, 48
Coping mechanisms, 194-195, 199
Core conditions, 49
Counseling. *See* Family therapy; Therapy
Counselor. *See also* Therapy contract; Therapeutic relationship
  asking about abuse, 73-75
  and human development, 12-13
  interventions for, 29
  joining with family, 58-64, 85t
  personal reaction to violence, 78-80
  role of, 45-46
Craighead, L. W., 43
Crisis intervention theory, 34
Customer relationship, 90, 90t, 108-113
  case example, 91, 110-111
Cutter, H. S., 6
Cybernetics theory, 13

Dakof, G. A., 4
Day treatment, 35
de Shazer, S., 9, 123
Deacon, S., 29
Deneault, P., 6
Denial, 42-43
Depression, 73
Destruction of property, 71
Determination phase, 92-93
Develop a vision of the future, 120-123, 138t
Development, human, 12-13
Diagram, sequence, 148, 149t
Diamond, G. S., 4
Dickey, M., 4
DiClemente, C. C., 48, 92, 93, 106
Difference punctuation interventions, 182-190
Direct activity, 29
"Directing traffic," session leadership, 59, 62
Disease, addiction metaphor, 31-32, 50, 172
Distance, family, 19-20
Divorce, 17
Domestic violence, 6, 69-75, 72t, 78-80
Donovan, D. M., 48
Drinking: A Love Story, 93
Dropout, of therapy, 89
Duncan, B. L., 39, 48, 52, 53t
Duncan, D. F., 5
Dyadic Adjustment Scale, 188
Dysfunctional family, 33

Elias, D. B., 43, 166
Emotional intensity
  lowering, 57, 64-66, 85t
  raising, 80-81
Empathy
  and absentees, 98
  and emotional intensity, 66, 68-69, 69t
  and opponents, 97
  and solution sequences, 150
  as therapy core condition, 49

Emphasis vs. absolute differences, 27
Enforcement, leadership and, 59
Epston, D., 51, 162
Exaggeration, 132
Exceptions to problem sequence,
    155-156, 157t
Expectations, therapeutic, 50-51, 53t
Expected challenges 195-197
Experiential family therapy, 24-25
Externalizing problem, 51

Falloon, I. R. H., 25, 29
Fals-Stewart, W., 6
Families Anonymous, 32, 35
Family, definition of, 17-18
Family centeredness, 37
Family functioning, 18-20
Family life cycle, 20-21
Family systems theory, 16-17
Family therapy, 11. *See also* Therapy
    after abuse, 77-78
    barriers to, 36-37
    communications, 24-25
    contract. *See* Therapy contract
    emotional intensity in, 57
    experiential, 24-25
    feminist, 25-26
    goals of, 26-30. *See also* Goals,
        therapy
    and interdependence, 12-13
    intergenerational, 22
    and joining, 58-64, 85t
    and metaphor, 28-29
    misunderstandings of, 30-33
    power in, 56-57
    and reframing, 23, 27-28, 66-68, 69t
    schools of, 22-26
    settings, 33-37
    systems theory, 13-16, 14f
Federal Bureau of Investigation, 73
Feehan, M., 6
Feld, S. L., 73
Feminist family therapy, 25-26
Fernandez, L., 7
Fisch, R., 29, 67

Fisher, R., 126, 127
Fishman, D. B., 22, 25, 29, 30
Fishman, H. C., 22, 30
Floyd, F. J., 6
Flynn, P. M., 43
Focus, 134-135
    case example, 135, 159-160
Foote, F. H., 4
Framing counseling, 82-83, 85t
Franks, C. M., 25, 29
Friedman, A. S., 4

Garrett, J., 7
Gelles, R. J., 72, 73
Genogram, 22
Genuineness, 49
Gerrein, J. R., 89
Gestalt influence, and experiential
    family therapy, 24
"Getting out of coming here," 102
Getting to Yes, 126
Goals, therapy, 26-30, 48-49, 69
    case example, 100
    changing, 136-137
    conflicting, 125-134
    finding meaningful, 100-101
    lack of, 137-138
    measurable, 123-125
    negotiated, 82
    and therapeutic success, 170-172
Goldbeck, R., 43, 112
Gomberg, E. S., 6
Greenwald, A. F., 89

Haley, J., 22, 24, 29, 140
Hare-Mustin, R. T., 25
Harlow, L. L., 5, 139
Harming pets, 71
Hay, W. M., 6, 139
Hecker, L. L., 29, 66, 69t
Henggeler, S. W., 4
Herman, S. A., 60
Hervis, O., 4

Hierarchy, family, 20
Holden, G., 43, 166
Homework assignments, 29
Hooley, J., 6
Hope, therapeutic, 50-51, 53t
Hospitalization therapy programs, 34
    partial, 35
"Hot button" issues, 57, 66
"How Is It Going?" session, 201-203
Hubble, M. A., 39, 48, 52, 53t
Human development, 12-13
Human systems, 16-21
Humor, 132
Husband, S. D., 51

"Identified patient," 32
Iguchi, M. Y., 51
Imber-Black, E., 29-30
Inaction, 169
Individually based therapy, 2
Inpatient therapy, 34
Intensity, emotional
    lowering, 57, 64-66, 85t
    raising, 80-81
Interaction, 12, 61-64, 140, 172
Interaction change, 168-170, 170t
Interactional sequence, 141-143, 148,
    152, 157t
Interdependence, 12-13
    and systems theory, 13-16, 14f
Interests vs. position, 127-131
Intergenerational family therapy, 22
Interpersonal process, 84-85, 140
Interventions, 29
Interviewing for sequence, 144, 146t
Intoxication, abuse and, 70
Intrapsychic processes, 12

Jenkins, L. R., 43
Joanning, H., 4
Joining, families and, 58-64, 85t
Journal, of changes, 193-194
*Journal of Marital and Family
    Therapy*, 2

Kao, C. F., 5, 139
Kavanagh, D. J., 43
Klassen, A. D., 6
Klerman, L. V., 5-6
Klion, R. E., 110, 111
Knapp, R. C., 93, 109
Kores, R. C., 43, 166
Krueger, D. W., 5
Kurtines, W. M., 4

Lamb, R. J., 51
Lambert, M. J., 39, 58, 112
Landau, J., 7
Landau-Stanton, J., 7
Langhinrichsen, J., 72
Leadership, establishing, 58-60
Lee, W. V., 70
Lewis, T. A., 4
Liddle, H. A., 4
Life change, reinforcement of, 51
Liftik, J., 89
Lipchik, E., 123
Listening, and success, 163
Livingston, L., 70
Long, C. K., 43
Longabaugh, R., 48
Lowe, J., 6
Lowering intensity, 57, 64-65, 85t

MacKune-Karrer, B., 60
Madanes, C., 23, 30
Maintenance stage, 93, 112-113
Maisto, S. A., 43, 112
Malone, J., 72
Mann, B. J., 4
Manohar, V., 89
Matthews, D. J., 76
McAuliffe, W. E., 139
McCollum, E. E., 48, 59, 60
McCrady, B. S., 6, 139
McGoldrick, M., 195
McKay, J. R., 43, 112
Measurable goals, 123-125

Melton, G. B., 4
Men. *See also* Case examples
    as addicts, 2, 6-7
    and domestic violence, 72-73
Menicucci, L., 7
Metaphor, 28-29
Miller, S. D., 39, 48, 52, 53t, 89, 90t
Miller, W. R., 93, 97, 106
Milwaukee Brief Therapy Center, 9
"Mind reading," 61
Minuchin, P., 12
Minuchin, S., 22, 30
Mitten, T., 24
Models, lack of, 37
Moltzen, J. O., 43
Monologues, 62-63
Morgenstern, J., 45
Morral, A. R., 51
Motivation, 45
    assessment of, 87-88, 117t
    definition of, 88-95
Mott, M. A., 43
Mullen, R., 4
Murphy, C. M., 6
Murphy, W. D., 43, 166
Mutual acceptance, 131-134
Myatt, P., 43, 112
Myers, M. G., 43

Nagging, 5, 15
Napier, A., 24
Narcotics Anonymous, 35, 44
Native American treatment center, 5
Negotiation, goals, 82, 126-127
Nelson, H. F., 6, 139
Nelson, T. S., 30
"New" family, 183-185
Nichols, M. P., 30
Noel, N. E., 6, 139
Noone, R. J., 5
Norcross, J., 48
North, W. C., 43, 166
Notebook, of changes, 193-194

O'Farrell, T. J., 6, 43, 112, 139
O'Leary, K. D., 72
Ongoing challenge, 196
Opponent, 96-98
Osborn, C. J., 9
Out-of-home placement, 34
Outpatient services, 34, 42
Overcloseness, 26
Overnight therapy programs, 35

Papp, P., 25
Parent blame, 30-31
Parents, of drug-abusing adolescent, 4.
    See also Case examples
Patch, V. D., 89
Pearlman, S., 139
Penicillin, 45-46
Perez-Vidal, A., 4
Peters, K., 5, 139
Pets, harming, 71
Pfenninger, D. T., 110, 111
Philadelphia Child Guidance Clinic, 22
Physical violence, 70-71
Piercy, F. P., 4
Positional negotiation, 126-127
    vs. interests, 127-131
Positive goal, 120
Posttreatment challenges, 195-200,
    208t
Power, and family therapy, 56-57
Precontemplation stage, 92
Preparation, stage of change, 109-111
Pre-posttest results, 188-190
Presence, therapeutic goal, 120
Prevention, abuse, 75-77
Problem sequences, 141-150
Problem solving, 44-45
Problem-focused view, 41-42
Process, 137
    adding to, 83-85, 85t
Prochaska, J. O., 48, 92
Property, destruction of, 71
Psychological violence, 71-72

Quantifying change, 123-125
Quinn, W., 4

Raising intensity, 80-81
Rape, 71
Raynes, A. E., 89
Real problem, avoiding, 136
Reduction, emotional intensity, 65-66
Reframing, 23, 27-28, 66-68, 69t
Reilly, P. M., 43
Reinforcement, life change, 51
Relapse, 6, 93, 172-180, 174f
   booster session, 203-207
REM approach, 66-69, 69t
Repetition, 148
Residential substance abuse treatment
   programs, 34
Respect, 49
Robinson, S. M., 43
Roffman, R. A., 43
Rogers, C., 49, 58
Role-play, 185-188
Roles, family, 18-19
Rosen, K. H., 60
Rosen, K. R., 79-80
Rosenbaum, A., 72
Rosenberg, C. M., 89
Rosenthal, T. L., 43, 166
Rotgers, F., 25, 29
Rounds-Bryant, J. L., 43
Rules, family, 18
Rychtarik, R. G., 93, 106

Sadowski, C. J., 43
Safety planning, 75-77, 77t
SAMHSA (Substance Abuse and
   Mental health Services
   Administration), 8
Santistiban, D., 4
Satir, V., 24-25
Sayer, G. P., 43
Scaling, 123-125
Schmidt, S. E., 4

Schwartz, R. C., 59
Segal, L., 29
Self-defense, 71
Self-efficacy, 43-44, 166-168, 169t
   case example, 167
Self-focus, 153
Self-help groups, 35
Separation, physical, 66
Seraganian, P., 70.
Serrano, A. C., 4
Setback. *See* Relapse
Sexual violence, 71
Shadish, W. R., 7, 48
Shea, R., 7
Shields, N., 70
Silent family members, 63-64
Silverstein, O., 25
Sitharthan, T., 43
"Slice-in-time," look at family, 20
"Small talk," 60
Smith, D. B., 45-46
Smith, L. A., 4
Snyder, W., 14
Social cost, 6
Social learning, 25
Solomon, K. E., 43
Solution sequence, 150-156, 151t, 157t
   case example, 154-155
Solution-focused therapy, 9, 89, 93
Sonis, W. A, 4
Sorensen, J. L., 7
Spanier, G. B., 188
Spousal abuse, 6, 69-75, 72t
Sprenkle, D. H., 4
Stages of change, 89, 92
Standon, M. D., 7
Stanton, M. D., 7, 48
Steinmetz, S. K., 72
Stellato-Kabat, D. 7
Stellato-Kabat, J., 7
Stephens, R. S., 43
Stets, J. E., 73
Stith, S. M., 60
Stout, R. L., 6, 139
Strategic family therapy, 22-24
Straus, M. A., 72, 73

Strawderman, E. T., 79-80
"Street people," 6
Strength, client, 40
Structural family therapy, 22-24
Substance abuse, as focus of treatment,
    134-135. *See also* Family
    therapy; Therapy
Substance abuse counselor. *See*
    Counselor
Substance Abuse and Mental health
    Services Administration
    (SAMHSA), 8
Success, therapeutic, 163, 164f, 165t,
    166t
    case example, 159-160, 165-166
Symbolic interventions, 29
Systems theory, 13-16, 14f
Systems Theory: An Ecology of
    Influence, 13-14, 14f
Szapocznik, J., 4

Technique, therapy, 26-30
    raising intensity, 80-81
Termination, 207-208
    interventions, 200-201
Terminology, 32-33
Thain, J., 43, 166
Therapeutic relationship, 48-50, 53t
    complainant, 90, 90t, 103-108
        case example, 104-106, 107
    customer, 90, 90t, 108-113
        case example, 91, 110-111
    visitor, 90, 90t, 95-102, 137
        case example, 114, 115
    to complainant, 113-116
    to customer, 99
Therapist. *See* Counselor
Therapy. *See also* Family therapy;
        Therapeutic relationship;
        Therapy contract
    and active intervention, 29
    and biologically based disorders, 31
    booster sessions, 199, 201-207, 208t
    client contributions to, 40-47, 53t

Therapy *(continued)*
    consolidation of. *See* Consolidation
    and the disease model of addiction,
        31-32
    goals, 26-30, 48-49
    including family members in, 4, 5
    including partners in, 6
    increasing success of, 161-172
    model, 52, 53t
    and parent blame, 30-31
    returning to, 198-200
    termination of, 207-208
        interventions, 200-201
    use of direct activity, 29
Therapy contract
    case example, 120, 122
    develop a vision of the future,
        120-123, 138t
    make goals measurable, 123-125, 138t
    problems with, 134-138
    resolve conflicting goals, 125-134
Thomas, F., 4
Thoughtful session, 67
Threat of force, 71
Time-out, 76, 77t
Todd, T. C., 7
Tolson, R. L., 6
Tonigan, J. S., 97
Toughlove program, 35
Trepper, T. S., 4, 30, 48, 66, 69t
"Triggers," drug use, 140
Troubleshooting, relapse, 178-179
Turner, J. A., 6
Twelve-step approach, 44, 45
Tyree, A., 72

Unexpected challenges, 197-198
"Unidentified patient," 32
Ury, W., 126, 127

Van Hutton, V., 6
Violence, domestic, 6, 69-75, 72t, 78-80
Visitor relationship, 90, 90t, 95-102, 137

Visitor to complainant, 113-116
Visitor to customer, 99
Vivian, D., 72
von Bertalanffy, L., 15

Walsh, J., 43
Walters, M., 25
Warning signs, 199
Watzlawick, P., 67
"We are stuck with each other," 99
Weakland, J. H., 29, 67
Weiner, N., 13
Weinstein, S. P., 70
Werk, T., 70
Wermuth, L., 7
Wertz, J. S., 43
Whitaker, C. A., 24, 58

White, M., 51, 162
Williams, C. N., 5-6
Wilsnack, R. W., 6
Wilsnack, S. C., 6
Win-lose situation, 126, 127
Women. *See also* Case examples
  as alcoholics, 1, 5-6
  and domestic violence, 72-73
The Women's Project in Family
  Therapy, 25, 26

Yates, A., J., 43, 166

Ziff, D. C., 43
Zweben, A., 93, 106, 139